ON THE SET OF
FELLINI SATYRICON:

A Behind-the-Scenes Diary

ON THE SET OF
FELLINI SATYRICON:

A Behind-the-Scenes Diary

 by Eileen Lanouette Hughes

WILLIAM MORROW AND COMPANY, INC.
NEW YORK   1971

To my daughters, Mary Larkin and Kathleen
To Tina, my housekeeper
To Sally Improta, who typed the book
To Federico Fellini, who dreamed the dream.

Table of Contents

Introduction

During the course of his twenty-five-year career, Federico Fellini's gargantuan fantasy and soul-searching autobiographical themes have earned him international recognition as one of the world's greatest and most sensitive film directors. *La Strada* and *Nights of Cabiria,* both starring his wife, Giulietta Masina, won him two Oscars, but the pinnacle of his success was reached with *La Dolce Vita,* a scathing dissection of modern society, and *8½,* a penetrating and anguished analysis of a man in crisis.

In 1965 Fellini made his first color film, *Juliet of the Spirits,* again with his wife in the principal role, and though the director displayed his customary flair for fantastic symbolism and psychological probing, the film was received with mixed critical reactions. A long period of creative uncertainty and personal crisis ensued, and Fellini fans wondered if the director's fabulous talent had dried up. Some even doubted that he would ever make another film.

Fellini's stubborn insistence on making his films the way he wants to make them has sparked legendary feuds with his producers. After *Juliet* the director became involved in a lengthy battle with Dino De Laurentiis, the producer of his two Oscar-winning films, with whom he had signed a contract for a picture to be called *The Voyage of G. Mastorna*. The producer insisted upon having Ugo Tognazzi, a popular and talented Italian actor, in the role of Mastorna but the director did not want him under any circumstances, preferring Laurence Olivier or Marcello Mastroianni. The preparation was completed and sets were built but the shooting of the film was delayed by months of discussions, recriminations, and litigation, culminating in the director's near fatal malady in April, 1967.

As Fellini tells it, "De Laurentiis forced me to take Tognazzi for *Mastorna* but I never wanted him. I was in a state of confusion and went to the hospital with a strange disease. I called it 'Tognazziitis,' but five top Italian doctors diagnosed it is inoperable cancer of the pleura. By that time, they had already taken five hundred X rays and all showed the same thing.

"I was in an oxygen tent under sedation, with all those tubes in me, and I couldn't breathe. I thought I'd had a heart attack. The first indication I had that I might be dying was when I saw a pile of telegrams, two in red envelopes which meant they were from the Heads of State. One was from President Saragat and the other from Pietro Nenni, the Foreign Minister, and they said something like, 'Dear Fellini, you must live not only for the Italian cinema but for the Italian people.'

"You can imagine how I felt; and the German nurse treated me very tenderly and this had already unsettled me. In my hallucinatory state, I woke up to see her sobbing as she watched the television. Totò, the great Italian comic, was dead and I dreamed he came to meet me with flowers, so I was convinced the end was near.

"Then a friend from Rimini came to see me, a laboratory specialist who insisted I had a very rare form of allergic pleurisy called Sanarelli-Schwarzmann. 'Only animals get it,' he told me, 'but you have it.' The doctors thought it was a fascinating theory but didn't accept it. My friend advised me not to take any more of the medication I was getting, and with the connivance of one of the nuns and a nurse's aide I was given a cortisone injection. In twelve hours I could breathe and in twenty-four hours I could talk. The doctors were amazed. One of them marveled, 'I always knew you were a very unpredictable type!' I spent two months in the hospital and another recovering."

After his recovery, the director was rescued from his dilemma by Alberto Grimaldi, a young Neapolitan producer, who got Fellini released from the contract with De Laurentiis by paying three-quarters of a million dollars to cover the expenses already incurred on the film. Meanwhile, Fellini continued to nurture his intention of making *Mastorna* but decided to shelve the film for a less taxing project. In less than two months, in November and December of 1967, the director filmed an episode, *Toby Dammit,* or, *Don't Bet Your Head with the Devil,* based on a short story by Edgar Allan Poe. An Italian-French coproduction with Grimaldi as the Italian producer, the episode was for Fellini an act of liberation. "I tried to make fun of myself," he declared, "to throw myself into the sea, to exacerbate my style to the point of parody and grotesqueness in such a way that I could never go back to it."

In the beginning of 1968 Fellini returned to *Mastorna* but still seemed unable to begin the actual filming. "It made me nervous and suffocated me so I decided to put an end to it once and for all, a little like the scorpion which kills itself." Bernardino Zapponi, who collaborated with the director on the scripts of *Toby Dammit* and *Satyricon,* recalls, "We talked about *Mastorna* but he didn't want to do it. He was like a horse skittering back, a beast feeling a storm in the air, because for him it was a film of death. He became ashen whenever we talked about it. It was much too serious a theme and, since an artist identifies with his work, the subject tortured him. For him, it was like standing in front of a tribunal giving an account of himself, and he was not ready for the judgment of God yet."

Having eluded death himself and with *Mastorna* interred, the director, then forty-eight years old, embarked on another voyage, a trip back into time to disinter the *Dolce Vita* of the ancient Romans, an idea that, he sometimes claims, had been germinating in his fertile imagination since he first read Petronius' *Satyricon* in 1939 and wanted to stage it as an anti-Fascist parody. In more whimsical moments, Fellini explains, "I decided to make the *Satyricon* because it was the only name that came to my mind when I signed the contract and had to fill in the name of the film."

Prologue

On November 9, 1968, after six months of intensive research and preparation, Federico Fellini began filming his eleventh film, the *Satyricon,* or "Fellinicon," as it came to be called. It was the director's first full-length film in four years, his first in costume, the most costly film he had ever made, and the first with foreign financial backing. Alberto Grimaldi, the film's Italian producer, had made a deal with United Artists whereby the American production company would provide a minimum guarantee to finance the film in return for world distribution rights exclusive of Italy.

Satyricon was shot in Rome, often described as "Hollywood on the Tiber," at Cinecittà, a nondescript complex of ochre-colored studios, offices, and workshops built on the outskirts of the city in 1936, during the heyday of Fascism. Not far away, ironically enough, is the old Appian Way where the crumbling ruins of ancient Roman mausoleums and aqueducts and the labyrinths of Christian catacombs still entice thousands of tourists. During the war, Cinecittà was bombed out and after the liberation of Rome served as a refugee camp. It was reactivated as a film center in 1947 and, by 1969, in its twelve studios—two of which are the largest in Europe—545 films had been shot, including such colossal depictions of ancient Rome as *Quo Vadis, Ben Hur,* and *Cleopatra.* The fact that they were all filmed in the same studio is the only similarity between Fellini's vision of ancient Rome and the previous portrayals of that dead civilization, distorted and romanticized by the enshrouding layers of two thousand years.

The *Fellini Satyricon,* to give its full title necessitated by copyright conflicts, is inspired by, rather than based upon, the *Satyricon* of Gaius Petronius, a courtier in the entourage of Nero whose refined tastes and pleasure-loving habits earned him the title of "Arbiter of Elegance." In A.D. 66, Petronius, through a plot devised by a jealous rival, incurred Nero's wrath and ended his life before the emperor could do it for him. With his customary savoir faire, the courtier calmly opened his veins, rebinding them to chat with friends, reward or punish his slaves, eat a good dinner, and write out a detailed description of the debauched emperor's novel sexual propensities, before finally perishing as elegantly as he had lived.

But Petronius was more than an imaginative pacesetter of erotic pleasures and stylish pastimes. The Roman patrician was also a gifted and perceptive satirist of the mores and morals of his time, which he wittily and acerbically chronicled in perhaps as many as twenty volumes of satires. Unfortunately only three of them have survived, and those only in fragmentary form. Nevertheless, what remains of the *Satyricon* is a vivid, explicitly bawdy, and often very entertaining account of the life and licentiousness of Neronian times, centered around the picaresque adventures and escapades of three surprisingly modern hippie-like characters "doing their thing" in pre-Christian Rome.

Encolpius and Ascyltus, whom Fellini describes as "two break-

neck kids with completely unhinged lives and pan-erotic dreams,"
are friends and rivals for the affection and favors of Giton, a beautiful young boy, whose name means "neighbor" in Greek. As in
Petronius' *Satyricon,* the youths encounter many characters as un-
inhibited and unscrupulous as they are: Eumolpus, a jaded old poet
who begins as a freeloader, becomes rich, and dies stipulating that,
to claim their legacies, his heirs must first eat his body; Lichas, a
sadistic shipowner who scours the world for monsters and beauties
to titillate the emperor's inexhaustable appetite; Tryphaena, Lichas'
lascivious companion in orgiastic pleasures; Trimalchio, a rich and
vulgar ex-slave with a fondness for young boys; Fortunata, his
greedy and voluptuous wife; Habinnas, Trimalchio's tomb-builder,
and *his* wife, Scintilla, Fortunata's lesbian lover.

Petronius is the departure point. "The film we have created from
it," the director has said, "is a panorama, a vast canvas with fantastic tone, a sharp and allegoric fresco of our present-day world."
The vast canvas Fellini has created sometimes adheres very closely
to episodes and characters described in Petronius, as in the famous
"Dinner of Trimalchio." More often, it includes episodes considerably altered from the original, like "The Ship of Lichas" where
Fellini has Encolpius marry the cruel shipowner. Several episodes,
such as "The Villa of the Suicides," "The Labyrinth," "The Garden
of Delights," and "The Death of the Emperor," have been completely invented by Fellini and his co-scriptwriter, Bernardino Zapponi, who shares the director's penchant for the grotesque. Some of
the weirdest characters also are completely new creations: the hermaphrodite, the nymphomaniac whose sexual torment must be as-
suaged every hour, and the beautiful sorceress who is forced to restore the fire her rejected lover takes from the villagers in a manner
resembling childbirth. So much of the original work has been
transformed or deleted that, as the director admits, "It is eighty
percent Fellini and twenty percent Petronius."

And the world that Encolpius and Ascyltus career through is a dark, hallucinatory world where the audience, as the director intended, "has the sensation of being surrounded by mysterious masks, ghosts, and shadows, the like of which they have never seen before." In a daring and masterful tour de force, the director has violated every cinematographic rule by producing a film with no pace, no psychology, no stars, and no story. The film begins and ends with a wall enclosing nine separate episodes, two of them containing bizarre tales-within-tales. It is a gigantic series of frescoes depicting depravity, decadence, impotence, and death, peopled with spectral faces disinterred from time and living in a murky void, waiting to return to the graves from which they have been summoned by the wizardry of Fellini.

Before he began the film, Fellini, with his circus barker's flair for gulling the public and press, announced, "The roles in *Satyricon* will be played by big names, people who represent myths today to identify with the myths of the Roman era," and unabashedly ticked off such names as the Beatles and their former guru, the Maharishi, Richard Burton and Elizabeth Taylor, Marlon Brando, Peter O'Toole, Mae West, Brigitte Bardot, Danny Kaye, Groucho Marx, Pierre Clementi, Terence Stamp, Lucia Bosé, Capucine, Alain Cuny, Salvo Randone, Anna Magnani, Lee Marvin, Mina (the Italian pop singer), Magali Noël, Lyndon B. Johnson, and Charles de Gaulle.

In the end, only Lucia Bosé, Capucine, Alain Cuny, Magali Noël, and Salvo Randone made it to the screen. Terence Stamp and Pierre Clementi, whom the director originally wanted in the roles of Encolpius and Ascyltus "because they are two heads that don't seem used to thoughts like ours," joined the roster of those innumerable myths who did not appear in *Satyricon,* and the stars of the film were three unknowns. Martin Potter, a twenty-four-year-old English actor, is Encolpius; Ascyltus is played by Hiram Keller, a twenty-four-year-old American actor from the cast of *Hair*; and

Giton is seventeen-year-old Max Born, a hippie from the streets of London's Chelsea district.

For the remainder of the fifteen-hundred-member, multiracial, multilingual cast, Fellini and his agents scrutinized the faces of about three thousand people in Italy and London, choosing paupers and millionaires, beggars and butchers, freaks and cripples, the beautiful and the ugly, the old and the young. For, as Fellini readily admits, "Faces are more important to me than anything else—more important than the set designs and the costumes, more important than the script itself, even more important than acting ability."

As crucial as his faces are, so are his collaborators, the "Fellinidi," as they are called. The cinema world is already a world apart. The cinema of Fellini is unique; and just as the director searches for strange faces, so he seeks out a certain type of collaborator, the best in Italy. He is the sun and they are the satellites orbiting around him, a very special breed fanatically devoted to *il Maestro,* who will give up more lucrative jobs just to work with him.

And so Fellini and his "Fellinidi" went into orbit to film what the director called a "documentary of a dream." Its cost, by Hollywood standards, was comparatively modest for the kind of film that it is. The regular troupe of approximately a hundred were paid $16,000 per week, excluding the director and production manager. Sixty studio workers placed at the disposition of the film supplemented the work of the steady crew, and additional technicians and specialists were called in as needed. Each day, between the work being done at Cinecittà and that done in outside laboratories, 270 people were occupied on *Satyricon,* and between $12,800 and $14,400 was spent on general costs. Set constructions for the film cost $560,000, and an equal sum went for technical expenses.

Satyricon cost four million dollars, a million less than programmed. It took twenty weeks of shooting, only two days over schedule, on 89 sets and used 262,480 feet of film of which 11,811 remained after cutting. In the first month of its showing in Italy, *Fellini Satyricon,* which runs two and a quarter hours long, earned almost a million and a half dollars.

To me, it was more like the documentary of a nightmare. From the day I first set foot on the set until the end of the picture, my dreams were filled with the faces of Fellini's masked monsters pulsating in front of my eyes as though permanently glued to my eyeballs. Strangely enough, though it was inspired by a pornographic book, Fellini's *Satyricon* is for me the most un-erotic erotic film ever made. It is also a visual masterpiece, a constant bombardment of the senses that is certain to arouse feelings from repugnance to rapture.

The Theater

November 12

I was walking along the Corso, one of Rome's main streets, in late October, 1968, and came across Fellini with his famous black fedora stuck on the back of his head. He was leaning up against a doorway. I hadn't seen him for about four years, but Fellini never forgets a face and greeted me warmly, "Ah, the American journalist! How are you?" When I told him I was interested in writing something on the *Satyricon,* he said, "You come out, Eileen, on the ninth of November when we start. I don't have any reporters on the set for the first three weeks because it is then that I really find myself in the film and see where it is going. But you come; and don't go to the press people. Come to me directly. You can come anytime you like and as often as you like."

A couple of brief token scenes were shot on the ninth but today is the beginning of the real shooting. As happens in all movies the filming does not follow the script but is shot out of sequence. Otherwise, it would take twice as much time and the cost would be doubled. The scene is the theater of Vernacchio, a bawdy, obscene actor who performs with his company of grotesquely masked actors on a rickety outdoor stage. Ascyltus has stolen the beautiful young boy, Giton, away from Encolpius. After a fierce battle in the Baths, Ascyltus confesses he has sold Giton to the actor, and Encolpius goes to the theater and demands the return of the boy. Vernacchio refuses, but is forced to relinquish him after an enigmatic magistrate in the audience threatens to burn down his theater.

Fellini is wearing dark grey trousers, a black sweater, and a mask covering his nose as protection against the smoke used to create a murky atmosphere. He is on the stage directing Fanfulla, a famous Italian variety-theater actor who plays Vernacchio. Fanfulla is horrendously dressed in a sort of loose blouse and a tattered animal skin with a long tail hanging between his bare legs which are covered to the calf by boots studded with long spikes. His wrists are adorned with spiked bracelets, and covering his head is a close-fitting cap with a flap extending down over his nose. A single horn sprouts upward from the top of the helmet like a phallic symbol. Vernacchio's speciality is a prodigious capacity for farting, along with other astonishing spectacles: catching and eating live flies, drinking fresh urine, and chopping off the hand of a hapless slave and replacing it with a golden one.

In the center of the theater, brilliant red coals glitter in an enormous brazier. The macabre audience of about twenty watches or ignores the spectacle. A blond, ashen-faced young man sits in a trancelike state in a little sedan chair, staring fixedly into space. No one can figure out if he is crazy, stupid, drugged or deaf. He sits for hours like a yoga and if he isn't ordered to go to lunch, he never moves. Next to him is a massive grey dog who begins barking. Fellini bellows, "Where's the owner of that dog? Put him behind those two women and make him keep the dog quiet." The dog continues to bark and Fellini yells from the stage, *"Madonna, quel cane!* Madonna, that dog! Take it outside."

The director turns again and shows Vernacchio how he must display Giton, who is made up as Cupid and has descended from a stylized cloudlike structure in the middle of the stage, to the audience. A buzz of conversation begins and Fellini screeches, *"State zitti! Che casino!* Shut up! What a whorehouse!" A prop man continues impassively strewing the bottom of the stage with spider webs from a special machine.

They run through the scene again. Encolpius enters the theater and vigorously demands the return of Giton. Vernacchio runs his hands lasciviously over the boy, saying, "He is beautiful and well-fleshed and I paid thirty-five *denari* for him." The director makes Fanfulla repeat the action over and over, then turns to Max Born and says, "You are a nice little prostitute. I mean in the film. Try to be a little elegant, Mox," as Fellini pronounces it.

"A theater like this never existed in Rome," Luigi Scaccianoce, the taciturn set architect, explains. "There were amphitheaters at Taormina and other places, but Fellini wanted to detach himself from these to make a traveling theater where rich and poor alike could participate. In the theater, he wanted a fire in a huge brazier to give the effect of light on the faces of the audience. The fire had to palpitate. We resolved this problem with plastic resin and alum, materials which are not ordinarily used for these things. Lights were placed underneath and give the effect of a fire all around. It seems like the real thing and has a sense of authenticity which one feels throughout the entire film, but it is made-up art. These actors perform on the rim of a mountain of granite by the light of the stars and the moon. The moon has to be artificially created to justify the effect of the lights."

The moon was created by Joseph Natanson, a special optical-effects expert, who made many of the skies for the film. "The moon for the theater scene," he sighs, "was hell. Fellini took a piece of paper and made a drawing. I made the moon entirely with lights. There is nothing painted. In the middle of the clouds, there are lights and the moon."

It is time for the lunch break, and Fellini clambers down heavily from the stage. His six-foot-two-inch frame, as skinny as a toothpick in his youth, has now filled out to a hefty 198 pounds. His face has become jowly and his lionlike mane of hair, once thick and black, is now thinning and beginning to grey, but his big, almost black, eyes are still as glittering and penetrating as ever.

"How do you like my audience?" he asks, gleefully surveying the monsters. "I have taken people from the slaughterhouse and from the insane asylum. They are more wise and obedient than normal people. I, too, was taken from there," he says with a sly smile.

"Who takes care of them?" I ask.

"Oh, they come with their nurses," he replies nonchalantly, as though mental patients worked every day in the movies.

We went upstairs to his comfortable but modest two-room suite near the production offices for lunch. Fellini likes simple things. In between bites of prosciutto and cold veal, cheese, salad, fruit, and sips of wine, the director talked about the *Satyricon*.

"What about all the big names?" was the first thing I wanted to know.

"Yes," he admitted, "first I thought of casting the picture with big names but it didn't work out. The actors wanted too much money or they were not free or they placed unacceptable conditions. I prefer to make the film with completely unknown actors. It was a choice of big actors who are modern myths, actually incarnations of old myths, or unknown actors. There is no big difference except that it costs much less."

Musing about Mae West, who was to have played the part of the emperor's mother, a role that never materialized even in the script, he confided, "I liked her when I was very young. She is a myth of sex inserted in a fabulous pastiche. I talked with her in Hollywood but she was busy with television. Sometimes, I say names to myself to make a picture like life—so many things that happened, that never happened, the lies you tell to others. At a certain moment, I thought she was good. Before the picture, it is always chaotic and I want that. Life is chaotic. It's a vital dimension. Things in an orderly manner are in a cold dimension, like offices."

Then he rambled on about the film. "For a long time, I've wanted to make a film on paganism. The first time I ever saw a picture, it was one of those Roman epics, *Ursus* or *Tiberius*. The first time I was at Cinecittà, I saw a Roman film being made and there were gladiators running over to the bar.

"This is a science-fiction picture projected into the past instead of the future. I want to make a film in which the audience can never feel familiar or at home. I have a crazy perception of this picture. If we should, by some magical circumstance, find ourselves back two thousand years in a Roman house, we would scare them. Maybe love was the same but the terror that pre-Christians would feel would be foreign to us. This is a journey into the unknown, where the people are unknown, their dreams, their sicknesses, their psychologies, their nervous tensions.

"They were much more open and free," Fellini insisted. "There was no moral judgment. To be a homosexual was just part of sex. All our information comes to us from the Catholic Church. The Latin texts were changed by the monks or censored, burned, condemned, or distorted. I did a lot of research but always with a great fear of being confused. I must make this film with intuition. I don't want to be tagged or categorized. This film can arrive at the right point if the fantasy is absurd, drunken; otherwise it will fall on its face every five feet. The dangers are infinite. One goes in the dark. Who knows what the Romans were like?

"What we know about Rome, we know from statues. The people

have died and come to us from minerals, from the earth, from excavations. There is a stone dimension to them. That is why makeup is the most important thing in this film. I need faces to be portraits, not just made-up faces. They have to be expressionistic. There are portraits in the faces I have chosen to express that mineral condition.

"As for the script, I am having to do a work of fantasy so it must be precise, mathematical," he said. "It can't be improvised. For *La Dolce Vita,* the scenes of the nobles and the miracle were never written because I already knew what they were like. This can't be done with the *Satyricon* because I wasn't there two thousand years ago. It has to be faithful to the images as they are born. It doesn't resemble any film I have ever made. Ah, but to talk about a film before making it is absurd."

"Would you ever make a film in a foreign country?"

"Oh, if I were less lazy and younger, I would make a picture in New York," the director replied. "It's like a living stage. Antonioni is making a picture in America but he has a particular eye. He is always outside a situation, detached. I have to be confused and involved. If not, I don't understand a damned thing. One needs to be open to make a film. At a certain stage, one is less open, more tired and less able to adapt. You need certain kinds of things. Perhaps when I am more empty-headed and need to have it filled, more desperate, I will go to a foreign country.

"Antonioni is a documentary director. He has the eye of a photographer. His talent is in the eye, not in the blood, and so it is easier for him to make a picture in a foreign country. The allure of his pictures is very exterior and very elegant. They have a strange result, like *Vogue*: sophisticated, but cold. Even if he made a Martian film, it would be a cold, detached film. He has everything to gain in making a film abroad." With that, the director donned his overcoat and black fedora and hurried off to the set, but urged me to stay and talk with one of his guests, Professor Luca Canali.

A teacher of Latin and Latin Literature at the University of Pisa, Professor Canali is a pleasant, impeccably dressed young man, a noted scholar and poet with no previous experience in the cinema world. "Fellini needed a person who was technically capable but not too rigidly academic, so I was hired as a consultant for all material dealing with the linguistic and historical aspects of the film in Latin and Greek. Have you been in the theater? Fellini dedicates much attention to the audience," the professor said. "It is a strange audience. They speak among themselves and you hear fragments of the conversations which I invented. They speak of the furs one woman is wearing, of the urinal disturbances of some man, in a purely invented Latin.

"Scholars of the language disagree as to how the Romans spoke but there is almost total agreement that the pronunciation of the Latin was different from ours. It underwent modifications with time but certainly in archaic times, *Caesar* was pronounced like *Kaiser* in German, *scienza* like *skientia,* for example. The change in pronunciation came about in post-Neronian times. In the *Satyricon,* we tend to use a pronunciation nearer to that of the harsh archaic language, which is arbitrary since already by the time of Nero, the Romans had begun to speak like us. But Fellini wanted to give a far-off quality to the language.

"Only about a half of the script is based on Petronius," the professor continued. "The other half is invented by Fellini; but even the parts not in Petronius are very beautiful and could have been written by him, always with this same sense of un-communication. Because what was there in the ancient world? Archaeology, History, Languages, Literature—all those things which we subdivide as specialists were all fused together. Consequently, we know a great deal about the ancient world but nothing about ancient man.

"Fellini is trying to unify the Roman man in his own world with all the elements which made up the world as it was lived by him. This will be the importance of Fellini—the synthesis of this man and his world. Only an artist can do it, but even an artist feels the mystery of that ancient world. Petronius was one of the greatest of the Roman writers and it is only a great modern artist who can bring to life again the experiences of a great artist of the ancient world but as though it were on another planet. Fellini has also seized on one of the essential aspects of the *Satyricon*—the presentiment of collapse, of the end of a civilization which is breaking up from the spiritual point of view."

Back on the set, I took a good look at the audience and Vernacchio's troupe. Fellini had brought part of the *Commedia dell'Arte* company from Naples including a very famous eighty-eight-year-old actor who is deaf and had just married his third wife the year before. Fellini kept quizzing him, "When did you last make love?" and the old actor quavered, "The last time was last week. You know how it is. I can't abuse myself." Because of his deafness, he never heard Fellini's directions and continued to shake the primitive musical instrument he had been given until the director finally screeched, "Shoot him! Stop him!"

Fellini found the dwarf, another of the actors in Vernacchio's company, watching cars for tips in Naples. Another old man is supposed to walk across the stage playing a long trombonelike instrument. As he passes, Vernacchio grabs it and pretends to stick it up the man's backside. Up to now, the old man had spoken in incomprehensible Neapolitan but, astonished by this completely unexpected bit of business, he leered in perfect Italian, "Ah, the mysteries of Paris, eh, Maestro?"

Chatting with Eugene Walter, the American dialogue coach, I said, "I've never seen such a bunch of freaks and monsters."

"Fellini," he explained, "wants to show that the neurosis of the modern world existed in the ancient world, that human nature and neurosis is universal and eternal. But he also wants to express individuality. Notice how in the audience, he makes each person terribly individual. Some turn their backs, some talk, some stare, some laugh. All the freaks come from Naples. I don't know why."

This was a very crucial moment in the film. Fellini had explained at lunch, "Makeup is the most important thing in this film." But neither Danilo Donati, the set and costume designer, nor Rino Carboni, the head makeup man, understood what Fellini had in mind. Extras would bounce like rubber balls from the set back to the makeup department because their faces were not "the portraits" Fellini wanted in his film. The solution came with the return of Piero Tosi, who had created the makeup during the fifteen-day preparation period before the shooting began, and then had left. Tosi, whom Fellini calls "Pierino, the only one of his kind," said, "Fellini created a crisis in the makeup just to get me back. With him, it's always work, work, work! I can only produce four hours and then I'm in a trance. He is incredible. He's quite capable of asking Picasso to come and make wooden clogs!"

Fanfulla, the fifty-six-year-old variety performer whose real name is Luigi Visconti, told how he got the part of Vernacchio. "I've known Fellini about fifteen years. He called me up and said, '*C'ho una bella cosetta per te,* I have a beautiful little thing for you.' Nothing more. I went out to Cinecittà for tests and they made me up but it was a completely different makeup from the one I finally appear in. He wanted a special makeup and Tosi and Donati spent ten days working on it. Fellini didn't like the eyebrows and they painted my body brick color and finally made me *quel personaggio,* that character.

"Fellini followed everything from the shoes to the eyebrows, and kept saying to me, 'You have to get fat. *Per l'amor di Dio!* for God's sake, don't lose a pound or you will ruin me.' He also told me, 'You are Vernacchio who has his company in the theater of the Subura. You are bad, wicked, perverse, and a pederast.'

"I was supposed to do a hundred farts and I had this tail that went up every time I farted or made a declaration of love. Fellini made all the farting sounds. He had great fun!

"He wanted me to say my lines in a kind of German Latin but I refused. 'Don't you know Latin?' he asked me, and I said, 'No, and I don't intend to spend a month learning the lines from the script in Latin.'

"The only thing I minded was that I had to act without a mask. I almost got poisoned. Imagine working for ten days in that smoke!"

That was my introduction to *Satyricon*, and I went from day to day like Fellini said he was going, "in the dark." I didn't have a script. They were carefully guarded because another director was making a quickie version of Petronius' *Satyricon* starring none other than Fellini's old bête noire from *Mastorna*, Ugo Tognazzi. A suit was pending and the court was deciding which director had the right to use the title *Satyricon*. The production people were afraid some of Fellini's ideas from the five-hundred-page script might be swiped and find their way into the other *Satyricon*. But maybe it was more fun that way. Every day brought a new surprise, or, more often, shock.

Interim

November 19–December 12

I have not been able to visit the set for over a month. Meanwhile several episodes have been completed or nearly completed except for bits and pieces.

Encolpius has given his lament in front of a wall covered with graffiti in the Subura, the slums of ancient Rome, the opening of the film. Giton has gone off with Ascyltus and Encolpius agonizes over the loss of his beloved and the perfidy of his friend.

Antonio Scordia, an abstract painter who did many of the paintings in the film, described how the wall was made. "One morning, I received a call and Fellini said to me, *'Caro Nino,* dear Nino, you must help me. I need a big wall full of writings and slogans, signatures and graffiti and nobody understands what I want. Please come here and do it for me.' I invented everything. When Fellini asked me to paint the wall, I painted it as a place where every Roman had left a sign of his passage. Fellini says the graffiti are dirty words like 'fuck' and things like that. I did the work of a thousand passers-by through the course of a hundred years all in one day!"

The scene of the boys dividing their goods, and the collapse of the Insula Felicles, a huge tenement in the Subura, has been completed except that, on the very last day of the shooting, a model of the building must be made to fall. This episode is in Petronius but has been somewhat transformed. The Insula Felicles existed in ancient Rome and because of its immense size was one of the most popular tourist attractions of that era. After Encolpius has rescued Giton from the lewd clutches of Vernacchio, the two return to their shabby room in the Insula where they make love with childlike abandon. While they sleep, Ascyltus returns and mockingly derides the two lovers. Encolpius decides they must divide their possessions. Ascyltus agrees and, at the end, insists they also divide Giton. Encolpius, confident of his paramour's fidelity, is stunned when Giton, choosing between the two, utters the only two words he says in the entire film, "With you," and points to Ascyltus. After they leave, the shattered Encolpius prepares to kill himself, but plaster crumbling from the walls warns of the imminent collapse of the building and he flees.

The Insula didn't fall the first time because the building had been prepared long before the actual filming and the plaster had all dried up. During the night, the Cinecittà workers re-did it, and today it goes exceptionally well and is very striking. It is done with stunt men, the best in Cinecittà. One has to hang on to the crumbling wall while dangling a nine-year-old child by the hand. Even though the bricks are made of light polystyrene and tiles of sugar and cork, still, several stunt men get hit on the head and come away bloody and scratched. The four horses in the pool in the courtyard go wild and run away. This occurs spontaneously and Fellini shoots the scene as it happens.

If it goes wrong the first time, the entire set will have been ruined. The workmen follow the shooting with intense anxiety and when it goes off well, they all run to the bar to celebrate. The scene is almost perfect. Only a small piece has to be reconstructed during the night to be reshot the next day.

Fellini has also finished a brief scene of the dwarf with the permanent erection from whom Encolpius seeks advice on how to regain his virility after he has become impotent, or, as it is delicately put, "lost his sword." The dwarf advises him to seek the aid of Oenothea, the sorceress, and recounts her story. (The tale of Oenothea is still in the film, but unfortunately the dwarf has disappeared in the cutting, thereby ruining one of the best cracks I heard about the *Satyricon*: "Where else but in a Fellini film could you find a hermaphrodite and a dwarf with a permanent erection?")

The young Oenothea, played by the American model Donyale Luna, attracts the amorous attentions of an ugly old wizard, actually a fish peddler from Naples. She invites him to her house, but keeps him suspended in a basket all night long. For revenge, the wizard takes the fire away from the villagers, and when they come to plead for its restoration, he tells them the fire is under Oenothea's skirts; and she is forced to give birth to the fire as she would to a child.

As Oenothea lies wracked with pain, the villagers arrive, each with a faggot, and extract the fire from between her long stork-like legs. Possibly the tall, skinny model reminded Fellini of the story children are told about babies being brought by the stork, and he is playing a sly joke. In any case, the episode is not in Petronius but taken from bits and pieces of medieval legends.

A unique device was created to make it appear as though the fire was really being extracted from Oenothea's body. Each of the faggots had to flame up in four seconds. A mixture of alcohol and benzine was used to make the flames. A battery inside the handle of the pole heated up a resistor at the end so that after two seconds, the torch turned red, and in another two seconds, burst into tongues of fire.

The ugly wizard almost went up in flames himself when the ashes from the cigarette he was smoking fell on his flimsy costume. Then, when he was hung in a basket for three hours, he became absolutely furious because he couldn't smoke, and kept screaming, "Let me down!"

The director had a great deal of difficulty with Donyale Luna who daily threatened to quit because she wasn't treated properly. She would arrive every day at the studio in an ancient car escorted by two wildly dressed hippie friends who were not permitted to enter by the gateman. And Fellini almost fainted when he saw her for the first time without make-up and the blue contact lenses she wears. "She looks like a mouse come out of a hole," he shuddered.

Encolpius is not cured by the young Oenothea but by the old Oenothea. However, as he sits in a drugged stupor waiting for the sorceress to appear, he sees, flickering through the flames of a fire in front of him, the beautiful, smiling face of the young Oenothea —which abruptly changes to the head of a skeleton, then back to the face of the beautiful witch. Fellini put Luna so close to the fire that her costume had to be dampened so as not to burn up.

As she fondled a beat-up white teddy bear named Enzo whom she considers a magic genie, Donyale explained, "I didn't know if I was burning up when I was sitting by the fire. I was being, not watching. There was everything, not just the fire, but the stars, everything. I don't know if Fellini thought of me as a stork. He wanted me to play myself, a stork, a grasshopper, a bird. Fellini doesn't play jokes. He is very serious. He only told me to be myself, to be free and not to have any actressy hang-ups.

"Fellini is incredibly wise," she continued in her almost inaudible voice. "He knows what you are and does not tell you to be something else. His main thing is purity. Whatever you are, he wants the pure you. He does a lot of purifying of people when he's directing and he wants you to forget all that bullshit you've learned in acting school or from your parents and to forget what you want to be and just be. Fellini used all of me. He's beautiful and I trust beauty. He's a genius and he flies very high and I love him. I could not love him without understanding him. I am sure I have met him in another lifetime. Where? In ancient Rome."

The old Oenothea is played by Maria Antonietta Belizi, a boutique owner from Bologna who is an old friend of Fellini's. The director had her completely painted black and her naked body marked with strange designs and made her wear an outlandish headdress. Her body is plump and her breasts sag and she is thoroughly repugnant looking, but not at all dismayed by either her nudity or her role. For me, it is a gross scene, but Danilo Donati objects, "It was a very difficult scene for the director but a very chaste scene. Fellini is never vulgar or pornographic. If you think of the old Oenothea as Mother Earth, a return to our origins, it is not obscene."

Martin Potter, the young English actor who plays Encolpius, confessed, "One of the most difficult scenes I had to do was at Oenothea's house when I must go to the Mother Earth figure. I was sitting against a wall and Fellini wanted something extraordinary as though I were numbed or under a magic spell. I knew he wanted my eyes heavy, like being drunk, but more refined. I saw a marabou walking in front of me and then I looked through the window and saw Ascyltus being killed. I had to act as though I didn't understand but at the same time as though I did understand. I was happy, smiling, my eyes closed, then open, then focused on Mother Earth, a black woman like out of a dream. I recognized my mother, went to her and mated with her saying, 'Oh, Mama, what a disgrace! I am impotent.'

"I understood what Fellini wanted but it was an extremely demanding scene because it included so many things under so many different mental states. I would have liked to do it again but Fellini refused."

One episode has been shot and reshot, the scene of the nympho-maniac who has been put under a curse so that her sexual tension must be relieved hourly. The role is played by Sibilla Sedat wearing a plastic nose fashioned by Rino Carboni, the head makeup man, to achieve the aquiline effect Fellini wanted.

The scene was first played on Sound Stage Fifteen, the largest of the Cinecittà studios, but the director was not happy with it. Origi-nally, the background was dotted with the trunks of thin white birch trees, but once he saw the set, Fellini realized it was too ordi-nary, like knowing a familiar country. He transferred the scene to a desert background where there was nothing to remind anyone of anything, and added a wind effect to create a more mystical, magi-cal climate.

This is the kind of expense that drives Fellini's producers out of their minds; but Joseph Natanson, the sky man, finds it completely understandable. "He has the great courage to try things, completely disregarding other people's work and efforts and the cost. If he has not yet decided how he will do a scene, he will make a big set and shoot for two days to be absolutely certain it was the wrong thing. Then he will start again. It's expensive but it's very good because then he knows he has taken the wrong road."

A mysterious cart pulled by a black horse is stopped in the wind-swept desert. The nymphomaniac's husband sits in despair. Ex-hausted, he can no longer satisfy his wife's sexual needs. Ascyltus, who has been invited to alleviate the wretched woman's misery, climbs up and sees the tormented woman tied hand and foot to the side of the cart. The husband abjectly unties the woman's fetters.

A journalist said to Fellini, "It seems to me you are shooting this scene with a sense of compassion, of distress."

"It's not true," the director replied. "The husband is distressed.

We look only with detachment at the affairs of these human beings who lived two thousand years ago and don't mean a damned thing to us."

Fellini coaxes one of the three Russian ladies who frequently appear in his films, "Nadia, it's your turn. Recite that prayer in Russian that you know. *Brava!* A little louder. Look here. Let us learn a little Russian too."

Then he turns to Sibilla, the nymphomaniac, lying on her back in a white pleated robe, damp and sweaty from her agony. "Sibilla, open your hand. Close it. Again slowly, like a vampire. Turn yourself from side to side. Make everything tremble. Again, agitated. Tremble. Arch your back as much as you can. Raise your head. Open your eyes wide." She sees Ascyltus with a sardonic leer on his face.

Ascyltus, played by Hiram Keller, is dressed in a short pleated tunic and a leather breastplate. He throws himself on top of the nymphomaniac. "Sibi, does he weigh too much?" the director asks, anxiously. *"Forza, Iram!* Go on, Iram, Iram!"—dropping the *H*, which is difficult for Italians to pronounce. "Sibilla, get excited. Turn your head and say, *Che vergogna,* what a disgrace!"

To one of the servants following the cart, a North African, Fellini says, "Describe at the top of your voice a dream you had." To a Senegalese girl, "Sing a song from your country. It should be a desert lament." She sings "Frère Jacques." Each is given an identity. There are no extras in Fellini's films.

The Villa of the Suicides

December 17

This is probably the most beautiful and harmonious episode in the entire film, even though it ends in death like so many of the others. The Emperor had been brutally murdered by rebellious soldiers, and the patrician owner of the villa, knowing he is in disfavor with the new emperor now triumphantly marching to Rome, prefers to kill himself rather than be executed. It is perhaps Fellini's tribute to Petronius, who also chose to kill himself rather than face death at Nero's hands. The nobleman frees his slaves and sends them off with his children to safety. At twilight, in a ritualistic ceremony, he opens the veins of his wrists while his wife tenderly watches. Afterwards, she slits her throat rather than be parted from him in death.

Fellini is setting up the suicide scene in the garden in front of the lovely country villa, which has a coat of arms suspended on each side, one for his family, one for hers. The sand in front of the house is pinkish, as is the crumbling wall on the left, opposite the villa. A cascade of water flows down the wall and a crude sundial stands in front of it. To the right is a willow tree with no roots, only branches. A hedge of fluffy pampas grass hides the road leading to the villa.

There have obviously been changes made in this set from the original plan. Luigi Scaccianoce, the set architect, is a little disgruntled. "We began with an outline but that's not the way it was carried out. One follows Fellini and the script is born. Everything is born from improvisation. Just as with a painter, you can't be precise and tell him what colors to use; but these improvisations cause difficulties.

"The entire scene of the 'Suicides' has an air of total purity and sweetness. It passes from sunset to night because we had to create an atmosphere which indicated that this was the fatal moment of this family, predetermined and serene. Everything had to correspond to a certain state of mind at peace—the colors and the plants. The sky is pink. The rocks are pink and the sand is pink—made of three-fifths tennis sand and two-fifths pulverized Carrara marble dust."

Fellini is sitting on the camera boom like a big black bear. His face is stubbled and he whistles softly to himself, probably a tune of Nino Rota's, the composer who writes the music for all his films. He is waiting for the lights to be adjusted. It's at these times, or when the scene is dull or repetitious or unimportant, that I scurry around the set talking with people and trying not to incur the director's wrath, which is always unpredictable. He has a thousand faces and a thousand moods and it is impossible to anticipate which one you may have to cope with at any given moment.

The wife is being played by Lucia Bosé, an Italian actress who gave up a spiraling movie career thirteen years ago to marry Dominguin, the Spanish bullfighter. She has now resumed acting after separating from her husband. Fellini chose her for the part because "I first thought of Lucia after seeing her photographs in the newspaper. It was the face of one who has suffered, impregnated with a peasant aristocracy. It seemed to me that she had so much of the rural and noble at the same time, of spiritual vigor, and of the remote and mysterious."

La Bosé said, "He didn't explain anything to me until I got on the set and then he told me, 'It is a gradual encounter with death, a gradual detachment from life, a walk toward the finishing line stripped of any spectral solemnity, completed with the air of a great beginning.'"

"*Allora*, Peppino," Fellini announces to Giuseppe Rotunno, the lighting cameraman, or director of photography in American terms. Rotunno is always called Peppino but Fellini, with his penchant for shortening or lengthening names, sometimes calls him Pepe or Pepos, depending upon his mood. "*Silenzio*," he bellows, glaring around. "*Pronti*, ready." Lucia emerges from the villa. The director settles his hat on his balding pate, peers through the camera, then goes and spreads out his arms, showing her how she must walk, on tiptoe, repeating it over and over again until he gets exactly the walk he wants. "*L'ultima*, Norma," he calls to Norma Giacchero, the script girl, "the last one." But it never is, and it is a refrain we will hear a thousand times.

Fellini sets up a new scene. The suicide, played by the American actor Joseph Wheeler, is sitting on the bench and Fellini is murmuring "very nice," which comes out "very nize." "*Pronti e fermi*," he yells, "Ready and still." Then he turns and shouts at Wheeler, "Turn your head to the left, then to the wall. Stay still. Lower your head and stick your hand out." He must slit his wrists with one of ten different daggers, each prepared with a little syringe inside which, when pushed, makes the fake blood spurt out so it seems like the real thing.

While he continued with this scene over and over, I chatted in subdued tones with Hiram Keller, who has come on the set to watch. The tall, brown-haired, green-eyed young actor, with his sardonic face, is the perfect character for the sneering, cynical Ascyltus.

"My father is a judge in the State Supreme Court of Georgia and he wanted me to be a lawyer," Hiram said. "I studied law at the University of Georgia but logic bores the hell out of me, and when I told my father I wanted to be an actor, he answered, 'You should be what you want in life but I won't help you.' I took off for New York, worked at part-time jobs, studied with Stella Adler and Lee Strasberg and got a part in *Hair* where I played everything but the two leads."

A friend of Keller's from NBC who was working on Fellini's television Special (a one-hour program the director made showing the preparations for *The Voyage of G. Mastorna* and *Satyricon*) was going to Rome, and the young actor asked him to take his photograph to show Fellini. Shortly after, his agent received a wire asking Keller to come to Rome. "I didn't even have to do a test for Fellini," Hiram marveled. "He's the kind of man who, with a look, can size you up with such accuracy. He just stared at me for twenty minutes and signed the contract.

"At the beginning," he continued, "Fellini said I had nothing to worry about, and told me, 'You are evil and vulgar and cynical and you lay everything in sight.' It's indescribable, like a dream come true. It's a bit like working in *Hair*. Fellini gives you everything you need to work with. He knows what he wants. You just know the position and the time. The rest he tells you at the moment you do it."

Thoughtfully, he sighed. "Playing for Tom O'Horgan in *Hair* and here with Fellini, I figure I'm going to have to pay my dues some place."

December 18

Joseph Wheeler, the noble suicide in the villa, first came to
Rome in 1965 with Langston Hughes' *Trumpets of the Lord*
and has been busy in films here and in Denmark ever since. "In a
way, it's a mystery to me how I got the part," he confessed. "I met
Fellini four years ago when he was planning to make *The Voyage
of G. Mastorna* and he wanted to use me but he never made the
film. I had a small part in *Toby Dammit,* and I played one of the
nobles in the theater scene. He saw me in the rushes, liked my face
and character, and gave me this part. I don't question destiny. He's
the funniest man in the world but he's also a genius. There's nobody really like him. To the unpracticed eye, it all looks like a
bunch of mishmash until it gets on the screen, and then one sees
where the genius lies."

Fellini stops to chat and confides that when he went to New York
for *8½,* a hat manufacturer asked if he could make a model of his
black fedora and sell it as the "*8½* Hat." This seems to tickle him,
and he slaps the hat on the back of his head.

Eugene Walter, the American dialogue coach, is telling me, "The
source of much of Fellini's inspiration comes from Robert Graves's
Hadrian's Memoirs and Jerome Carcopino's *Daily Life in Ancient
Rome.* There's a million things he found in those two books." Fellini, ever the busybody, saunters over and adds, "and *La Mia
Rimini,* written by me. Of course it costs twenty-four dollars but
you ought to get it if you want to understand this film."

Eugene continues, "After his modern films came the intermission,
the film he didn't make, *The Voyage of G. Mastorna.* This is Act
Two of his career. But the world behind the camera is more important than what happens before the camera. What happens off
screen is why Fellini's films are Fellini's films."

Since there seems to be an interminable delay in setting up the scene, I decide to scurry around and see what is happening behind the camera. First I stop by the casting office to see what Lya Consalvo, the casting director, is doing. Blonde and harried looking, she is surrounded by strange types with even stranger stories to tell, but philosophical about it all since she has already worked with Fellini on *Juliet of the Spirits* and is quite accustomed to chaos.

"For five months before he began the picture," she explains, "Fellini saw everyone who came into the office. A week before word of his production gets published the news goes round by word-of-mouth, and all the extras, the beats, everybody comes. He keeps photographs of everybody. He has all the photographs from the first movie he ever made, divided in envelopes, and on the back of each photograph, he writes what he thinks about them, the way he sees that face and how he can use it."

The envelopes are bulging. Some of them are labeled "Filthy Ugly Mugs" or "Beautiful Old Maids." On the backs of some of the photographs are Fellini's scribblings: "He is rather vile," "A crazy criminal," or "That one has the eyes of a snake," or "A type who would slit children's throats"; "Too sly," "Too modern," "Sensual," "He looks like a bubble of air," "The eyes of an assassin," or "He seems like a chicken."

"All is possible with Fellini," Lya sighs. "We don't know until the night before what scene is to be shot tomorrow. Before he goes away, he says 'Call this actor,' or 'I want this or that one.' Many of them have worked in other Fellini films. When I tried to reach some, they had died or married or changed their jobs or moved away. But whatever he asks, I find it normal. He could ask for the Pope and it wouldn't surprise me."

Wondering which role Fellini would have given the Pope, I drive down to see what that little wizard, Danilo Donati, is concocting.

His one assistant and five helpers are housed way off in a corner of Cinecittà in some dilapidated old sets left over from a long-forgotten western. One shabby frontier building has a sign over the door saying "Saloon." The one next to it is "Forrester's Meat Market." Donati hangs out in the saloon and I find him there hustling around, with a cigarette in a long holder dangling from his lips and a scarf thrown around his neck, his eyes red-rimmed from lack of sleep. A short, pudgy man with the expression of a badgered dog, he is surrounded by the clutter of props of past scenes, scenes in progress, and scenes to be shot: dolls with wooden heads and raggedy hair for the children of the suicides, a Roman chair for the villa, busts of the ancestors of the suicides copied from statues in Roman museums, a sacrificial altar to be used in the villa, copied from an ancient model but reworked so it is not precisely authentic. At the moment, Donati is busily designing the jewelry, inspired by Roman artifacts, which the rich guests will wear at Trimalchio's dinner.

"All directors are different," he sighs. "There are different roads they travel with different intentions. Fellini is very precise in every detail. We have the epoch but according to the way he wants to make it. He didn't want things copied. That would not have served his fantasy. He has his way of seeing the ancient world, a very personal approach, which gives it the Fellini authenticity.

"Have you seen 'The Villa of the Suicides'?" Donati asks in his rapid Italian. "This is a rather happy scene but a little funereal— the villa with the lead door, the peacocks, a symbol of the cemetery in Italy. The lack of people in the scene and the big open space are intended to give the effect of silence in space. The plants are those that grow in a swamp because the villa is near the sea. There is a sense of sadness, a lack of time, not sorrow, of people who are going to another country. It is a little bit like the famous cemetery in Genoa, and one doesn't speak in a cemetery. The water serves to make just a little noise and also gives a sense of time that continues. The clock symbolizes the passage of time. The tree has no roots but it doesn't have to be naturalistic. You only have to see the leaves.

"All the house is empty. The masks of the ancestors will accentuate the sense of death, which is not a death but a detaching from the world without our Christian fear of death. The colors are muted because Fellini doesn't want any disturbing colors and the light is the light of the sunset. It took ten days to make the set." He sighs again and hurries off to consult with one of his workers. Donati runs constantly throughout the filming.

On the way back to the set, I stop off at the painting workshop to see what the artists are up to. Paola Mugnai, a pretty young painter who rides around Cinecittà on a bicycle trailed by two mongrels, is surrounded by the paintings to be used on the wall next to the pool of the villa. "They were very difficult to do because Fellini wanted Pompeian paintings that weren't Pompeian. We had to make several tests and they had to be changed four or five times until finally he saw a piece he liked and that was it."

The paintings, inspired by frescoes at Pompeii and Herculaneum, were made using the ancient Greco-Roman encaustic technique—painting with pigments mixed with melted wax. The sketches for these paintings were made by Antonio Scordia and painted by two people in five weeks.

Back on the set, they are finally ready to shoot the scene of the children of the suicides being sent off to safety. The shooting has been delayed because the extra who was to play one of the women slaves has not shown up. Liliana Betti, Fellini's young assistant, was made up with long white robe and black wig to substitute. "It happens all the time," says Norma. "Liliana is always filling in for someone. Doesn't she look like an old Roman?"

The five children are loaded into the cart. The horse trainer has also had to be dressed as a slave to drive the horses and control them as they clatter off past the willow tree and behind the hedges while the children wave good-bye. Fellini makes them repeat it two or three times and, when the scene is over, kisses each of the children good-bye. He is always very sweet with children.

I remember there was a very similar willow tree in *Juliet of the Spirits*; here too is a willow tree. And the basket in which the ugly wizard was suspended outside Oenothea's house is not unlike the basket in which Juliet is hoisted up to Sandra Milo's tree house in the same film. Like every artist, Fellini has certain symbols which appeal to him and recur, consciously or unconsciously, in his works.

Professor Canali, looking strangely out of place on a movie set, arrives and talks with me while Fellini is preparing a new scene. He has suggested some brief passages in Latin and Greek to be recited by the suicides before they kill themselves and the director has selected several. I ask him why Fellini wanted this episode in the film.

"Of course, there is a realistic explanation for the suicide, the political change," he explains, "but there is another less realistic explanation. The film is a representation of the entire existence of man, one aspect of which is suicide because suicide exists, like love, like politics, even if it is a negation of life itself. It is one along with all the other aspects of life which Fellini presents. And the history of that period is the history of suicides. Even the emperors would send orders to have themselves killed. Seneca killed himself, too, as well as Petronius."

I laugh to myself because everybody has a different idea about "The Villa of the Suicides," but the funniest explanation I ever heard is probably the most accurate. Bernardino Zapponi told me when he and the director were writing the script together, "I said to Fellini, 'We must have a noble family with children playing in a reborn climate,' and he said gleefully, 'Yes, that is very beautiful; and then let's kill them all off.'"

Fellini starts another scene, with Encolpius and Ascyltus arriving at the villa where they find the dead bodies of the suicides sprawled on the rosy sand. It is nightfall and they are to come up the hidden road behind the pampas grass and stop, terrified by what they see. Encolpius is dressed in a short gold tunic and carrying a knapsack. Ascyltus is in grey and walking along with a stick. We don't know where they have been or why they have come to the villa.

Fellini is sighting through the camera and saying, "Martino, come. Move again. Again. Now go." The boys are walking behind the grass and can't be seen.

"Fix the grass," Fellini orders. "That part there." It has been broken a bit when one of the boys peers through to see what Fellini means.

"Go, Martino. Go, Keller. Stop." Fellini shows Martin how to walk. Then he shows Hiram. "Now, look there," he commands Hiram. "Look at him, now. Remember you are together. No, no. You have-to-start a step back. No," he screams, impatiently. "Wait, Martino."

Fellini leaves the camera and demonstrates again how Martin must walk. "No, you don't have to run, Martin. Don't do that, otherwise we lose your pretty face. You have to go stealthily and you go like a soldier marching in. Tell him, Eugene," he begs the dialogue coach.

This goes on over and over until one wonders how Fellini can stand it.

Giulietta Masina, the director's wife, has arrived to watch, and, admiring the set, comments: "These creatures, this ambience. It can be old Rome but it can be a thousand years ahead. They are suspended in time. They have already lived but they can live again in the future. This could be a lunar landscape if you took that willow tree away. It is a fearful modernity but at the same time, of ancient times.

"There are all the elements of life," she says as she glances around. "Water that runs, sand that gives off the light of the sun, the sundial which indicates that time is passing, that a sense of humanity is passing; but life continues in all its elements. The wind is like an element of human life. Federico doesn't think of these things purposely but he does it intuitively."

At lunch I have a long talk with Peter Ammann, a tall, lanky Swiss psychoanalyst of the Jungian school who is a volunteer assistant on the film, helping Norma Giacchero, the script girl, keep track of the continuity. He also helps interpret on the set in English, German, French and Italian since Fellini has actors of every nationality in the film all speaking in their own languages. It's like the Tower of Babel sometimes.

In 1965, Peter came to Rome with the vague intention of working in films and six months after his arrival met the director, a great admirer of Jung's psychology, through a mutual friend, the head of the Jungian school in Rome.

"It was a strange coincidence," the psychoanalyst recalls. "At that time, Fellini was preparing *The Voyage of G. Mastorna,* and Mastorna, in the film, was a cellist. I also am a cellist. Fellini said, 'Maybe you can help me'; so I showed Mastroianni—who was to play Mastorna—how to play the cello for the tests that were made. After that, Fellini and I became friends and I worked as a volunteer assistant on the *Toby Dammit* episode to get some experience.

"This will be the turning point in Fellini's style and work. The period from *La Dolce Vita* to *Juliet* is now closed. Something new is beginning. This film is completely different in his approach to the material and in the manner of expressing himself stylistically. It is a part of the development of the maturity of the man, maybe not so much in the story itself but in the way he handles the material. There is a certain detachment. He doesn't identify so much as he did in *8½.* Here the protaganists are young men. The identification he had in his films of the last ten years is gone. It is another layer.

"Fellini is a gamut of extremes," the psychoanalyst explains, "of psychic possibilities. For example, his voice—it sometimes is a very male voice and he can roar like a lion; but it can also be a very female voice, like an angelic being. This large scale of sensitivity, of receptivity, of fantasy, of ability to take in and be conscious of so many things, is one explanation of his genius. Some people say that he is not cultured or intellectual; but he does have culture, not a cerebral culture, but one connected with instinct and intuition. Anyway, it doesn't matter whether Fellini is cultured or not. He creates culture."

After lunch, Fellini continues with the same scene. It's taking forever to get the two boys up the road and into the villa. A new arrival appears on the set already crowded with visitors: twenty-one-year-old Hylette Adolphe, who comes from the island of Mauritius and is a photographer's model in London where she lives. She has fantastic black eyes, gorgeously fringed on the upper and lower lids with false eyelashes. As she looks around, bewildered, she explains, "I arrived this morning from London. Two weeks ago, I had an interview with one of Fellini's casting representatives and I was called last Thursday. I haven't a clue as to what I have to do. I think I have to play the part of a fourteen-year-old girl but I don't know how."

What she has to play is a slave girl left behind in the empty villa who is found by the two boys in the cellar. After a wild chase through the villa, the three end up first in the pool together where the Pompeian paintings Paola talked about are reflected in the water, then in the bedroom where the boys make love to her and finally abandon the slave girl for each other.

Hylette plays the part bare-breasted and speaks an incomprehensible language invented by Eugene Walter. (The director decided her eyebrows had to be shaved off and they fought for two days before he finally convinced her by saying all great models shaved their eyebrows. They were shaved at least twice.)

After frolicking in the pool, Ascyltus carries the slave girl off, leaving Encolpius staring at the sky and remembering Giton—who has been carried off by a soldier. The sky for the pool posed an almost insoluble problem for Joseph Natanson, the sky creator, who said, "The sky where Encolpius lies in the pool and looks up at the heavens and thinks of Giton, that awful pansy, was very difficult because he has to see a starry sky. To photograph real stars is very hard because the light is so slight and the earth moves all the time. Astronomers have special cameras built on a base moving with a clock to move the camera at the same rate as the earth is rotating. I wanted to make a sky with a well-known constellation like the Milky Way shimmering. It was almost impossible, but I did it."

Fellini, intrigued as always by a newcomer, comes to greet Hylette and says reassuringly, "You must not worry. Nobody here has ever acted before. Nobody here has ever directed before and we are always tripping. Can't I offer you some LSD, some mescaline, some pot? No, only water?" and goes back to the camera with a big chuckle.

"Have you ever seen any of Fellini's films?" I ask Hylette. "I've seen *Blow-Up*," she answers. "I wouldn't mention that here if I were you," I advise her, without telling her she had the wrong director.

December 20

The boys have now entered the villa of the suicides and are down in the cellar. It is very dark and desolate and there is a suggestion of long passageways off to the right leading to the slave cubicles. At the moment, they have come across a haunch of prosciutto ham in the kitchen and are eating ravenously when they hear a wailing noise which frightens them.

Fellini is bellowing at them, "Gnaw it ravenously. Yes, like that, eat like that," as they tear the meat like two dogs with their teeth.

Martin farts, with sound effects provided by the director, and Hiram says, "You dirty dog, breaking wind," and laughs lasciviously. Fellini is very dissatisfied with their performance and keeps at them. Over and over again they do it until the prosciutto is coming out of their ears and still Fellini isn't pleased. The more the director bellows at them, the more tense they become. He stomps back and forth, from the actors to the camera, and his face gets heavier and his voice higher. Part of it is the language problem. But he also expects them to know what he wants without ever having explained it to them.

Finally, after about twenty times, he breaks it down into even smaller sections, "Eat. Look happy. Laugh," providing the sound effects himself. "Very good, Iram," he says at the end.

Hiram is jubilant and confides, "I've finally found a relationship of working with him today. He told me to use my own ideas if I wanted. He was telling me I had to be more fluid. But I'm so cold and I feel this tension."

Fellini comes to kiss Giulietta affectionately as he always does, when she arrives on the set. After twenty-five years of marriage, they still seem completely devoted to each other. She is a small, compact, charming, and outgoing woman with the same wistful expression that made her so endearing in *La Strada, The Nights of Cabiria,* and *Juliet of the Spirits.* Practically every day, she comes on the set to watch the shooting, sitting quietly knitting or studying English from the book she carries around with her. Although she still acts, Giulietta is very much the housewife, loves to cook large dinners of homemade pasta for friends and relatives, and looks with maternal care after her innumerable cats at their lovely villa by the sea in Fregene, about twenty miles from Rome.

"Federico is a simple man," she says in her deep voice. "He eats simply—cheese, fruit, fresh vegetables. He loves Chinese cooking and likes to dress comfortably, not elegantly. He doesn't smoke or drink, goes to bed early and gets up early and doesn't like parties or socializing.

"When he is directing me, we know each other so well that it's not necessary for him to tell me what to do. He makes the character for me as an actress and wife. However, Federico is not only a director, but also a writer. He writes his story, selects the actors, and tells his tale with comments. To tell his stories, he has selected the cinema because it is more modern and more popular than novels. As a writer would put words on paper to describe the characters he has in mind, so, in the same way, Federico sees his actors as characters and imposes a certain personality on them.

"As a director, he has an extraordinary patience to teach and show the actors until he gets what he wants, which is perfection. He is not happy with halfway measures or approximation. He has this incredible tenacity to repeat and repeat."

During one of the innumerable lulls in the shooting, I sit and talk with Martin Potter, the English actor who plays Encolpius. He is huddled in a blue terry cloth robe to keep warm, with his hair up in pin curls. A classically handsome, blue-eyed young man, his normally brown hair was dyed blond for the role, and he was sent off to a gym to fatten up his slender frame for three weeks before the film began. He is an intelligent, sensitive, and reserved person, with a tentative smile that masks a strong will. After studying at the Central School of Speech and Drama in London, he toured with a repertory company and played on television but never in a film.

"My agent introduced me to one of Fellini's agents in August and he took photographs of me back to Rome for Fellini to look at," he says. "About a month later, my agent phoned me and said I had an appointment with Fellini at the Savoy Hotel. I saw him, lunched with him, and we talked. I shall never forget that meeting at the Savoy. For what seemed like an eternity, Fellini looked at me. Then he explained certain things about the part, that he was looking for a young man who was completely modern but didn't go into too great detail at that time. The next day, Fellini went back to Rome and I was getting very excited about the whole thing. I took my wife and baby daughter down to Cornwall for a holiday and while I was there my agent phoned and said I had to fly to Rome. It's fantastic to start at the top!"

Ettore Bevilacqua, whose last name means "drink water," bustles around the set dispensing espresso and mineral water to Giulietta and other visitors. He speaks in a rasping rumble that seems to come from the bottom of his feet—perhaps because he is deaf. With his bushy hair curling down onto his neck and Tartar-like moustache, he looks like Genghis Khan. Watching *il Dottore*, as he calls him, limping around with a pulled muscle, he remarks, "He's like a caterpillar tractor. He seems tired but it is the others who fall apart. He, never!" Bevilacqua is a kind of factotum for Fellini, serving his meals, handing him his coat and hat and generally mothering him.

"I am also Fellini's trainer," he announces proudly. A former fighter, he is also a master gymnast, and began working with Fellini fifteen years ago as his masseur to keep the director fit. He also puts the actors through their paces in the morning and occasionally acts in films.

"Fellini is marvelous," he whispers in a highly audible tone that can be heard throughout the entire studio. "He likes to have his work come out well but doesn't like to talk about the cinema. We never talk about it, only about the weather, what I am doing, the exercises. He is never absent from the set because he's very strong." Then he leans over and hisses loudly into my ear, "He is on a diet."

The Temple of the Hermaphrodite

January 9

This is one of the first episodes written into the script. It is not in Petronius, but Fellini felt it was part of this pagan civilization and thought of the hermaphrodite as strange and magical and striking. Encolpius and Ascyltus have been told about the Temple of the Hermaphrodite by a young girl slave in the caravan of the nymphomaniac whose husband is taking her there hoping for a miraculous cure. Somewhere along the way, the two boys join forces with an unscrupulous thief, and the three decide to steal the hermaphrodite, worshipped as a demigod in a ruined temple of Ceres in Magna Grecia in southern Italy. The albino demigod oracle must be kept constantly wet or he will die; but the thieves, who plan to take him to the city to exploit his mystical powers, do not know this. Only the interior of the temple is seen. Against a glowing white crumbling wall, the hermaphrodite lies in a queer cradle attended by two old men. Lining the steps down to the pool, which separates the demigod from the worshippers, is a motley group of suppliants, not unlike modern-day pilgrims to Lourdes.

Fellini, dressed in a beige sheepskin-lined suede jacket and his black fedora, is sitting on a stool by the camera. About thirty extras are clumped around gas burners below the stage of the temple, some lying on wooden benches sleeping, completely oblivious to the ruckus around them. It is freezing cold in the cavernous sound stage and the contrast of their weird faces above modern overcoats is startling. Many of them are pitifully crippled or deformed or afflicted with some disfiguring disease.

Fellini is very nervous, as always when he starts shooting on a new set, and his outbursts will be frequent and voluble until he feels at ease in this strange environment. He is like a cat sniffing around a new house before it decides to stay. The director is screeching in rage at some of the crew banging behind him. He hates noise when he is setting up a scene. Yet clamorous confusion is what he thrives on.

While he works with a small group of pilgrims lined up on the steps, Eugene Walter, the dialogue coach, comments on the set. "The tree roots are falling into the temple and the walls are caved in to show ancient times within ancient times. Every past has a past. The very green grass growing around the temple is due to blood from sacrifices and piss. Where grass grows greenest, it is usually on a battlefield where there has been much bloodshed. Only Fellini knows what the floor plan of the temple was. In every Fellini film, he has a way of using the set, moving in and out so you never see the complete thing."

Fellini sets up a scene with Encolpius and Ascyltus and the robber, played by Gordon Mitchell, an American actor, greedily watching the pilgrims deposit offerings for the hermaphrodite. It is not a very exciting scene. The behind-the-scenes drama of how the temple was put together is much more fascinating. It has taken so long—a month—to construct this set that they are now behind in the shooting schedule. Whenever there is a delay, it is because of the complicated sets, since everything has to be made at Cinecittà rather than farmed out to specialized companies. Many ideas for the temple were tried and discarded and parts were done and redone before it finally materialized into the image the director had in his mind.

Fellini didn't want the entire temple, only the parts that interested him. He wanted a very green little valley, like a road toward an unreal world, similar to one he had seen on the Aurelia, an old Roman road still in use. The grass was made of fibers of glass wool dyed green, each fiber attached to a line with reflectors above and below to create a transparent light. The lights could be subtracted or added as needed.

The director insisted upon having a transparent wall behind the hermaphrodite's cradle, and Donati finally hit upon the idea of using rock alum, the same substance used as an after-shave styptic, which could be broken up into crystals and lit from behind. Once the material was found, the problem was to construct the wall. The alum wall was inclined to enable the crystals to be glued on one by one, but there was no glue to be found to stick the crystals to the solid piece of alum. Liquid glucose worked for half the crystals, but then production announced the wall had to be ready in two days and the tedious process had to be speeded up. During the night, everything fell down and they had to start from the beginning with another system, gluing the crystals with sugar or glucose and fixing them with transparent plastic. About six and a half tons of rock alum were used, and about nine hundred pounds of sugar to stick the wall together. Everybody was sure it would fall again or melt under the heat of the lights, but it got so hard it couldn't even be destroyed. In two days the wall had been done and re-done and no one could believe it, including Donati himself, who said, "Everything was an attempt at new things. We were always unsure of what would happen because nobody had ever done these things before."

Fellini wanted the columns to indicate a half-buried temple, not of a god but of a monster, something alien to Rome, an exotic Oriental cult. After various models were tried out, Fellini settled on Persian-looking ones, covered with tiny pieces of tinplate painted blue and green. The temple cupola, designed to create an optical effect in the water of the pool, is made of 4,852 pieces of hand-cut brass coated with tin, and glued together one by one in twenty days at a cost of five thousand dollars.

"Fellini," as Donati pointed out, "creates images which disturb, offend, fascinate or assault the senses. Architecturally, the temple is absurd, but cinematographically, it is absolutely effective."

After lunch, Fellini has changed his suede jacket for a black raincoat and, with his dark, heavy face, looks like Mephistopheles. An old man in a shabby overcoat and beat-up old sailor's cap shuffles up to him. His arms tremble continuously and he can only mumble incoherently. An ex-beach attendant, he is an old friend of the director's and is called simply Marinaio or "Sailor." Every time Fellini makes a picture, Marinaio is on hand to run errands, do odd jobs, and even bit parts. The director is very fond of the old man and even fired an extra who made fun of him.

Fellini is creating a fresco of the pilgrims who are dressed in muted colors—greys and blacks, dull purples and greens, dark blues and browns—to harmonize with the subdued and solemn atmosphere of the temple. This is the first time I have seen him organize a large group of extras and it is amazing to watch him arrange them with incredible rapidity, getting them all to play the same tune even though none of them knows the score. He shows a one-legged man with a crude crutch where to stand, demonstrates to another how to limp, then places the others, about twenty in all, sitting, standing, or sprawling on the temple steps facing the demigod. He takes two extras out of the scene. Maybe he doesn't like their faces.

When he gets them all placed, he yells to Lamberto Pippia, the young and efficient production inspector, "Bring the sheep," and to Adriano Pischiutta, the special-effects man, "Prepare the smoke"; then he discards his hat and coat and works in a grey sweater to which his eye-glasses are attached. Suspended from a black cord around his neck is a tiny light filter (used to check the lights) which he often twirls in times of nervousness or impatience.

Three sheep are dragged onto the set and placed in front of the green valley by the pool. One of the pilgrims looks familiar. She is a woman called Lea Favi who was one of the audience in the theater scene, who died in the Insula, and who is now in the temple in southern Italy. Fellini frequently uses the same faces in different scenes to give the audience a sense of familiarity.

A new character appears, bare-chested and bare-legged with bloody bandages swathed around his head and behind. "He ain't very well," Eugene quips, as Fellini shows the man how to act like a spastic or epileptic. When he is finally satisfied with the epileptic's performance, he shouts to a special-effects man up in the rafters above the cupola, "A drop of water every once in a while in the pool."

The rehearsal begins, "*Dai, dai,*" he urges Barozzi, the epileptic. "Come on, make a sound like 'whoo, whoo, whoo,'" and the director reels down the stairs, whirling round and round sounding like a drunken hoot owl. The man is made to imitate the director's actions over and over again. "You," he orders, pointing to an extra, "on your knees, and you and you," pointing to others. Then he puts a tray of cheese in the hands of an old pilgrim by the pool explaining that he must place it on the ground as an offering. Exasperated because he doesn't do it exactly the way he wants, the director pleads with Maurizio Mein, the roly-poly assistant director, to explain it to the man.

"It's a Folies Bergères," Giulietta Masina remarks as she sits in a fur coat and yellow bandanna, calmly knitting a pink baby blanket.

Fellini then makes the short, white-haired old man named Gulà sit down to the right of the hermaphrodite's cradle. Standing on the left side is a tall skinny man with a gaunt face that looks as if it had been chiseled out of granite. The flat, broad-brimmed hat he wears accentuates his beaklike nose. Originally, there was to be only one attendant for the hermaphrodite, but Fellini has split the character in two, the short man to interpret the incoherent mutterings of the hermaphrodite-oracle and the tall man to keep him continuously sponged. (This is the second time Fellini has done this. The girl who recounts the story of the demigod to the two heroes was not in the script either. It was to have been told by a grotesque male slave, but the director divided the role when he saw the girl's face.) Fellini became enamored of the face of the old man, whose name is Capitani, and he appears in many of the episodes, always in a different role but with the same unmistakable features.

The sheep which has been placed by the side of the pilgrim at the pool is bent with its front feet down as though bowing in adoration to the demigod. "*Pronti,* ready. Go with the fog," and the smoke rises up out of the green grass like a thick mist. The pilgrim grabs the sheep by a cord but it balks and wants to return to the other two in the corner. "*Motore, a posto!*" and the horn indicating the camera is grinding honks raucously. The second take is halted in the middle because the sheep keeps butting the old pilgrim in the backside. Fellini tells him, "Don't just stand there like that. Speak to the hermaphrodite. Barozzi, try a leap. No, do it like before but with your back turned. Be as crazy as you can, as though you were infused with an electric current." And the director plods wearily up the temple steps to show him again what he wants.

On the sixth take Fellini becomes furious because the pilgrim doesn't put his tray of cheese down; but he protests it's the sheep's fault. The sheep is banished to the corner and Barozzi is also ban-

ished. While another extra shows Fellini how he is going to play
the part of the epileptic, one of the crew cracks, "That sheep is an
atheist. He doesn't want to go near the Baby Jesus." It does seem
as though the director is either evoking or mocking the birth of
Christ since the way the scene is set up, it looks remarkably like the
traditional Christmas manger scene—except there is no St. Joseph
and no Madonna, only two characters who resemble Don Quixote
and Sancho Panza. Fellini has insisted that there will be an absence
of Christ in this film but this episode certainly rings a Christian bell.

There is a long pause while Fellini waits for the new epileptic to
be bandaged, an opportunity for me to chat with Gordon Mitchell,
the thief. A former professor of science in high school and junior
colleges in Los Angeles with a master's degree in counseling and
guidance, he has been living in Rome since 1961. He has made
about forty pictures and has known Fellini, who asked him to do
this part, for several years. "I was trying to figure out the message
of the bandit who comes to steal the hermaphrodite," the actor
muses. "It is actually good versus evil, but Fellini also uses a lot of
astrology. The masculine is Mercury and the feminine is Venus
and the hermaphrodite represents the masculine and feminine in
all of us. The feminine is the spiritual part of you which tries to
guide you but there are always evil people like the bandit around
who are trying to destroy the good. This film can be shown a thousand years from now and the message will still be there."

The rumor is going around that the picture is a week behind
schedule, and I try to find out if it is true from Eugene Walter,
Fellini's English dialogue coach, who replies airily, "Since so much
of the film is what comes out of the head of the master, it is very
difficult to say what the schedule is or to stick to it or even to say if
it's ahead or behind. The film is supposed to be out in the spring of
1970, but he could decide to shoot through August. In any of Fellini's scripts, certain things get shortened and certain things length-

ened. He might decide to make it a two-part film and go on shooting for two years."

"Oh, God," I groan to myself. "Two years with these monsters and I'll be carried off in a strait jacket."

Fellini turns his attention to a lovely blonde girl who must walk down the steps on crutches. She is Hungarian and her name is Georgia Lillik but the director calls her Lilli. He shows her how to breathe hard, as though she were suffering from terrible asthma, but smile at the same time. On the second take, he admonishes her, "Listen, Lilli, don't look at me. Look at him," and points to a French photographer crouched under the camera platform, which has been moved up onto the steps of the temple. Then he whirls and yells at an old crone by the wall, "Ragusa, don't bat your eyes. Okay, Lilli, smile, Lilli, smile, a beautiful little smile. You are so beautiful when you smile," coaxing her on in a soft voice. "When you get here, stop. Smile but don't straighten up. Breathe like a dog. Smile. Come on. Smile. Breathe hard. Stop. *Va bene, è questa.*"

Leaving the set, I walk along with Pietro Rifori, the pilgrim with the tray of cheese by the pool. He is a seventy-five-year-old farmer from a village near Rome who has never acted before. "At my age, it isn't so easy to be an actor," he grumbles. "Fellini said he was going to hit me on the head if I didn't do it right; but what could I do with that sheep butting me in the backside?"

January 11

The director has finished with the pilgrims and is now setting up the scene of the two heroes and the robber stealing the hermaphrodite, who is asleep in his cradle. It is night and most of the pilgrims have left except for three slumbering on the ground near the temple wall. The camera will sweep past them down to the action at the cradle. The temple is filled with mist and the two attendants, Capitani on the left and Gulà on the right, lie sleeping also. Mitchell comes running in on the left, throttles Capitani from behind and pushes him into the water. The old man, who didn't know he was going to be pushed into the water, is indignant. "Did you get hurt?" Fellini inquires solicitously.

Piero Tosi, the makeup consultant, comes on the set and Fellini embraces him effusively, kissing him on the ear. (Fellini is constantly kissing everybody, or patting behinds or whatever is handy.) While Piero is retouching the hermaphrodite's makeup, I talk with Pasquale Baldassarre, the twelve-year-old albino who was found by one of Fellini's scouts in Naples. One of six children, he has never gone to school because his mother doesn't want him sent to a special school, but the director finds him "one of the most highly intelligent boys I have ever known."

Pasquà, as Fellini sometimes calls him, arrived in the care of his uncle, who told him only that he was to be in an acting contest to see whether he or a five-year-old albino girl could act better. "I like to work in the cinema," Pasquale tells me, "because I make money and I have fun. I like Fellini very much because he is like a father and he plays with me."

(There is an amusing story about how the albino was found. A secretary in the production office telephoned one of Fellini's scouts in Naples to ask for an albino between ten and fourteen years old, very pale and blond. After two or three days, a call came from Naples saying a search had been made through all the barracks of the *Alpini,* Italy's crack ski troops, but it was impossible to find an *Alpino* of that age because the Corps didn't recruit boys that young.)

They are waiting for the lights to be adjusted before doing a close-up of Ascyltus picking up the hermaphrodite. Fellini pats Pasquale's head lovingly as he lies in his cradle and calls out, "Bring a cover for this poor thing. He is trembling." The next moment, he screeches at a technician about some blades of grass which have been displaced in the valley. "*Là*, there, *quello stronzato* there. That shit there." Fellini's eagle eye can spot the slightest detail that isn't the way he wants it. They say he is so keen that when he looks through the camera, he is quite capable of saying, "The seventeenth tile on the left column has too much light on it."

Rino Carboni, the head makeup man, inspects the hermaphrodite and remarks, "Fellini can ask for the craziest things from one minute to the next. For the hermaphrodite, he said I had to have a little penis ready in case he selected the five-year-old girl albino. So I made it. For two days we had to make breasts for the boy and also for the girl. Fellini has to see the actors under lights. When he sees them in the proper ambience, then he decides, because a character has to function in a scene. He decided on the boy only when he saw him on the set." Pasquale doesn't know yet that he has been chosen for the role since the little girl is still on the set as a possible stand-in. Pasquale thinks the contest is continuing and is giving his all.

The director starts the close-up of Hiram picking up the hermaphrodite sitting off-camera, but next to the cradle, looking at Pasquale with a sweet smile on his face as though he were gazing at a baby. "*Motore.* Action. Iram. Look around. Good. Go," and Hiram picks up the child with a look of wonder on his face. "Another take. *Motore.* Iram, look at him like a baby. Then look around."

There is a pause for another light adjustment and Fellini cackles contentedly over some joke with Pasquale, shielding the boy's eyes with his hands. The albino can't see in the light and should always wear dark glasses; the strong lights are very painful for him. The girl albino has just been sent away and Pasquale crows jubilantly to his uncle, "I have acted well. I won the contest."

On the third take, Fellini says to Hiram, "Now look here. Look stealthy. Look to his face. Go away with him." While he is giving these directions, the director has a crafty look on his face as though he were stealing the Vatican treasures. They do a fourth take, and this time he says, "Iram, go down. Look at him and smile at me. Look at him and smile. Look at him and go, fast." Each time, Fellini adds something new to his directions.

Fellini now moves in for a close-up of Capitani, the hermaphrodite's skinny attendant, getting strangled by Gordon Mitchell. The old man is paralyzed because he knows what's going to happen to him. Fellini teases, "Ah, you refuse to work?" Pippo Spoletini, the man in charge of the extras, is irate because he didn't know the director was going to have Capitani pushed into the water, and complains, "These people come for me personally and now, whenever I call them, they'll say, 'He's calling me to get killed.' The man is old and thin. Fellini shouldn't have done it."

When he calms down we talk about his job and where he finds all these strange types. Pippo, who has the swarthy features of a brigand, worked as a stunt man in *Nights of Cabiria* and *The Swindler* for Fellini. He and his brother, Antonio, a former actor, have been rounding up extras for seven years.

Every week Production gives him a certain amount of money and he goes out and finds the characters Fellini wants. For this picture, he and his brother searched all over Rome and Naples and in the country villages. "I found a huge fat man sleeping in the Colosseum at night," Spoletini boasts. "Some I found in the shanty towns by the old aqueducts near the Appian Way and some in the slaughter-houses, the big general food markets, the flea market on Sunday, and in Trastevere across the Tiber where *i veri Romani*, the true Romans, live. I come from Trastevere so I know all the characters there.

"Fellini will say to me, 'I need a fat type, a monstrous type, or even a torso' and I find all of them, but he is very difficult to work with because he wants strange faces. He screams but he is not a bad man. He knows everyone around him, and the extras like to work for him.

"I gathered over a thousand people and he selected seventy or seventy-five percent. I was to have worked on the other *Satyricon* but I prefer to be paid less and work with Fellini. He always tries to make everybody happy. Sometimes he doesn't send away extras he doesn't need because he sees their faces imploring him and he can't refuse."

The close-up of Capitani and the thief is finished and the old man comes off the set, shivering and furious. While he is getting iodine poured over the cuts on his scrawny arms, he quavers out his story. His name is Alfredo Capitani and he is a seventy-two-year-old house painter from Rome who has worked in ten or twenty films but never with Fellini. "I am not afraid of the water. I would throw myself into the Tiber from a bridge if I had to, but I don't like it. He told me to do it and I did it but they are going to have to pay me extra for this. I was hired to be a farmer, not a sailor."

January 14

Fellini is preparing the scene where the two attendants raise the demigod up so that he is revealed as a hermaphrodite. While he is setting up the scene, I ask Eugene why he wanted a hermaphrodite in the film. "Why not," he shrugs, "since he's got whores, transvestites, gluttons, drunks, homosexuals, and all the other extravagant characters? Nowadays, if a family had a hermaphrodite, they would keep it a deep dark secret or have an operation, but in these times, it is a magical thing, a gift of the gods, and the child becomes an oracle."

Fellini explained to Pasquale only that he was going to be kidnapped and that some men were going to be killed because of him, but he never told the boy he was going to be nude and have breasts. In the beginning Pasquale was ashamed when his body was exposed. Now he rather enjoys the sensation he is creating.

The director demonstrates again how the hermaphrodite must be lifted. "Abandon yourself," he tells Pasqualino, who should be limp; but the boy has difficulty understanding and only giggles. Fellini in desperation turns to the boy's uncle and says, "Tell Pasqualí that he must be like a dead weight. How do you say it in Neapolitan?" The uncle speaks to Pasqualino in dialect: "You are half sleeping, half dead, as though you were drunk. You don't have to do anything."

Then Fellini turns to Capitani. "All right, show me how you have to take the veil to show the breasts and *pisellino*." Fellini does it for him. "Do you see how you are supposed to do it? Then after you've done everything, look at the people here who've come to see it. Mind you, Capitani, do it well or you won't get paid a lira tonight."

They are ready to start shooting. "*Apri il cielo*, turn on the sky," the electrician calls. It was to become another familiar and oft-repeated phrase, meaning turn on the lights.

"Go, Gulà," Fellini urges, "go, Capitani, delicately. Lower your head. Open the front. More. Open your eyes, Pasquà. Lower your head, slowly, slowly. Lower him gently. Put him down slowly, slowly. Now cover him with the veil like two mamas."

The photographers are clicking frantically and the director screams, "You've already got forty million shots. Why do you want more?" He does another take with the same urgently repeated directions, while an old crone sleeps peacefully on a bench with just two fang-like teeth hanging out of her open mouth. Fellini relents and sets up the scene again for the photographers, making Pasqualino laugh. Pasquale announces proudly, "*Adesso tutto il mondo ha visto il mio pesce*. Now all the world has seen my pisser!"

January 17

Before going on the set, I stop by the makeup department to check on what's going on there. Piero Tosi and Rino Carboni are making up the face of the young albino to look parched and deathlike. After the hermaphrodite has been stolen by the two heroes and the robber, they trundle him off in a cart through a mountain pass and end up in a desert where the demi-god dies from lack of water. Pasquale's normal pallor has been accentuated even more with white powder and his lips are scabbed and crusted with pieces of latex. Piero admonishes the boy gently, "Don't touch anything, Pasqualino. If you are going to be an actor, you have to suffer."

Over in the sound stage, everyone is on the set including Franco Pinna, the photographer who is photographing the entire film for a book, and Gideon Bachmann, a writer and documentary film director who is preparing an independent one-hour television show on Fellini and the filming of the *Satyricon*. The set is built like a crater enclosed by a wall of pale, flaky sand extending all around except for a huge chunk gouged out on the right side. The land is barren and cracked as though from a blistering sun. A rickety cart is in the foreground in front of the camera. The hermaphrodite is dead and the robber is furious and blames Encolpius and Ascyltus. He is going to kill them. They are running through the very difficult fight scene which Gordon Mitchell and two stunt men have been rehearsing for two weeks.

Fellini is perched, facing the desert, high on the steps of the amphitheater which leads to the Lupanare, or brothel, where the next scenes are to be shot. Liliana Betti, his assistant, and Norma Giacchero, the script girl, are sitting up there too, and there is plenty of time to talk while the stunt men demonstrate the fight to the actors. Norma and Liliana did extensive research on the Romans, reading twenty-five books in French, which Nino Rota, Fellini's composer, loaned the director on the customs, holidays, feasts, children's games, everything that indicated how the ancient Romans lived. After they had translated the more essential points and also digested Carcopino's *Daily Life in Ancient Rome*, the most important source, a twenty-five page treatment was prepared; and then the script written very hastily in about two months. Liliana says, "The preparation is the most important time for Fellini because it is then that he thinks about the film and creates it. It is the most creative phase."

Liliana talks about the director. "He only gets along with people who are on the same psychological level. He is very generous but never carries money on him, partly because Giulietta doesn't want him giving it all away and partly because he doesn't want to feel it on him. It annoys him."

Norma adds, "And he is not a liar as everyone likes to think. He transforms reality. He's very precise and can't stand to be thought of in that aspect. He only says what he thinks people want to hear. It's a kind of defense. When he gives an affirmative answer, the thing ends there, and he doesn't have to argue."

Liliana confides, "Fellini has become much more mature. He is very different from two years ago, probably because of his illness, when he was at death's door. He understood he was gravely ill when even his enemies came to see him."

They are now finally ready for a take, with Fellini still directing from the steps. "Move more, make wider movements," he calls to Martin, and to Gordon, "When you go to see if the keed is dead, go faster and shake the keed. After that you look at Martin and you become furious. Pasqualì, move your head to the other side. No, that's too much."

The director climbs down the steps and shows Pasquale how to lie in the cart and the actors how to fight, demonstrating for Hiram how he must kick Gordon in the groin. Then he takes the cart handle and shows him how to bash the robber's head in viciously. Even though he has experts, Fellini always ends up doing everything himself. He makes Nenno Zampella, the Master of Arms, rehearse the fight again, then returns to sit on the steps and watch. He is pleased, and marvels, "They are all full of bruises." Still not satisfied, he goes down to give new directions to everyone. Giuseppe Maccari, the camera operator, is behind the camera, Peppino Rotunno is behind him studying the lights through a little glass lens, and Fellini is on a stool beside the lighting cameraman with a megaphone in his hand.

The scene starts. "Action, Gordon," he calls, and the thief walks up to look at the dead hermaphrodite. Then the fight starts, a brutal battle beginning in front of the cart. Encolpius breaks away, runs to the left and tries to scrabble up the side of the crater with the robber chasing after him. The youth breaks away again but the thief catches him in the center of the wall and is about to kill him with a knife. At that point Ascyltus, who has been dazed by a blow, stumbles to his aid, dragging the wooden handle of the cart which has broken off during one of the rehearsals. They wrestle the robber down on his back and while Encolpius holds him, Ascyltus smashes his head in. These are the wide movements that Fellini wanted ranging over half the large set. At the end, everyone claps. Fellini calls, "Bravo, Pasqualì," and goes to shake Gordon's hand.

Nenno Zampella, the Master of Arms, sighs, "In five minutes, Fellini ruined two weeks of work. He rearranged the whole fight, which had been set up like a ballet; and then he decided to bust the robber's head with the handle of the cart, rather than with a rock as it was originally."

Fellini is over inspecting the Lupanare, which is being prepared for next week's shooting, and then strolls up to me to announce, "It's a whorehouse of two thousand years ago and I've got Padre Arpa [one of his clergy friends who is visiting the set] to come and advise me because he is an expert on the whores of two thousand years ago." Chuckling over the bewildered expression on the priest's face, he returns to have an animated conversation with Antonio Scordia about the paintings on the wall of the Lupanare, gesticulating wildly in his customary fashion.

Lupanare is a Latin word, which is also used in Italian and means *brothel,* but this is a rather peculiar brothel built on the top of an ancient amphitheater. The steps leading up to it are made of small broken and crumbling yellowish bricks. I suppose it's that "every past has a past" idea Eugene has talked about. The wall of the Lupanare is made of ochre-colored plaster. From left to right, there are big drawings of Oriental gods, then a door, then a drawing of Priapus and another door which leads to the interior of the brothel, then a nude man and woman in a circle and a final door over which the figure of a rampant bull is painted.

As soon as Fellini leaves, I race up the stairs to talk to Antonio Scordia, who explains, "All these things except the bull, which is modern, are from Pompeii but re-elaborated. Fellini told me not to put nude women on the outside because he was going to put some fantastic whores, very sexy and vulgar and exciting, inside. He wanted something symbolic and not too realistic for this scene."

Scordia, a fifty-year-old abstract painter, was born in Argentina of Italian parents but has lived and worked in Rome for many years. So as not to confuse his abstract style of painting with the classical paintings Fellini needed for the film, Scordia painted them with his left hand, reserving his right hand for his own works. "I have known Fellini for thirty years since we worked together in 1939 for a newspaper," he says. "Fellini was like a stick then and wrote comic stories for the paper and made sketches. How afraid of everything he was when he was young! Now, he is more mature, more confident and more shrewd.

"When Fellini started preparing the film," the artist continues, "he wasn't happy with the things the production people came up with. When he asked for Hellenistic, they gave him Baroque. Never in his other films has he needed consultants like a professor and a painter. The important people in this film are the director and the collaborators, not the actors, who are all unknown. He has a professor and an artist because they are fresh forces for him, far removed from the world of the cinema.

"I can't say that he has no weak sides," Scordia admits. "Sometimes he is a little mawkish and he has a weakness for certain surrealistic things which is just a little too convenient. I can say so many things but I absolutely must say that he has made some extremely interesting and beautiful films, but he is a little hammy. He is continuously alert to take advantage of everything that is useful to him, expecially publicity for himself and what he does. But these are weaknesses. I can't judge them so harshly, even his lying. Fellini is a liar but not one who really lies. He invents one situation to hide another because he is very sensitive and has very rapid reflexes. Everything he does is based on intuition."

After lunch, since they are only doing details and close-ups of the same scene, I stop by Makeup. Rino Carboni and Piero Tosi are doing a makeup test on Mario Romagnoli, the proprietor of "Il Moro," a restaurant near the Trevi Fountain popular with cinema people. He is to play the part of Trimalchio, the coarse ex-slave and the most important part in the picture. A sixty-nine-year-old Roman, he is six feet tall, weighs one hundred and ninety-eight pounds, and has the face of a sad mastiff. Il Moro, as he is called, is not very happy. "I've known Fellini for twelve years," Moro rasps in his croaking voice that sounds like a bullfrog with laryngitis. "He always used to come to my restaurant but now he doesn't come anymore because he got too fat. In October, he asked me to be in the picture. He pestered and pestered me but I didn't want to do it because I didn't want to leave my restaurant. For somebody like me who is accustomed to yak with my clients, it is absolute agony to come here and sit for four hours without doing anything." As Tosi and Carboni keep trying different swatches of hair on his head to make it larger, Moro grumps, "Fellini wants an Onassis. Onassis would be ideal."

Maybe Onassis would have turned him down but his wife's sister, Lee Radziwill, was very anxious to be in the film, and called the director several times from London. They were to have met in Rome but it never came off. It's probably just as well, because Fellini would undoubtedly have made her one of the whores in the Lupanare.

January 18

"Why are there so many monsters in this picture?" I ask Fellini.

He replies, "But they are not monsters. They are innocent. You are less innocent."

Fellini examines the still-unfinished amphitheater again and has an animated conversation with Luigi Scaccianoce, the set architect, and Scordia. He is not happy with the murals yet. "They look like posters from Mussolini's era," he complains. He wants the paintings less distinct and more blurred and blended into each other, as though they have withstood centuries of wind and rain.

Scordia sighs, "I did them right the first time. He made me do them over and now he wants them back the other way." This is typical of Fellini, not knowing exactly what he wants until he sees something in front of him, at which point he realizes he doesn't want that. When he saw the steps leading up to the amphitheater perfectly made, he insisted they be broken and scuffed. The horrified carpenter, whose idea of Roman architecture is geometric and perfect, moaned, "See, it was so beautiful and now it is all ruined."

Surveying the set, Scaccianoce morosely explains, "The amphitheater existed before this time. The frescoes are an evocation of that preexisting world. It looks like a collage. Fellini is trying to tie it all together, to give the idea that it represents preexisting society in the Subura. With him," he says resignedly, "it always has to be reworked. Yesterday, he put gold on, today, yellow paint and dust.

It will not be finished until it reaches the true evocation of what he has in mind."

I lunched with Piero Tosi, a shy and retiring Tuscan who has been working nineteen years in the theater and films as a makeup expert and costume designer. He studied painting in Florence, then began working with Luigi Visconti and Franco Zeffirelli. For Fellini, he did the costumes for *Toby Dammit* and the preparation for *Satyricon,* the fifteen-day period preceding the film when various makeups were tried for the few actors already selected, like the three boys and Fanfulla. Tosi, who is not officially a member of the crew but only works on a consultant basis, is a meticulous perfectionist, accustomed to working with great deliberation, and finds the chaotic conditions on the *Satyricon* unsettling. The director's last-minute decisions and constant changes of mind keep everyone on tenterhooks.

"I want to make clear," Tosi explained in his soft voice, "that I am not part of *Satyricon.* I only came for a week and I am still here but I am ready to run away at any moment. Why? Because I want my own life. When you work with Fellini, you have no life. You work from six in the morning until eight at night. Then he takes you out to dinner or calls you up in the middle of the night to talk about the picture, the costumes or something. He lives the picture and he sleeps only four hours a night. I was supposed to do *Juliet of the Spirits* but I ran away because I was terrorized."

To circumvent these nocturnal intrusions, Tosi worked out an elaborate telephone code for his friends—so many rings, pauses, and rings. The friends all forgot the code but Fellini found it out and remembered it only too well.

Tosi continued, "Fellini wants a Neronian imposition in the makeup, but how can you get near this unknown world? Only through paintings and sculptures, to maintain that fragmentary character. During the preparation period, I went to museums to study the epoch, to detach myself from the modern world, to assimilate the ghosts of that era in order to prepare a platter to serve Fellini.

"These hairdos and faces are apparitions seen in a museum or in a tomb as though they have been discovered by an archaeologist. It is the astonishment you feel when a tomb is opened—that mysterious moment when it is unearthed. It lives again, like an image you dream and then forget immediately.

"Fellini selected a gallery of faces for me, all of which are in certain categories—men, women, scene for scene. My job is to make them appear in their defects and in their qualities. Defects can also be a quality. Necessity creates the makeup. Every character presents a problem to resolve. I invent things as I go along. You can't foretell a makeup. After so long, it's become a picture game on faces.

"Every minute has its problem. Time is my big problem, and money. When I have a face in front of me, I don't know what is going to come out. I begin and I paint the face. The face itself suggests something to me. All those faces," he shuddered, "but it is never the numbers that count in Fellini's film. He could make 'The Dinner of Trimalchio' with only three faces."

After the lunch break, which usually lasts an hour, Fellini is back for a close-up of Pasquale in his death throes. Piero Tosi looks on with a contented expression on his face. "If we hadn't had the good fortune to find that boy, looking as he does, we would have had a big problem," he confides.

I got bored watching Pasquale open and close his mouth and say "pa-pa-pa," and went up to the production department to talk to Enzo Provenzale, the production manager. A short, red-haired, blue-eyed Sicilian, he likes to call himself "the Mama of the directors." Provenzale is cool, taciturn, and reserved, with a mind like a computer when it comes to totting up figures, the complete opposite of the common conception of the swarthy and volatile Sicilian. His first film with Fellini was *The White Sheik* in 1952, and he also served as production manager on the *Toby Dammit* episode.

"This picture, which is more than a colossal, should have taken at least two years to prepare and shoot, but we will shoot it in one hundred and forty days," he announced. "It is always a question of color and the complicated sets, the costumes and the faces, because Fellini wants to give to the audience the sensation of a dead world.

"One of the biggest difficulties of the film is the sets. There are sixty sets and every two and a quarter days we must have a new one ready. We use mostly Sound Stages Five and Fifteen, six theaters and the lake and five constructions outside on the Cinecittà grounds.

"Each day, we consume enough electricity to light a town of thirty thousand people. We use fifty-seven miles of cables, almost enough to stretch a line from here to Viterbo. This has never happened before in Italy," Provenzale said.

"We have had to set up our own dye plant to dye the cloth used in the costumes. Some costumes have twenty yards of cloth, handwoven because Fellini wanted to have a material that was not modern and which the Romans might have worn. Nobody knows how many yards of cloth are being used. It is treated in a special way, pleated, sewn, and then pressed to give the crinkly effect Fellini wanted. To press the cloth, we had to make an iron over seven feet long.

"Each time a person is made up, it costs seven dollars. This has never happened before. The usual cost is twelve cents. The makeup alone will cost sixteen thousand dollars. The frescoes will cost over a hundred thousand dollars, and seventy tons of clay will be used for the statues."

Provenzale finds the origins of *Satyricon* in *The White Sheik*. "It's a fantastic transfiguration," he said. "Fellini is still the same but he has evolved in these years. All of us have. He is farther away from reality, but he has never been realistic. He is trying to disinter a dead world in this film, and to do so he is using an immobile system of shooting. All these faces he has put in this world, he discovered himself; and in them he finds himself. They are fragments of himself.

"The common denominator in all his films is his distorting fantasy, more profound than it was before. His films are always seen through a deformed lens, but it may be the true lens. Fellini has always been interested in psychology. He has been examining himself since the day he was born."

Outside the Lupanare

In the bowl of the amphitheater, a ritualistic ceremony is being enacted in front of a small bronze statue of Venus with a garland of flowers draped around it. A flame is burning and a woman dressed in dark robes is kneeling before it, praying. To the left, her husband, with a garland of flowers on his head, sits on a step anxiously watching while at the bottom of the steps a diviner, attended by his assistant, reads the liver of a small lamb. The woman is barren and has come to consult the diviner to find out if she can conceive. The diviner's assistant is none other than Capitani with a wreath of flowers incongruously perched on his head over his craggy old face. Encolpius has retrieved Giton from Vernacchio and the two are now on their way to their room in the Insula Felicles. To reach the towering tenement in the Subura, they pass through the Lupanare where a variety of exotic and gross whores peddle their erotic wares. The fertility rite and the whorehouse are sights which Encolpius and Giton see along the way home.

Donati, the set and costume designer, has the final say on the amphitheater: "It is really like a cup," he insists. "An empty space where a rite has to be performed inside. It was done to give a strangeness to the scene, which is really an initiation into the rites of love. You have to accept it. You can't ask what it is or why."

An old man in a purple robe is sitting in a chair with his face garishly made up and two lotus blossoms stuck rakishly over his ears. His name is Luigi Battaglia and he is a seventy-five-year-old actor who has worked fifty-seven years in the theater and films and had a role in the *Toby Dammit* episode. "They told me I was an old pimp but I don't know what I am supposed to be doing," he quavers. "They dressed me up like this and here I am. What's the name of this film, dearie?"

Fellini is sitting on the steps of the amphitheater saying to the woman's husband, a young Australian hippie, "Robert, go to your left. Zmile. Mox, look to me. Martino, you too. Come, Robert. Stop. No, don't look at the sign." A sign has been placed in the white sand to show him where he must stop. They do another rehearsal with Fellini pretending to be the diviner, repeating the line over and over again: "This liver is dark." Fellini gets exasperated with Robert. "*Che cazzo di lingua parla?* What the prick language does he speak? Eugene," he pleads, "tell him to smile a bit." After another rehearsal, Fellini stops to make some drawings for Donati.

Painters are still coloring the inside of the central corridor of the Lupanare a bright blue. This is the corridor which leads to the interior of the whorehouse. Norma Giacchero, the script girl, announces, "This scene does not exist in the script. It was invented yesterday evening so even I am going along in the dark. But," and she gives one of those eloquent Italian shrugs, "by now we're accustomed to it."

"What was in the script?" I asked.

"Oh, the scenes that were supposed to be shot were of a man kneeling in front of an enchanting Negress and saying, 'I am your slave,' and then another of an old pimp leading a big shepherd dog into a room for a client to make love to."

Fellini starts with Robert again. He is annoyed and his temper flares frequently. "All right, go, Robert," but he doesn't move. "Which language do you speak?" Fellini enquires in English.

Robert replies, "English."

Fellini gives him a withering look.

The soothsayer, a big man dressed in orange, has the liver in his hand and says, "The liver is dark. It's a good sign."

"All right, Robert," Fellini commands, "go to your wife."

She is praying in front of the statue, "Oh, Mother Venus, take pity on my barren state."

Fellini tells her, "Move your head, Luisa, and stay on your knees," and shows Robert exactly how to lean over Luisa so as not to cover her head.

He shrills at Luisa, who has moved out of position, *"Ma che cosa c'hai nella capoccia?* What have you got in that big head? Stop. Robert, try to walk a bit softer," he says gently. "Don't go like this," and he demonstrates clumping along and plunking himself down. "Go down soft." After four excruciating takes, the director leaves for a long talk with the producer and the production manager.

There is a long delay and I sit and talk with Robert Blake, the husband of the barren woman. A twenty-one-year-old Australian, he explains, "I'm another flower child. One day I walked into Cinecittà and I was standing in the middle of this set. A man asked me what I was doing here and I said, 'I heard Fellini was looking for people to work.' The man said, 'I am Fellini.' That was a month ago. They took pictures of me and here I am. I heard what Fellini said to me, those dirty words, but I couldn't care less. He still has to pay me thirty-two dollars anyway. The rent is the only absolute in the situation and I've still got a cave in Positano. This is the first time I've had a job in years."

Max Born pricks up his ears at this. "I've never worked for more than a week either," he announces, "except for playing the guitar on the streets around Marble Arch or in the tube stations." Max is perfect for the part of Giton, whom the director describes as "a whore with the face of an angel." A seventeen-year-old hippie from London, he is dark-haired with large limpid brown eyes and the face of a wise cherub. To dig what life was all about, he skipped out of his proper English public school to roam through the streets of Chelsea without a penny in his pocket or a pad to bed down in. Fellini had advertised in the Roman papers, attracting hundreds of boys all wanting the part of Giton, but none suited him, and his search took him to London.

"In early August Fellini's scout went to a model agency in Chelsea looking for boys and all kinds of freaks," Max says. "A friend who had a small hairdressing shop under the agency suggested I go upstairs where I met the model agent. She arranged an appointment with Fellini's scout, who took some pictures outside because I didn't have any. When I left him, he said he'd let me know in a couple of weeks but he didn't."

Max left London and went to the country. When he returned a month later, he was told that Fellini was coming and wanted to see him at the agency. There the director talked with him briefly, surrounded by hundreds of other people, and invited the young hippie to lunch at his hotel, the Savoy.

"I went the next day and Fellini asked me who I was and what I did," Max continues. "Martin Potter came to lunch too but they wouldn't let us in the hotel restaurant because we didn't have ties on so we went to a Chinese restaurant.

"We talked about loads of things including films. I'd seen *Juliet* a number of times. It was one of my favorite films. I liked it because it wasn't straight. Other people make fantasies but most of them are such god-awful fantasies. *Juliet* is like a Godard film. Fellini doesn't mess around with anything real. He's got dreams and visions and fantasies. I knew from watching it that I would like Fellini.

"I felt very close to him because I knew he was a very aware person that I could get across to. I'm one of the flower children, not really a hippie. Say that. Make it beautiful. We said 'good-bye' and Fellini said he'd let me know in three weeks. He never told me precisely what the role was but said the film was about ancient Rome and people freaking out but very much like now. They were all doing their own thing, but decadently."

Three weeks went by while Max waited around in London. Then the agent received a letter saying Fellini wanted the boy for a role without specifying which one, and only a week later did he learn he was to be Giton. Max had to go to Rome for a screen test and arrived on November first with his stepfather. "He came because he just felt he ought to and I didn't mind," Max goes on. "They did a makeup test and cut off all my hair. It was halfway down my back and beautiful.

"My mother was very pleased but, at the same time, she keeps trying to say something to me. Like, at the last moment, she said, 'I guess you've sort of made it but what would have happened if you had a normal face?' Like, who's got a normal face? All faces go through changes depending upon what's inside them. They're sometimes ugly, sometimes beautiful, but never normal."

Max Born, who never read Petronius' *Satyricon* but read the script several times, says, "I'm working for the first time. It's a groovy game. Working for Fellini is more or less what I had imagined it would be like. Fellini is straight. I get very strong vibrations from him. Like he's aware of everything much the same way I am. He has a kind of cosmic awareness.

"I look through everything and I find the real me. The real me is quite close to Giton, in the sense of being basically innocent but at the same time very wise. Giton knows a hell of a lot and kind of flows along because he knows so much and doesn't get messed up. He's found his own scene, without any morality, without any hang-ups. He's always doing what he wants to do without being nasty.

"What do I think about when I act?" Max thinks a moment and answers, "Fellini takes me just like a puppet and I have to adapt. At times, when he's impatient, I don't get enough vibes from him. That does get difficult, but it doesn't bother me. When we started the picture, Fellini said, 'It's a trip, this one, and we're going to have fun!' It's the other people who take him too seriously."

Fellini does a close-up of Martin and Max walking up the steps of the amphitheater. "Look at the balls of the bull," he commands. He orders the small statue of Venus, which was made overnight, placed back in the center of the set, tells Martin to go to his second position, and then goes to look through the camera, whistling.

When the close-up was finished, I went off to lunch with Peppino Rotunno, a black-haired, dark-eyed, gentle man with the face of a sad monkey. He has a serene nature, never raises his voice or displays temperament, the exact opposite of the volcanic Fellini. Now forty-five years old and one of the best cameramen in Europe, Peppino has worked with some of the world's greatest directors, including Vittorio De Sica, Roberto Rossellini, Stanley Kramer, Luigi Visconti, and John Huston, for whom he shot *The Bible*. For Fellini, he filmed the *Toby Dammit* episode, then continued on with the *Satyricon*.

"It's going very well," he said. "With Fellini's method of work, nothing is ever finished. When he has a subject in hand, he wants to update it always, every day, every hour, every second, always to improve it. But, in a certain sense, all the great directors are alike.

They are forever looking for perfection. They all make different films but their way of arriving at perfection is very much alike. I construct a bridge between the screen and the public to allow the director to reach the public in the fastest possible way and to permit the public to understand in the quickest way.

"My problem is to keep the lighting technique from being obvious," Peppino explained. "The public must not be aware of the lights and the illumination of the settings, but feel more of the atmosphere and have the sensation of luminescence. The spectator must have the feeling of actually living in that epoch and then we return outside again to look at it from far off. It is a way of using a technique: the technique of not using technique. It's an original idea for this film and the first time I've done it. Fellini suggested it to me not so much in words, but I understood what he wanted from conversations he had with others, with the set designer, the archietect, the makeup people, and the actors."

The cameraman believes Fellini is trying to detach himself from his other films with the *Satyricon,* and to remain detached and feel the film from the outside. "Each ambience is a new film," he said. "He changes the atmosphere, the mood, but there is an invisible thread that holds it all together. Fellini has even put himself in a certain mood, a certain state of mind. I try to stay inside the director and condition myself to follow that mood with the lights. There is a very close collaboration. I tell him what I am going to do. Sometimes he agrees; sometimes he wants something a little different. I have always maintained that the director and the cameraman must be the same person or be so united that they are the same person. One can't take one road and the other another. I'm not here to make a beautiful display of photography. I am here to make Fellini's film.

"Fellini is always nervous when he goes into a new scene," Peppino explained, "because he is looking for the right road. He always selects faces but he doesn't know how they are going to react. They don't understand and he gets mad but, in these frescoes he is preparing, he sees those faces and he has to have them.

"It is not true, as you hear so often, that he improvises as he goes along, that everything comes by chance. Instead, he is very well prepared in his mind, but always leaves the door open to give himself the possibility of changing the scene, of improving it; and this I find very beautiful. Fellini has a personality that will never limit his intelligence. It is always open to new ideas. He can think of a film and make it twenty years later. He is always evolving, always updating himself because he has a fundamentally youthful foundation. What he does today, he won't do tomorrow. He pretends to be unprepared, but he is a monster of preparation. This is his strength. His impatience, enthusiasm and nervousness spring from this.

"Fellini is a real man of the cinema," Peppino concluded. "He understands the camera very well. As the pen is the instrument of the writer, so the camera is Fellini's instrument as an artist."

After lunch, Marcello Mastroianni, spiffily dressed in black overcoat, black Mao jacket and tight blue trousers, arrives on the set. He has just come back from Russia, where he went to discuss a new film he was to make with Sophia Loren. He sits by me and Capucine and Giulietta Masina in one of the camp chairs. Fellini, like every director, has his chair with his name marked on it, but he rarely sits in it; so it's always occupied by a journalist or visitor or even an extra.

"I have such a weakness for Fellini," Marcello confides. "I am always enthusiastic about what he is doing. I saw *8½* the other day after about five or six years. It really is a beautiful thing. Films being made today, which are supposed to be so modern, are just abortions compared to it. It's a confirmation of the art of Fellini."

Fellini comes over to embrace Marcello and kiss him exuberantly on both cheeks. He laughs and jokes and then reports to me that

Mastroianni has said I am very erotic. Mastroianni has said nothing of the kind, but Fellini is always making little jokes about sex, or inquiring about your sex life, or wanting to know if you are curious about his. One day, he asked me, "Will you write about my sex life in zis buk, Eileen?"

"If you want to tell me about it, I suppose I could include it," I twitted; but he didn't venture any details.

A new scene begins up at the top of the steps with four pimps at the entrance to the brothel. Battaglia, the old man with the lotus blossoms behind his ears, is sitting in the central doorway. Behind him stands a fat man with a flabby paunch and flowers stuck at his bosom. Another man, this one young and exotically made up and costumed, is standing in the left doorway. In the right door is a horrid old lady dressed in bright red with very black hair and black rimmed eyes painted on her white face like a crooked mask. The colors of the costumes pick up those of the murals and the wall. Fellini really displays his mastery of improvisation in this scene, because he has three different situations going on simultaneously and only he knows what he intends to do.

Max and Martin are at the bottom of the steps and must pass the barren woman and her husband in front of the statue of Venus, then climb the stairs where they are importuned by the four pimps. Fellini starts the rehearsal. "Go, Martino, Mox. Come, Battaglia," to the old man with the flowers. "Go, Domizi," to the fat man with the jiggling belly, a food vendor in the general market. "Battaglia, go to Max, pat him and make a hammy movement. Turn Giton around and show him off."

He's had a second thought and comes over to report to Mastroianni, "You know she had a tremendous advance to write a book." He's always asking me if the money has arrived yet and when he is going to get his cut. It's his standing joke.

Then he's back directing: "Martino, you zmile at zee beginning because it is funny but then you go and pull Mox back." He decides the fat man must sit and calls for a stool. "Go sit," and he sits inside the corridor, which the painters have just finished.

Fellini is working himself up into a fit. "Zambon," he yells at the painter who is still frantically repainting the steps. "Please stop it." He screams at Martin, "Pass on the other side of Mox," without explaining to him that he wants him to do it so he won't block Max's face from the camera. To Battaglia, he rages, "You are a pimp. Come out like you are one." He hollers at Alfredo, whom he has now seated on the floor, then yells at Elisabetta, the lady in red, "Hard, grab him hard." She must grab Martin and try to lure him into the whorehouse.

"All right, let's try it again. Alfredo, remember you are a pimp. Say anything you like, but speak. Everybody in place. Battaglia, turn him around like a *ballerino*. Alfredo, you don't have to act like a policeman. You're a pimp." To the old woman, he shouts, "Seek him out. Smile." Her face breaks into a hideous leer. "Stop."

Wearily, he calls Maurizio, the assistant director. "Explain to Alfredo." Alfredo is a gypsy horse trader who doesn't even understand Italian. He must stick his tongue out in lascivious little jerks and beckon the boys with his head. Fellini admonishes Elisabetta, "You mustn't come to Martin like you are a Madonna. Touch him, kiss him, anything. Martin, zmile. You are having fun. You are in a comic situation."

They do it again and he screeches, *"Che merda, che fa,* Elisabetta? What shit, what are you doing? Come to him; pull him hard, hard, toward you. Alfredo," he implores, "you must look at the blond man. He is very beautiful.

"Pronti, ready. Let's try to shoot this one." He shows Alfredo how to make a rude gesture. "Elisabetta," he screeches, "pull off his arm. Mox, don't stand like a statue." He changes his mind. "Elisabetta, start from inside the corridor. When I call you, come out and do what I told you before. Alfredo," he pleads, "you must not look at us. We don't exist. Look at them."

On the third take, Battaglia anticipates his action again and they do another, but Fellini is still not content and decides to change the scene. He now has Elisabetta sit down. "Tell Alfredo to stay where he is," he shouts through the megaphone at Maurizio. "We will try a new way. Maurì," he screams with frustration, "make her sit down. *Madonna!*"

They start again, this time with Robert and his wife in front of the statue of Venus. "Robert, talk with the lady. Take her hands, both of them." Then he notices there is something wrong with Elisabetta's earring and tries to fix it, but can't, and calls for Gilda, the hairdresser.

On the next take, he is bellowing through the megaphone to Eugene, "Tell that Englishman how to speak and stroke her hands. *Che cazzo ha in testa?* What the prick does he have in his head? *Cretino,* why are you laughing?" he shouts at Robert, who is giggling.

Gideon Bachmann, who has been waiting for a moment like this as an example of the director's uncanny talent for intuitive directing in the television documentary he is shooting, explains, "Fellini's greatest asset is that he always knows what is the right thing on the spur of the moment, when it happens and without thinking. Like here, he can tell an actor standing there like a block of wood, in a landscape that somebody else has created for him, how to move his shoulder or his head, in order to make one thing out of that actor and that landscape to express what he is thinking at that moment, without the actor ever knowing what it's all about. It just happens then and there and he probably couldn't tell you before how he was going to do it. There are no camera directions in the script. It is absolutely intuitive.

"But the intuition doesn't really begin to work until the set is built and there in front of him and he's got to face the reality, invented essentially by others, and work inside it. That's when the force begins to work. Fellini needs the whole world there first, in order to be able to begin adjusting and controlling. I consider him a genius in this very specific sense of knowing more than one would assume naturally possible, the right thing at the right time. That's the same thing as knowing what another person is thinking. There's some mysticism there. You don't know how it works but it's a fabulous force."

The Whorehouses in the Subura

January 22

Stage Number Five is a beehive of activity. Overnight Fellini has changed the script and combined two scenes. Originally, Encolpius and Giton run through the streets of the Subura, the gamier section of Rome, catching glimpses of the life, the people, the streets, the houses, the taverns and the shops. They run into a house of prostitution only to avoid the insistent summons of the magistrate who has forced Vernacchio to relinquish Giton to Encolpius. For some reason known only to himself, the director has inserted in the scene not one brothel but a whole series of them and omits the sights of the Subura. Stretching the length of a long canal, which resembles the Cloaca Maxima, the ancient Roman sewers, are the prostitutes' cells.

Fellini is following along as the set is being assembled by the distraught Donati and his assistants. The costume designer is hurriedly scribbling graffiti on the wall while the director is telling a painter how he wants a fresco. Giggling mischievously, Fellini takes to scratching his own graffiti like a naughty schoolboy. *"Ego hic facevit amorem,"* he scrawls, "Here I made love"—bad Latin, but intended to convey the impression of an unlettered client who has left behind the crude trace of his visit.

Beside each door, the name of the prostitute, her price, and a symbol denoting her specialty is crudely and incorrectly written: *Philaenium XXX nummis; Bacchis XXXVI nummis; Bacchis II, XXXVII nummis; Delphium XV nummis; Anterastilis LXX nummis.* The names of the prostitutes are taken from Plautus, and *nummis* indicates pieces of no specific money. Fellini chose it so as not to pinpoint the epoch.

The director is on a raft in the middle of the thirty-foot-long canal surveying the scene with a sublime expression on his face. (It takes eighteen pumps to move the dirty, fetid water in the canal.) To the right, at the end of it, is an arch, the only Roman arch seen in the film. The painters are painting, the carpenters are hammering, the prop men are scurrying with furnishings for the cells; and a line of extras is waiting below, in the rear of the big darkened studio, for the director to choose his characters for this scene. They are millionaires and beggars, ugly and beautiful, young and old, fat and skinny, tall and short.

The big lights are being set up, but only a couple of scenes will be shot today, and not until much later in the afternoon. Meanwhile, there is nothing to do but sit and watch the frenzied activities of the crew and talk with whomever I can catch. Luigi Scaccianoce, the set architect, is sitting glumly watching the bustle. A small, sad-looking man with the air of a perplexed professor suddenly transported from the classroom to a crazy house, he has had twenty-five years' experience in the cinema working with such notable directors as Roberto Rossellini, Orson Welles, Pier Paolo Pasolini and Joseph Losey. This is his first experience with Fellini, perhaps not one of the most gratifying of his career since he became increasingly gloomy as the picture progressed and left a month before *Satyricon* was finished to work on another film.

At the moment, Scaccianoce is explaining how the sets are made. "Fellini makes designs accompanied by explanations. Then small models are made or the designs reworked until, little by little, we arrive at the actual construction and find the color tones and the richness or poverty of the materials. Sets always present difficulties, whether technological or ideological. These sets don't have a realistic construction in any way, either archaeologically or historically. It is a style of scenery invented by the imagination of Fellini. He is the real set designer. The idea is completely his and we must construct the idea and put it at the disposal of the camera. The work will stop only when his brain stops working."

Maurizio Mein, the assistant director, comes and slumps exhausted in a chair. A squat, stubby man with sideburns growing almost into his mouth, he is astonishingly agile, running all over the set like a marathon racer, intently studying Fellini's face to see if he is doing what the director wants. Fellini's instructions are not always too precise and most of the crew are always second-guessing what he means. Maurizio has been working in the cinema twelve years and worked with Fellini on the *Toby Dammit* episode and the NBC television special. In *Toby Dammit* Fellini invented a scene in which the hero is conducted onto a set where four westerns are being shot simultaneously. Fellini needed someone to organize the four troupes and called Maurizio because he had worked on so many spaghetti westerns.

"Meeting Fellini," Maurizio recalls, "I had the strange sensation of being with a man who had no problems. The cinema is no longer a technique for him, nor a job, but rather a way of life. Talking to him was like hearing a voice I had heard during my infancy but then never again. It was lucky for me because talking with a great man like him, with my shyness, I would have been paralyzed.

"Fellini creates on the instant, a kind of instant film, and gets impatient because he is afraid of losing the image in front of him. He wants to achieve what he wants and to bring to life immediately what he feels inside himself.

"He hardly ever says anything to me," Maurizio continues. "He expects a certain form of collaboration, that you immerse yourself completely in the film. Before beginning, he talks about what the film is to be like—the faces, the atmosphere, the costumes, the color. Once that's done, he expects you to live in this atmosphere and follow in the wake of his intuition. It is a collaboration based on sensations rather than precise facts.

"We know from one day to the next what we must do, from the technical point of view, but never what he will film. No one knows, and this is the fascinating part, otherwise it would be terribly boring. Every day there is a new climate of creation."

January 23

Donati is still reworking the sets from yesterday, hastening from cell to cell to supervise the work in progress. A painter in blue smock and black beret is calmly plastering a square of gold paint beside the red room. The director leaves the camera, where he is setting up a fresco of the denizens of the Lupanare, and crosses over to the opposite side of the canal where all the spectators are standing, opens the robe of a woman wearing an elaborate gladiator's helmet, gives her a satisfied smile, and tells her to "stay covered."

Back for another rehearsal, he shows Carlo, the man in purple, how to walk to the canal. "Look. Come on. *Coraggio,* courage." To the soldiers, he warns, "Lower your heads. Stand like statues. Look directly into the camera and keep your eyes like balls. Rossi, walk looking into the camera." To Carlo, "Put your head against the wall, but look into the camera."

Fellini uses this technique of having people look directly into the camera throughout the film to give the audience the eerie sensation of being spied on by ghosts or extraterrestrial beings.

"All right, undress the woman," he orders. She is a plump, Reubens type—the kind Fellini likes so much—sitting in front of what looks like a primitive organ. Black cords crisscross her bulging bare back, holding up a piece of flimsy red tulle which scarcely covers her naked behind. Inside the blue room, lying in a niche in the wall is another scantily clad woman, with smoke rising up in front of her from the vases on the floor.

Water is now made to gush out of the gutters into the canal, and an extra called Lauretta has had the yellow robe she was wearing stripped off to reveal her in a filmy pink gown over bare breasts. "Carlo, smile, and Lauretta, look like a madwoman," Fellini orders, and zooms down the track behind the camera, yelling, "Carlo, scream, scream. Forward, soldiers," and screeches at the naked woman playing the organ, "Play that thing, and stick your behind out more." A pot of black smoke is brought out by Adriano, the special-effects man, and it billows the length of the canal. Shouting directions to each extra, Fellini is carried down the track, and on the fifth take is finished.

Later at lunch, I chat with Enrico Rossetti, the Vice President of Cinecittà, who remarks, "This film could not be made in any other studio in the world, and especially not in countries where the work is done only according to set hours regulated by unions. Here we have continuous, extraordinary needs. Scenes are redone with incredible rapidity by the workmen. If we followed a rigorous routine, the film would last two years, but the Italian works as an *artigiano,* or craftsman. When he is asked to do something unusual, he is happy. The worker feels a direct participation in the success of the film. It gives the artisans a human rapport with the director. They even go to see the film to see how their particular part of the film turned out."

Back on the set, Fellini is escorting a member of the Italian parliament around, gleefully describing the three-hundred-and-fifty-pound woman he is planning to use as a whore. "Rita is a baby compared with her," he brags. "She is a *bella cicciona,* a lovely meaty one." Then the director takes his guest from cell to cell explaining the specialities of each occupant, and even has his picture taken, with Rita, the lady who whips a soldier, standing behind him and the Deputy for a prank.

Fellini starts the afternoon scenes. There is now a raft in the middle of the canal with the Empress and a group of slumming courtiers on it. He places five extras against the wall by the arch of the sewer.

Luciana, who plays the depraved Empress, isn't getting off the raft the way Fellini wants, quickly and crazily, and he shows her how to do that. He has been acting all day. He returns to the camera and watches her. Still unsatisfied, he staggers wearily down the length of the canal and places her on her knees, palms down, with her rear end sticking up high. A final adjustment to the old man in grey near the camera and he is ready. "Who the hell's pulling that raft?" he yells as it wobbles into view from under the arch.

"It's like the tunnel of love through the fun house," quips Eugene.

When this scene is finished, Fellini brings out his treasure, the grossly heavy prostitute whose bare breasts flow like lava over a flimsy aquamarine skirt. He seats her on the floor and makes her tuck one of her legs up with the other stretched out.

"That's Mount Crisco!" cracks Eugene.

"No," Enrico Rossetti disagrees, "Fellini feels nostalgic for the

days when there were brothels in Rome. That's Saraghina from
8½, the mother of all whores."

"No," Franco Pinna, the photographer, objects. "Like all Italians,
he is obsessed with sin and sex from his Catholic upbringing. Everything is sin, so naturally he turns to forbidden sex with whores.
That's why he puts all these whores in his movies." No two people
can ever agree on anything Fellini does.

The director has placed a tall, glistening, almost naked Negro
man behind the fat woman, whom he urges to jiggle her body,
but she is too shy and embarrassed to do it. Fellini searches around
and after three tries finally finds a man small enough to crouch
behind her and shake that mountain of flesh.

Before shooting, he goes down to the group of extras and chooses
those he wants for the next day. He pats one on the fanny saying,
"You did well. You can be in another scene but in a different
costume." He thanks another sweetly and kisses another on the
cheeks.

I chat with an extra, a thirty-four-year-old transvestite from
Perugia who calls himself Clara and plies his trade on the Lungo-
tevere. He has already appeared in thirteen films, but this is his
first time working for Fellini. "I don't work," he boasts. "I lead an
easy life and I am very happy. Already I have more clients because
I am a pimp in a Fellini film!"

January 24

Fellini is calmer today because there are fewer people on the
set. He wants a veil half covering the door of the cell with
a hoop-like sex instrument hanging from the ceiling, and fiddles
around with it until he gets it right. Now he concentrates on the
sex instrument. The director is furious with the extra who is rais-

ing it and lowering it from the ceiling with a rope and makes him do it over and over again, saying, "Show me how you do it."

He places an old woman and two soldiers against the wall outside, saying, "Look into the camera as though into a void." To the soldiers, he orders, "Still, like that." To the old woman, "Say numbers, anything, but speak. More exaggerated. Open your mouth."

They have hoisted a girl up in the leather contraption. It is Susanna, or Susannona (big Susan), the same one who played the organ yesterday. "But this basket is broken," she protests.

"Exactly," Fellini replies with an angelic expression on his face, "it lets your buttocks jut through."

"My, weren't these ancient Romans complicated!" Susanna retorts, as she swings crazily around in the hoop.

"Look happier," the director orders, "you are going to make love."

Below her, the man lying on the ground has had his black robe removed and is naked except for a codpiece. Fellini covers the girl's bottom with a piece of green tulle. "Susanna," he implores, "sing while you are being lowered. Don't you know a song? And move your legs." On the tenth take, the director suddenly strips the green cloth off Susanna's bottom and leaves her with her bare behind sticking out of the hoop. Everyone gapes as she is lowered to the client stretched on the floor.

Horrified, Bob Herrington, the English press-relations man, gasps, "My God, I think we're making a pornographic film."

(These scenes of whores and erotic sexual romps may titillate Fellini's sybaritic fantasies, but they are curiously un-erotic, even boring, to watch. I feel sorry for the poor wretches who have to go through these things—which seem humiliating to me—and wonder whether this is art or exploitation. Susanna Limongelli, the girl in the hoop, a thirty-one-year-old extra who has worked in many films but never before for Fellini, told me, "He didn't tell me what I had to do, and this is the first time I have ever been nude in a film. I did it because I have to make money, not because I like it. Certainly, it's embarrassing, especially for someone who is over thirty; but for someone who needs money, *beh,* well," she shrugs. "I don't know what the film is all about anyway.")

Ruggero Mastroianni, who will edit the film with the director, sighs, "He will reinvent everything in the cutting." Fellini comes up, gives Ruggero the usual buss on both cheeks and says to me, "Why don't you go sit on that bench over there? Go. Be an American journalist interviewing the ancient Romans." I hide behind Ruggero as he tries to push me into the scene. It might have been amusing to play a bit part to see how I would react to Fellini's screeching and hollering, but at this particular point, I have the awful fear I will end up with my clothes stripped off swinging in some kind of strange contraption like Susanna.

Later, when things were calmer, Donati described how this whole episode came about. "Overnight, Fellini decided he wanted to make a street of pleasure, of little whorehouses. The set had to be made in two days. In two hours, each cell had to be painted, and we had to make twenty or twenty-five because they all had to be different. Even though the street is only about thirty feet long, he wanted to stretch it out to make it appear as though it were very much longer. So each of the six cells had to be repainted and in the same two hours we had to dye the costume to go with the wall of the newly painted cell.

"Fellini wanted the street of the prostitutes in an area that was black and filthy like the rest of the Subura. He chose the Cloaca Maxima because he wanted a thing of rats and vermin, where vice is better placed. This kept him from touching on the monuments and the settings he didn't want. He never intended to portray the monumental zone of Rome. And, after all, he couldn't do a thing like that in a temple or a public square, could he?"

The Dinner of Trimalchio

This is the longest fragment in Petronius' *Satyricon* and the one which Fellini reproduces most faithfully, though still filtered through his cosmic imagination. Encolpius has met an old down-on-his-uppers poet, Eumolpus, in the Pinacoteca or art gallery. The poet, a great freeloader, invites his young friend to a banquet at the villa of Trimalchio, whose name means "thrice blessed." An ex-slave, he has, by pandering to the sexual appetites of both his master and his mistress, not only gained his freedom but also inherited great wealth, which he has parlayed into an immense fortune—so many slaves he can't count them; so much land he can't walk over it. A coarse nouveau riche, he delights in flaunting his wealth and treasures at interminably long and lavish feasts to servile friends and hangers-on. He considers himself a poet and philosopher, but his only philosophy is the accumulation of more goods and his only poetry is cribbed.

Fellini thought of discarding this episode completely but then reconsidered. "To try to follow the images suggested by the text," he declared, "means to fall into the most trite and conventional depiction of a Roman banquet which the cinema has worn out by now: columns, silver plates, triclinia, ample bare breasts, orgies. How can one restore to this image a virginity, a new aspect?

"In the total reinvention I am making of the *Satyricon*," he explained, "the fragments of which are only an excuse to unleash the imagination to reconstruct an unknown world, I thought immediately of eliminating the dinner but I would have been accused of arbitrariness and alteration. So I looked for a different key. I made Trimalchio a rich landowner, a peasant himself, who lives in a country estate that stretches out in heavy, humid air. His table is that of a hoarder of agricultural foodstuffs. In his house, the only serious thing is food. All the rest is trimming, a joke.

"The banquet which Trimalchio offers actually was inspired by childhood memories of certain appalling dinners of the peasants of Romagna where I was born, which lasted from noon until two in the morning while guests challenged each other to eating contests. For example, here is a feat of eating, on a bet, worthy of Trimalchio: three chickens, twenty-two feet of sausages, and one candle. The candle was to show that the peasant had the stomach of an ostrich."

Though the dinner began today, everyone was barred from the set because Fellini was so nervous and the set was small, noisy and cramped. Even Bob Herrington, the English publicist for the picture, was refused admittance. "It's the first time in forty-two pictures I've ever been barred from a set," he fumed. "Imagine! Me, the publicist on the picture! I f——d that doorman out. It's the first time I've ever done it in all these years."

The day culminated in a stormy fit of temper when the director called for a knife to cut a mammoth turkey made of plaster and tripe. A prop knife was brought and broke. After four others failed to do the job, Fellini finally screamed for a real knife from the restaurant, but that didn't work either. The director stomped off the set, railing, "I am not going to continue working with this band of dilettantes." Betting was heavy among the crew that *il Maestro* would reappear after having a coffee, but he fooled them all and didn't come back, probably because it was near the end of the day anyway.

I wasn't too upset at not being allowed on the set. There would be plenty of other days since this became one of the lengthiest, dreariest and most revolting dinners in history. The shooting lasted three weeks, fifteen days for the "Dinner" proper and six days for the remainder of the episode. Meanwhile, I went off to talk with Bernardino Zapponi, the director's principal collaborator on the five-hundred-page script. Not far from the Spanish Steps, in the Caffè Greco, famous since the nineteenth century as the hangout of artists and writers, Zapponi talked about the script and the director.

A young Roman ex-journalist, the dapper, dark-haired Zapponi has written several scripts, including the one for the *Toby Dammit* episode, and published many short stories. It was through his book of bizarre short stories, *Gobal,* that Fellini came to meet the writer. Fellini read Zapponi's book in 1967 and asked the writer's collaboration on an episode based on an Edgar Allan Poe story. He really preferred to do one of the stories from *Gobal* but the film's French coproducer said it was impossible to do two episodes from Poe and one of Zapponi. "It had to be all Poe," the writer laughed, "but there is nothing of Poe in Fellini's episode. It is all invented except for the title and the ending.

"We began to talk about the *Satyricon* when I first met Fellini," Zapponi said. "He thought of it as limpid, Mediterranean, as the joy of exploration. Immediately during our first meeting, Fellini found the right approach. He abandoned himself to adventure, to detaching himself from the world we know."

Before sitting down to write, Zapponi met with Fellini every day to map out various sequences. They wrote in August and September, spending more than two months on the script. "We had a great time together," he remarked, "like two kids in a stolen boat who had put out to sea without knowing where they were going. De Mille would have documented ancient Rome, but we took ourselves away from concrete things to invent absurd things, to recreate the far-offness of the epoch.

"The *Satyricon* is a science-fiction film of the epoch, not of space," the writer continued. "Everything is seen in an optical illusion. After the joy of invention, the tiring part was to make something distorted, unrecognizable, in order to give it a sense of the unknown. Even the dialogue is incomprehensible and the characters laugh when they should cry. Each of us made suggestions, just yakking away. One of us would say, 'I remember when I was a kid . . .' and the other would recall something else or suggest another thing. There were no well-defined roles. But Fellini has a very exact sense of the spectacle and he is the one who gives the frame to every scene. It was a bestial job!

"Fellini hasn't changed the script but, during the shooting, he cuts or adds because he may see things in his own way. He can't be chained down by a script. It is only a guideline for him. For example at 'The Dinner of Trimalchio,' nobody is plucking at bunches of grapes or having wine poured down his throat. It is much more chaste and anguished, with little gaiety, like a funeral banquet.

"In the dubbing, Fellini will make everything even stranger and more incomprehensible because the rhythm couldn't be modern. Things had to finish jerkily, incoherently. We took some dialogue from Petronius, put it in a strange and different Latin and in an archaic Roman dialect of the seventeenth century.

"His films are always Fellini," Zapponi asserted. "There are no similar or recurrent themes from his previous films, just his way of looking at humanity, with compassion and pity. He is full of a warmth which I didn't suspect, and expresses his pity and love for the next person, but also his tender cruelty. He is now more pitiless and cruel than ever before. Fellini is a Christian atheist. His hatred for the Catholic Church is like that of a child for a bad mother who puts him in the dark to punish him."

January 28

The set is still closed today so I went to talk with Alberto Grimaldi, the producer of the film, in his tastefully furnished office at Largo Ponchielli in the center of Rome. Grimaldi's production company PEA (Produzioni Europee Associati) made a deal with United Artists for four pictures in which the Italian company serves as producer and Italian distributor, while United Artists serves as world distributor and provides a minimum financial guarantee for each picture. Two of the films are *Satyricon* and *Burn,* a film being shot concurrently in Colombia by Gillo Pontecorvo and starring Marlon Brando. I was curious to meet the man who had the courage to take on Fellini, one of the world's most mercurial directors, and Brando, one of the most temperamental actors, at the same time.

Grimaldi, a forty-three-year-old Neapolitan with a degree in law, is an attractive, shrewd, and enterprising man with a keen nose for scenting out new trends in the film world. His first efforts in the cinema in 1961 were restricted to historical quickies for the Italian market, which earned swift financial returns but no critical acclaim. In 1963, the perceptive Grimaldi began making a series of low-budget westerns, "spaghetti westerns" as they came to be called, including two highly successful ones—*For a Few Dollars More* and *The Good, the Bad and the Ugly,* both directed by Sergio Leone

—which made a star of Clint Eastwood and millions for the producer.

"Step by step," Grimaldi affirmed, "I tried to improve the quality of my films. After the westerns, I thought I had to begin doing pictures of very high artistic quality. But I also decided that a picture must be a spectacle because it has to reach the greatest audience, not just the small elite group.

"I decided to make pictures of high quality because during the past ten years the taste of audiences has been improving. For example, years ago when a so-called 'art picture' was shown at a festival, it was synonymous with commercial failure. It won a prize, but didn't earn any money. This, however, has changed in the last eight or ten years. The prize winners have also enjoyed good financial success."

Grimaldi met Fellini in the spring of 1967 and asked him if he had any projects in mind after *Mastorna*. When he discovered the director had intended to do the *Satyricon* for a long time, the contract was signed, in July, 1967. "I thought the *Satyricon* was sensational and exciting because it had never been done before," Grimaldi said. "United Artists just read the treatment and approved the project. They put in trust and money. The control is ours. The activity of the producer, especially from the Italian or European point of view, is not the same as in the United States. There, the producer is actually an employee of the distributing company. He doesn't take any risk in financing the film, whereas in Italy, the producer finances the picture totally or partially. He takes a big risk and has to pay if the picture is over the budget. His real role is very similar to that of a book publisher."

I asked if having to cope with Fellini and Brando simultaneously had created any difficulties. He smiled wryly and explained, "I never intended to do *Burn* and the *Satyricon* simultaneously but, for reasons beyond my control, they started five days apart—*Burn* on November 4th and Fellini on November 9th. Brando's script

was not ready for a few months and the film had to be postponed
and Fellini's picture was pushed ahead."

If he had any problems, Grimaldi didn't intend to discuss them,
but I wondered what kind of response he would have to a remark
I overheard after Fellini's tantrum on the set—"Anyone who tackles
Brando and Fellini together deserves what he gets."

January 30

The set is open today and visitors are tolerated, if not exactly
welcome, at Trimalchio's feast. The dining room is built on
Stage Two, a much smaller studio than either Five or Fifteen, and
is jam-packed with at least two hundred members of cast and crew.
It is an ugly and drab set. The high walls are painted a flat, luster-
less orange, the floor a dull purple. Fellini had preferred a lower
ceiling so the tons of smoke which will be used in this episode
would remain inside longer, but it had to be raised to accommodate
the lights. On three sides the couches have been inclined so the
heads of the guests are higher than their feet. Surrounding the three-
sided triclinium is a second, higher level or corridor. On the left
wall is an enormous, unfinished mosaic of Trimalchio, based on a
blown-up photograph of il Moro's mournful face. On the right
side, an upper gallery has been built to accommodate the drably
dressed poor relations and scroungers. The entire set, which took
twenty-three days to build, was designed in this simple, stark style
to accentuate the gorgeous costumes of the guests and their macabre
faces, which are intended to leap out at the audience.

Donati has outdone himself in inventing the jewelry, costumes,
and props. The base of the enormous golden urn behind Trimalchio's couch is ingeniously encrusted with millions of tiny lentils
sprayed with gilt to create the impression of gold pellets. What appear to be basalt urns are actually alum coated with tar. Plastic is
made to resemble lapis lazuli and malachite. Rough chunks of alum

serve as rock crystals and several quartz vases and urns are actually painted glass. The unfinished portrait of Trimalchio is being put together with thirty thousand Charm candies.

Donati moans, "For Trimalchio, Fellini couldn't decide who it was to be. He wanted Mario Romagnoli, but il Moro didn't want to do it. Finally, after Fellini persuaded him, you know what he said to me? He told me I had to do a huge mosaic of Trimalchio in three days. I said, 'But it's impossible! What do you expect me to do, make it with candies?' And as I said it, I realized it *could* be done with candies so I ran around and bought all the Charms in Rome. Can you imagine!"

Trimalchio, with a lugubrious face and air, is dressed in a blue velvet robe with a mauve and gold stole and a gold crown on his grey hair. Heavy gold bracelets adorn his arms and the large ruby brooch glittering on the right side of his robe has been fashioned from a big red lollipop. His crown, like many worn by the guests, is made of real holly leaves dipped in gold paint. Other crowns have been devised from bits of macaroni and various shaped pasta tinted gold.

Next to the host is Fortunata, his shrewish, avaricious wife, played by Magali Noël, gaudily jeweled with earrings and bracelets and dressed in a gauzy green robe revealing her bare breasts and backside. The heavy, elaborate coiffure she wears is lavished with gold bands and gems. Her sister, Mara Krupp, sits beside her in an orange robe with a fancy two-foot-high headdress. At the left end of the triclinium is Fortunata's mother, played by Fides Stagni, whose wig has been made up in long, sausage-like rolls of curls similar to those seen on ancient busts of Roman matrons.

The ghastly guests are all intricately coiffed and bejeweled, with their spectral faces made up in colors to match their costumes: blue faces, orange faces, yellow faces, green faces, ashen faces, gold faces, and red faces. While the host and his family sit in regal splendor on the center triclinium, the guests all lie facing each other, and below them, on a kind of ledge, are brilliantly colored goblets. The camera crew is crammed into the center.

All the food being eaten is real: *polenta* (a kind of pudding made of corn flour), dates, raisins, cooked egg yolks, boiled potatoes, candied fruits, nuts, *ricotta* (a soft white cheese), marmalade, and mashed beets, all set out on flat plates before the diners. Condo, a massive Great Dane with a golden collar and a gold star glued on his forehead, snoozes by the side of his mistress on one of the ticking mattresses which cover the hard, uncomfortable couches. The breed didn't exist then, but Fellini liked the dog's face and insisted on having him in the picture. Condo and his mistress, a young French actress, were signed up together for thirty-two dollars a day.

Trimalchio is monotonously reciting a list of his silverware, a passage taken from Petronius. Offstage, to the left, behind the host's couch, a man is making shadows on the wall with his hands. The director stops the scene and wants to know whether the smoke from the grotesque turkey placed in the center can be seen in the camera. He lies prone on his stomach on one of the mattresses on the triclinium next to a guest with a blue face. On the second take, Fellini says to il Moro, who has been repeating numbers in place of lines, "Instead of separate numbers, say them all in sequence." Magali Noël has nothing to eat and Fellini orders something to be brought to her. All the guests continuously gorge themselves with food and drink. After seven more takes, Fellini peers through the camera and says, *"Va bene, è questa"*; but, of course, it isn't.

Trimalchio recites his numbers again while the man off-camera makes shadows, saying, "Once there was a rich man and a poor man who had a quarrel." Trimalchio interrupts to ask, "What is a poor man?" then calls for the potty. Two black slaves, a girl and a man, heave him upright as he morosely announces, "I am going to make *cacca*."

Bob Herrington, his nose covered with a mask, is on the set watching and frets, "They send these bloody buggers all the way from

America and then I'm never sure I can even get them on the set.
Five journalists are arriving from Japan on Monday. Just imagine,
five! I wired them not to come, but they're on their way. What am
I going to do with them? Maybe I can put them on one at a time.
They all look alike. Fellini will never know the difference."

Fellini yells for Donati, who comes running with his plaid scarf
trailing behind him. "You never give me a chance to breathe," he
complains.

Moro lumbers back onto the set and grumps in his grating voice,
"I have never worked in the cinema before and I never will again.
Fellini kept pestering me, 'Do it for me, do it for me,' but the shop
earns more than this and I can't even go near the restaurant because
I have to be here for makeup at six. And all my patrons tease me.
He told me I only have to work fifteen days but I have a contract
for seven weeks." This is to compensate him for the time spent
away from his restaurant.

At least fifty people are crowded around the director and the
noise is building up to a loud buzz. "*Silenzio,*" he bellows, echoed
by Pippia and Maurizio. The director is concentrating on a detail
of Martin and the fat guest in yellow next to him, carefully placing
goblets on the triclinium. A big golden urn is carried over to Martin, who takes the long-handled dipper and helps himself to the
wine (cold tea colored with fruit syrup). Fellini samples a bit of
food from Martin's plate, teasing, "Is it good?" knowing full well
it has become revolting by now.

"Action, Martin. Eat. Stop. Martin, you are eating like a British
girl just out of school." He screeches at the extra in yellow, "Eat
like a pig!" then stomps over to Martin and pushes his hands down
into the plate of gooey food. "For a moment, act as though you are
a baby." To the extra, he yips again, "Eat like a pig, not like a
signorina. Stop. *Va bene,*" then adds, "Belch, it's not a sign of bad
manners. And Martin, you must talk louder. Belch. Do whatever
you want."

From the sidelines, Eugene Walter says quietly, "Martin, you may burp if you like."

"Martin," Fellini is still fussing, "talk louder, Martino. Make your hands messier." Martin is speaking in English to the Italian extra next to him, who doesn't understand a word of what is being said, but he nods and smiles and finally gets up an explosive belch.

Fellini now begins the scene where Eumolpus, the poet, is pelted with food by the derisive guests. A group of Greek poets have entertained the diners with recitations of Homeric verses and when the tattered old poet, now half drunk, hears them, he bestirs himself from his sodden state, climbs to the upper level behind the triclinium where he has been reclining next to Encolpius, and begins to recite poetry. But the vulgar and gluttonous guests are not interested in culture and jeer him down. Eumolpus is played by Salvo Randone, one of Italy's greatest classical theater actors, and Fellini explains with expressive gesticulations how the poet must stagger up, begin to declaim, then cover his head with his shawl when the pelting starts and return to his place with an air of injured dignity. Fellini goes through every movement and gesture, making Randone watch him, then stands and watches Randone imitate him to be sure the actor has caught every nuance. The two of them look like Chinese shadow boxers or some kind of comic vaudeville team. The director returns repeatedly to demonstrate exactly what he wants Randone to do even though Randone is a consummate actor. Fellini is like Toscanini directing an orchestra. He destroys the personalities of the actors, even the most skilled, to get one style of acting—his.

While Fellini goes on for half an hour instructing Randone with the precision of a ballet master, the prop men, the makeup people, the photographers and the television people clamber all over the scuffed set which Zambon, the painter, is hastily retouching because the white plaster is showing through. Bevilacqua, who is trying out for a part in a gangster film, appears shorn of his leonine mane of hair. "It's worth it to cut your hair for ten thousand dollars," he rasps, "and they said it didn't matter if I couldn't speak English."

Since Fellini was still occupied with Randone, I went on one of my scouting expeditions. Magali Noël, Trimalchio's strumpet wife, a pretty, red-haired French actress, played the part of the prostitute in *La Dolce Vita* who takes Mastroianni's father home where he has a heart attack. She hadn't seen Fellini since *La Dolce Vita,* but when she ran into him last August in Venice, the director told her he had a surprise for her, a part in *Satyricon.*

"I didn't ask which one because to work with him is a great honor for an actress." Magali said. "To work for him twice is an almost impossible dream. In Makeup they shaved off my eyebrows and did one side of my face one way and the other side a different way so Fellini could select the one he preferred. But he looked at me and said, 'Let's leave it like this.' I have one side that smiles and one that cries. One is all up and the other all down. With this makeup, I wouldn't even have to speak. One sees, one understands everything he has in mind."

I thought of a remark Gideon Bachmann had made. "Fellini always makes two films with the same actors. The first time, he opens them up. The second time, he finishes them off. Look at Anita Ekberg and Marcello Mastroianni and Anouk Aimée!" It made me wonder if Magali were being finished off.

January 31

The day is warm and sunny with a hint of an early spring in the air. When I arrived at the door this morning, it was firmly shut in my face by the harassed doorman. Fellini is nervous again because the set is so small and the din sometimes beyond belief. I protested vehemently to Enzo Provenzale, the production manager, who claimed the order wasn't intended for me; and I am back on the set again in the afternoon.

In the morning, the guests were still throwing food at the poet. Fellini donned a robe and hurled the first fistful of some kind of black mess. You see his hand in the camera and the blob of food he threw is still plastered on the column where the poet had been declaiming. (I asked Eugene Walter why Fellini never appears in his films. "Oh, but he does," he protested. "He plays the part of the camera.")

Marinaio, the old man with tremors, was given a small part by Fellini. He was rigged out in pale blue tulle and mauve and gold and put into the scene to tremble while the other guests crammed themselves with food. It was his moment of glory. The guests also helped themselves to a pot of writhing live black eels swimming in ink-black sauce, a sight I was glad to have missed.

The pan of pig heads is still on the set. Alongside it is a huge frying pan with raw eggs and real cow udders from the slaughter-house, which are already beginning to smell. ("The Romans were great for sow udders, pig udders, and cow udders. They were great for stuffing udders," Eugene—an authority on Roman dishes—said solemnly. "They also loved things that weren't what they seemed to be.")

Fellini, dressed in a black raincoat and his usual fedora, is going to do the scene with the cow udders. Two slaves have carried the frying pan into the dining room and he is giving exact instructions as to how they are to be distributed. Trimalchio and his entourage must look on greedily as they are passed around, but Moro has a pained expression on his face. "You're not sick, Moro. You're happy," Fellini reminds him.

The prop man is handing out Turkish taffy again. Hundreds of pounds must have been consumed already. Most of the guests must constantly chew and there's nothing like Turkish taffy to keep your jaws working. Fellini is directing the slaves, "Go down on your knees every time you take something from the pan; and talk. Say numbers, anything you want, but don't stop talking. And you, in the corner, Edmondo, and the others, chew, chew, chew."

Now he is ready to shoot. Trimalchio has returned from relieving his bowels and this is a new dish brought in to bedazzle the guests. "Moro, move your head to the right. Your head straight and down a little," Fellini commands. "Begin to speak, Moro. Stop." The slaves have toted the udders in but are not distributing the plates as Fellini demonstrated. "You did it like a cretin," he yells at one slave.

On the second take, Moro starts off saying, "For several days my stomach hasn't functioned," going into explicit details and advising his guests, "If anyone needs to, there are hot towels and hot water available outside. I think there's no greater torture than holding yourself in."

Trimalchio turns to Fortunata and asks, "Why are you laughing? You won't be able to sleep tonight," a quote taken directly from Petronius, with Moro delivering his lines, deadpan, in a deep, gravelly voice.

Fellini notices an olive on the floor and goes down to scrape it away with his foot. Nothing escapes those sharp eyes of his. The slaves drop the huge frying pan with a thundering clatter and he asks, "What's the matter? Is it too heavy? Moro, don't stop; talk all the time," he orders while he inquires into the difficulty with the frying pan. The slave has a sore hand. "Why didn't you tell me before?" Fellini demands and changes him for another. Meanwhile, Moro drones on saying whatever comes into his head, like, "Finally, I am liberated." "Stop," Fellini calls and changes the slave again, this time bringing in Barozzi, the skinny epileptic from the temple scene.

Professor Canali is looking on, and explains: "Normally, the Romans had beds on which they lay or reclined with little tables by them. This is an invention, but we cannot exclude the possibility that a triclinium like this actually existed because we are not informed."

Fellini works on a close-up of Moro describing his bowel trouble. He wants two slaves to make shadows on the wall with their hands and screams at them, "Watch what you are doing so you can control your movements. Look at the shadows." He bellows at one who is rehearsing, wearing a pair of pants and a hair net, "You've been doing the same thing for four days and you still haven't got it."

Then he prompts Moro, "Why did your friends die?"

"Because they didn't liberate their intestines and it went to their brains," Moro replies, and the director breaks up.

He frequently prompts actors with questions just to get them to speak, because it doesn't matter what they say. All their voices will be dubbed later.

Scordia, the artist, comes on the set and confides, "I am preparing a private collection for the house of Trimalchio where there are many works of art from Greece, Egypt, Persia and Sumeria in a big room. Sometimes they are taken from a painting on a plate that is only a foot large and I make it six feet high. I get them from museums and books. It's not difficult, only amusing." He looks around distastefully and remarks, "I regard them as an homage to classicism. I hope it will be a noble moment in the film in the midst of so much vulgarity. It has taken me two weeks to do the frescoes." Then, catching sight of the mosaic of Trimalchio, he shudders, "It's a horrible thing. One can see from a mile off it's a blown-up photograph in spite of all the cunning. It has no style and no beauty."

Fellini finishes with Trimalchio's bowels and turns his attention to another small scene where the slaves hand out long gold knives to the guests. The tray of knives isn't working too well and the director orders it nailed onto a dolly so it can be pushed around, because it is too heavy to carry.

Bob Herrington, who also had difficulty getting on the set, whispers, "This is a crazy house. If Grimaldi himself came, they wouldn't let him on."

A journalist keeps asking me what they are going to do with the knives. I don't know whether they are going to shave, or cut their throats. I hope the latter and leave for the day.

February 7

Betsy Langman, one of the guests, whose protruding eyes have been accentuated to make her look like a staring statue, tells her story. A twenty-seven-year-old American actress and a grandniece of Henry Morgenthau, she was introduced to Fellini by Carlo Ponti, Sophia Loren's husband and one of Fellini's former producers. "I love it," she coos. "Everybody counts here and there is respect for each individual. It's not like New York. Here, if you have a quality, they use it. The makeup man takes pride in you and is proud if Fellini is pleased with what he has created. I don't even mind working for twelve dollars a day."

The Italians are intrigued by Betsy, whom Fellini calls "Baaytsie." They can't possibly imagine a millionairess working for twelve dollars a day in a bit part; but, as Betsy explains, "Just because your family is rich doesn't mean you are."

Fellini prepares to shoot the scene where the rich Cinedo insults Encolpius. Yesterday, Martin's reaction was filmed. Today, we see what he is reacting to. Genius, a famous fortune-teller who plays the rich old pederast, is exotically costumed in a black velvet skirt with plates of copper over his chest and stomach, a gaudy necklace, and big copper earrings. His eyebrows and cheeks are painted gold and on his dark brown curls is a gold Juliet cap topped by a garland of colored flowers.

"In your place," Fellini says to Genius. "Look here, *gioia*, joy." He is directing sitting in the center of the triclinium and tells

Genius, "Say dirty words, numbers, anything you want." Exasperated, he screeches at the man reclining next to Genius, "Throw away your cigarette and take off your glasses." Another guest, dressed in orange, is brought to stand by the pillar behind Genius and a prop man is busily spreading white paste to simulate cheese on a board in front of a squatting slave near the wall.

Fellini yawns loudly waiting for all this activity to stop. Genius twitters, "Oh, *Dio*, I've forgotten all my lines I learned this morning." Fellini comforts him. "It doesn't matter. Just as long as you don't keep silent." To help him, since Martin is not there, he places the psychoanalyst, Peter Ammann, in front of him so he can direct his insults at him.

Fellini demonstrates again the nasty, sarcastic face he wants Genius to make. "And then, when you have insulted him," he explains, "go 'Ta-ta-ta' with your fingers. No, no, not the *cornuto's* sign. [This is a very insulting Italian gesture made with the index and pinky fingers extended out from the fist and signifies that the man at whom it is directed has been cuckolded.] Like this you must do it." The director shows him how to put his middle finger over his index finger. "Both hands," he says.

Genius launches into an impromptu tirade. "But you are still laughing!" he says scornfully. "At fifteen you were already a fag. You were a fairy at five." Fellini gleefully prompts him, talking like a machine gun, asking him suggestive questions which elicit hilarious answers. "You are a ragpicker. Pooh! *Per carità!* I have known King Alfonso of Spain. I knew Mussolini long ago. And whom have you known? *Oh, Dio mio!* Oh, my God! You stink. Away. Away. Away." "Stop," Fellini calls and places Genius' head against the pillar and goes to look through the camera saying, "Get down more, Genius, and when I say go down, tell him off but good —fairy, fag, anything you want."

On the second take, Fellini prompts him, "Does he know Latin?"

"Latin!" responds Genius, "he doesn't even know Italian!"

Fellini is on his knees on a mattress in front of him, feeding him insults. "You are ugly, ugly, ugly, *brutto, brutto, brutto*. I hate you pretending to be a gentleman."

On the third take, sitting on the steps of the triclinium, he prods Genius again with questions. "Don't you think he has a certain class, a certain elegance? Why is he so unpleasant? He is a handsome boy. Count," he orders, when they have both run out of the litany of insults. Then getting his second wind, Genius starts in with "*stronzo*, shit, *froscio*, fag, the faggiest of all fags, invidious."

Fellini sets up a final detail. Looking through the camera, he says to the woman next to Genius, "Move your can. Genius, look at my hand and count. Don't bat an eye. Count. Open your eyes, more wide open. Nod your head. Say all the insults you want. Stick out your tongue. You are mad, mad, mad. Open your eyes again."

While they set up lights for the next scene, I talk with Eugenio Mastropietro. Known professionally as Genius, the Mago of Rome, he has been a fortune-teller for thirty years and known Fellini for twenty. Besides appearing in other films, he was in *Juliet of the Spirits* as a mago and *La Dolce Vita* as a rich eccentric.

"Fellini doesn't believe in fortune-telling," he says. "He makes believe he does on purpose, although he believes in me because he is afraid of me. He asks me if the film will have success, if people are sincere, and about his health. I told him *Juliet* would not win an Oscar, but this will be Fellini's greatest film and it *will* win an Oscar.

"What is he like? He is obstinate and has a very strong character, great courage and imagination and a very broad outlook. Human? I wouldn't say so. Everybody is good for him and nobody is. Fellini is for himself."

The director turns to the scene where Trimalchio's notary reads a list of the host's newly acquired lands and slaves. Both the previous scene and this one are in the original Petronius. Peter Dane, the American actor who plays the notary, is hastily going over his part.

His face is pallid, his eyes red-rimmed, and his chin covered with warts. It has taken six hours to make him up. Fellini is lying prone on a mattress on the floor peering at him through the camera. The musicians, one of whom is old Capitani from the temple, are standing in the pit. Fellini says, "Give the musicians something to eat," and they are given platters of food. Behind the notary, he places two ladies and the hunchback in yellow on the triclinium. Gilda is summoned to comb Peter's hair, after which Fellini commands, "Go," to Peter.

Peter begins reading out the list of Trimalchio's property. "Stop," Fellini orders. He takes the hunchback off the triclinium, substitutes a man in red, and warns the musicians in the orchestra, "Pails of water will be thrown at you and the water may reach you but you must not even notice it. Go on eating and saying 'Pa-pa-pa' like chickens."

(Eugene Walter is sick and will be away for the duration of the picture. Fellini is on his own now with his English, which is picturesque but sometimes confusing, although he manages amazingly well when he wants to. Eugene says, "When I'm there, he speaks perfect English. When I'm not, he can't. I'm his other battery.")

He now concentrates on a close-up of Peter reading the list of Trimalchio's property. Peter begins, but Fellini whistles him to stop. Sitting in front of him, off camera, he asks him questions to make him respond. Peter protests, "I wasn't given that part," but Fellini replies, "It doesn't matter, you just look afraid."

"When did you bought these Pompeian gardens?" he asks, and they go through the list. No matter what Fellini asks him, Peter meekly answers, "Yes sir" or "No sir." It's the first time I've ever heard anyone address him like that. Foreigners usually call him Mister Fellini. It's funny to hear him addressed as "sir." After two takes we are liberated for the day.

I asked Peter Dane why he addresses Fellini as "sir" and he said, "Because he terrifies me. He's the only director who does."

Trimalchio's Pool and Tomb

February 15

This the first day of shooting at Trimalchio's outdoor pool where the guests arrive to be bathed and beautified before they enter the villa for the long orgy of eating and drinking. The scene is being shot in the immense Stage Five. In the center is a large pool surrounded by candles of varying heights and thicknesses. To the left are clumps of real grass and back of the pool is a large expanse of dark furrowed earth. The scene is very static, a fresco which Encolpius and the poet see as they arrive at sunset for the dinner.

It has taken three weeks to prepare this set. The water of the specially constructed pool has to be cleaned every night by passing it repeatedly through a filtered pumping system. A gasoline heater maintains the temperature at an even ninety-five degrees to keep the one hundred and twenty bathers comfortably warm. Two thousand plastic candles immersed in wax stick up like spikes around the pool, and two thousand arc lights illuminate the set. Besides the bathers, there are fifty guests, two young boys, five slaves, five pederasts, five masseurs, and ten peasants in the scene. Thirty-five litter chairs, which look like sarcophagi, stand in the tall grass to the left of the pool. Around the three sides of the set, a black curtain has been hung so that Joseph Natanson, the special optical-effects man, can create the blood-red sky.

Fellini is sitting on a stool next to the camera on a high platform in front and to the right of the pool. Sometimes he yells through his megaphone and sometimes just bellows directions. He is telling Maurizio Mein, the assistant director who is way in the background, to line up some farmers in the furrows of earth, which has been mixed with dye to make it blackish. Some slaves and guests have already been placed by the pool. Other guests are being borne to the pool in litters.

"Haven't we got any farmers?" he demands.

Maurizio shoves the ten farmers into the scene.

"Maurizio," Fellini yells, "now there are too many farmers. The second, third, and fourth on the right can go, and get me one in a sheepskin and make him kneel down."

Moro rests placidly in a chair, dressed in his heavy robes, and jokes, "I'm not going to take a bath today. I take mine at night."

Bevilacqua, Fellini's masseur and general factotum, saunters by with a crew cut and a small beard pasted on his face. He is dressed in a blue terry-cloth robe. "I play the part of the head masseur," he brags in his gruff voice and marches up to present himself to Fellini, who looks at him and chuckles, "*Che pancia!* What a belly!"— which irritates Bevilacqua because he is very proud of his physique.

Fellini is now back up on the platform next to the camera, leaning over talking to the group he has arranged below in front of it. "You must be absolutely immobile and look up directly into the camera." To the bathers, he yells, "You must all be motionless as though you were posing for a family portrait." To the slaves standing near the guests, "Pretend you are cutting their nails." When he gets the scene all composed, the director bellows, "All right, ladies, take your bras off." There is a horrified gasp. The ladies, who had not expected this, are very disconcerted because they are lined up in front of the pool with all the men behind them. "*Ragazze*, girls," Fellini bellows in a wheedling voice, "take off your bras. *Coraggio!*"

Joseph Natanson is there with his camera to take the approximately fifty-five feet of film he needs for the matte shot of the sunset sky he is to make for this scene. Fellini must wait for him to finish shooting and he hates it. "Can I go now, Natanson?" he asks impatiently. "I have put everything together forty-five times. Ready? Let's shoot. Natanson, are you ready?" he demands. "Tell me when we can start the action." He shouts to the bathers standing immobile in the pool, "Don't move and only look at me. Only the masseurs move." Exasperated, he calls again, "Natanson, can I go?" Undaunted by Fellini's impatience, Joseph finally responds, "Not yet." Fellini takes out his frustration on the pool people. "Stay still. *Che cazzo!*"

Finally, Natanson says he can start and Fellini calls for action. On the third take, he screams, "Take your hands off your breasts, girls, you don't see anything. *Coraggio.*" Not happy with the man in front of him, he calls down to him, "Raise your chin. Can't you stay like that, *gioia?*"

Fellini climbs up on the higher platform to look at the scene, then calls, "Blow out the candles and get out of the pool, one by one, calmly." The women refuse to get out without their bras. Many of the ladies in the pool are mortified, especially the younger ones. The older ladies don't really care and some of the younger ones, once they get used to the idea, nonchalantly pose for the photographers who have rushed in and are shooting their heads off. The men, naturally, try to get as close as possible to the women, making frank or rude remarks and comparisons about the women's figures, and sneaking a feel wherever they can.

At the end of the morning shooting Fellini leaves the set for a short lunch break, and I get the chance to talk with Clara Baldassarre, the set seamstress, or wardrobe mistress. A sweet woman with the patience of a saint, she is a grandmother who has been a seamstress in the cinema for twenty-five years. Her hang-dog face gets more and more tired looking as the picture progresses, and it's very understandable. Every morning, she has to get up at four-thirty to arrive at Cinecittà at six, and sometimes works as late as ten o'clock at night. Two dressmakers and two tailors make all the costumes, supplemented by extra help brought in for the crowd scenes.

"The costumes are made continuously," she says. "The unique thing about them is the way they are made, the dyes and the materials." Cotton-linen, a soft and delicate material, is used for some robes, stiffened muslin for the stoles, and for other robes and shawls the coarse interlining normally used in fur coats.

"Donati thought of it," Clara adds. "No one else would have used such materials and made such costumes. They wear out right away, but they produce the desired effect."

After lunch, the director concentrates on details of the slaves and guests while the bathers stand transfixed in the vaporous pool. A man who looks oddly familiar comes to speak with Fellini. He is a young Austrian actor and night-club entertainer named Herbert Andreas. Fellini makes him go through his mechanical-doll act for me and then I realize he looks like Danny Kaye—whom Fellini had originally wanted for the part of Lichas but wasn't able to get. He is now considering Andreas, but in the end, after weeks of waiting hopefully, he was given no part. Probably what intrigues Fellini, besides the actor's resemblance to Danny Kaye, are his eyes, which are small and blue and set close together, with a slight cast in the right one.

On the way back to town, Andreas tells me, "Fellini said he'd like to do something with my eyes. It's funny, they've always bothered me the most because they're so little. He told me Lichas is cruel and asked me to lose about six or seven pounds. My agent introduced me to Fellini in September, but Fellini just looked at me and walked away. I prepared a large telegram saying, 'To my dear son, Roberto . . . I sent you one of the best actors.' It was signed 'God.' I walked on the set as the mechanical doll, went up to Fellini and delivered the telegram without saying a word. It broke him up, and he told me to come on the set and watch how he works. And then he said, 'My name is Federico, not Roberto.' "

February 17

Fellini is arranging a detail of the pool scene and orders a little hunchbacked slave dressed in yellow, the hairdresser for Fortunata's mother, to walk from the stool where he is sitting, get up on the edge of the pool, and jump in. He rethinks and decides he wants the little slave to walk over to the edge of the pool, sit facing the camera and swing his legs around into the pool. From a collection of goblets and vases on a small table to the left, the director selects the ones he wants and places a Negro slave to the left of the camera to pour water from one pitcher to the other.

The director is restless and leaves the camera to saunter around the Dantesque scene he has created. He chats with an elderly extra dressed in orange named Cabella. An amused smile lights up his face as the sixty-nine-year-old man, an entertainment director on a cruise ship, relates the story of one of his current love affairs.

When they begin shooting the scene, Fellini unexpectedly says to the little slave, "All right, naked." The boy removes his loincloth and leaps into the pool. The women become hysterical and everybody moves in to see. Fellini explodes. "I am leaving," he rants. "Put up a rope and put all the people behind it. The production does nothing to protect me. From tomorrow on, I don't want anyone on the set. I can't stand it any longer. Closed doors to everyone tomorrow!"

A taut silence descends over the set, but everyone knows he doesn't mean it. Fellini is full of contradictions. He invites the whole world to come and watch him film, then expects them to act as if they're in a cathedral. But he needs people on the set. It stimulates him and gives him a chance to let off steam. Martin remarks, "Well, he didn't tell me I had to be nude either in the pool in 'The Villa of the Suicides,' but I did it and I don't see anything wrong with it."

Mercifully, there is a break for lunch while Fellini calms down. During lunch, Joseph Natanson, the sky man, explains why the director is always carping at him. A tall, distinguished-looking, Polish-born painter, he made his first matte shots in England for *The Red Shoes* in 1948. For the past fourteen years, he has been living and working in Italy and provided special optical effects for hundreds of films, including the *Toby Dammit* episode.

"Fellini," he says, "has one great defect: he thinks that in order not to lose his inspiration, he should be completely ignorant of all the technicalities of making a film. But that's not right. A great pianist should know how to play scales but Fellini absolutely refuses to play scales.

"He has never asked me why I needed a certain amount of time to photograph the scene he is doing. For him, it's just a nuisance, like having to eat when he's hungry. He doesn't mind waiting for the lights to be set up because he's more accustomed to it and has to do it every day.

"Also, he likes teasing people. He's very friendly but if he's tense, his friendliness is very often shown in this form of ragging people. It can be almost nasty and I sometimes find it annoying because my work is very difficult.

"I work always on the original negative to have the most perfect definition," he explains. "Even if I make a very long footage for tests, after all the experiments which Fellini would like to see and I would like to see, finally I have exhausted my capital. He always wants to try different things. People are so eager to work for him that he always thinks he can ask for something which no one would do for anybody else. But he is extremely invigorating and can force you to do things you wouldn't do for another director. That's his personality. You feel he is somebody you can criticize but whom you have to admire. Every director has his defects. Fellini's is impatience. But if he changed, many of the things which happen by accident would be destroyed, and many accidents in his films are extremely good.

"You should not give in to Fellini if you are absolutely dead certain you are right," Joseph insists. "You always have to wait, because Fellini's first judgment is usually not complete artistically. When he sees something which is not as he imagined it, he is terrified. The second time he sees it, he has already digested it and it has merged into his vision. Then he gets terribly fond of it. If you are too quick or not very sure that what you have done is absolutely the best, then you are tempted to change it. Sometimes this can be very dangerous because you lose the freshness of the approach. Things are not so spontaneous, and in a Fellini film, spontaneity is the most essential element."

Much later, after the film was finished, Joseph described his difficulties with the pool skies which provoked the only quarrel between him and the director. Fellini maintained the pool sequence was so brief that all the skies should be more or less the same. Natanson opposed this idea. "Even in the shortest sequence," he said, "a sunset should be a succession of light, of effect, of the climax of the sun producing the last rays of light and then dying into darkness. That was the first version I made but Fellini didn't like it and asked me to redo it. When I made it, he went back to the original version which is the one used in the film.

"But," he confessed ruefully, "I never did really understand what Fellini wanted me to do for the scene of the swimming pool. I just did it. This is always the thing with Fellini—somehow you do it." He chuckled, "And then when I brought one of my best skies to show him, we had a silly conversation. I said, 'But look, this sky is fantastic! It's an El Greco!' Fellini replied, 'It's not an El Greco, it's a Fellini!' I was very annoyed because, after all it was *my* sky and I said, 'No, it's a Fellini-Natanson!' "

February 20

The dinner is over and the pool scene is finished. We are now in Stage Eight in the Tomb of Trimalchio where the crass host has escorted his sodden guests to show it off and stage a mock funeral to hear how he will be mourned.

This morning there is wailing and vomiting and, for good measure, lesbian kissing is thrown in. Trimalchio enters with his entourage saying, "Pretend I am dead and say nice things about me. Play lovely music." Fortunata and Scintilla, played by Danica La Loggia, arrive late and, seeing everyone's attention riveted on Trimalchio now lying in his casket, they slip behind a slab of marble and kiss passionately. The director is concentrating on details of the guests before getting to the kissing scene. Morgana, the catlike prostitute from the Subura, is there dressed in green, and Fellini is making the man in blue by Trimalchio's casket wail and moan over the death of his friend along with the Negro slaves.

On the set, everyone is bored to death. An ancient extra in his yellow robe is fast asleep on a bench. Another is writing a letter. Still other extras sit scrunched together on narrow wooden benches and gossip or stare glumly into the darkness. Fellini has just finished another vomiting session and it is all too much. This is black comedy at its blackest.

At lunch, Mara Krupp, Fortunata's sister, whom the director calls "Dentona" or "Big Tooth," makes a dreadful scene. "I am tired of being insulted and called 'Dentona.' I don't give a damn about Fellini," she rants. "I am a great actress and here I am playing a bit part." It's true she does have large, prominent teeth emphasized by a receding chin, and it isn't pleasant to be reminded of one's defects. However, it is precisely the defect that impels Fellini to select a certain actor and she ought to thank God for her teeth, because he certainly hasn't chosen her for her beauty.

In the afternoon, Fellini continues with the macabre make-believe funeral. On a ledge on the left wall of the tomb, high above and overlooking the casket, he places several slaves. The orchestra is positioned in the center of the tomb with their primitive instruments and Capitani, the hermaphrodite's attendant from the temple, is to lead the orchestra around Trimalchio's oblong vault. The old man cuts a ludicrous figure in a short yellow tunic, which reveals his toothpick legs, and a dainty little crown, perkily decorated with four flowers, stuck on his head. The director hands him an odd-looking kind of tiered brass rattle and shows him how to shake the instrument and wail as he walks. Fellini has fallen in love with Capitani's face with its sunken, toothless mouth and beaked nose.

More slaves are placed on the ledge. A brown stole is brought to cover Capitani's scrawny legs and Fellini makes him throw back his head and wail in his quavery voice. The old man looks like a living corpse as he rattles his instrument and stalks like a stork around the casket. On the fourth take, Fellini yells at the slaves on the ledge, "Those three slaves on their knees looking down have to cry too. Capitani, throw back your head more. *Va bene, è questa,* Norma. All right, it's this one."

Waiting for the next scene, Genius does an impromptu cancan with his skirts held high, revealing brief bikini panties. Fellini is delighted and makes him repeat it.

Giulietta is visiting the set and confides, "Federico sleeps only four hours a night. He wakes up very often because he is so tense and sometimes he doesn't get home until ten or twelve. On Sundays, he sleeps later, until ten; but for lunch, we go out with Tosi or Donati to talk over the work. He is always working."

Fellini spends two hours more wailing with Moro in the tomb. Moro is crying, everybody is crying. It's been an agonizingly long funeral. During a break, Piero Tosi trots out two stalwart young men, dressed as Roman soldiers, onto the set. Fellini scrutinizes them intently and chooses one, whom Tosi warns, "Don't cut your hair, not even a smitch." Bernardino Zapponi, the co-script writer, arrives and receives the usual embrace and kisses on both cheeks. Then the director turns to the two lesbians, egging Magali on to kiss Danica more passionately behind the slab, cackling away like a madman.

When the scene is finished, Magali confesses, "I've never kissed a woman before, but he asks you to do it and you do it. He comes up to you jokingly and tells you what to do and then you find you are doing it. Only for Fellini would I do it, because in his hands, it won't be vulgar."

While all this is going on with rehearsal after rehearsal and delays for lights and makeup-retouchings and wig-recombings, I have been sitting with Martin Potter in the darkness, listening to what he thinks of Fellini and his role of Encolpius now, after almost four months have passed. "Sometimes I feel perhaps a bit frustrated," he confessed, "in that I am not doing the same kind of acting as in the theater in England or in television or even in some other film. Fellini does direct up to a fine point. He's willing to listen to my ideas but there is no time to discover anything. However, I don't feel in a strait jacket, because it doesn't go against what I want to do or am able to do. I have a clear idea about Encolpius but Fellini said, 'No, it's not necessary to talk about the part because you *are* Encolpius.'

"Maybe with more takes, we could get the part more polished, but he doesn't mind lack of polish," Martin said wistfully. "He wants a natural and real Encolpius, a bit ambiguous, because it helps what he wants in the film. So far, there has been no perform-ance in this film. Even Randone is not giving a performance."

February 22

It is a cold, gusty day and Fellini, bundled in his sheepskin-lined jacket, his black fedora clamped firmly on his head, is directing the scene of Trimalchio and his cortege arriving at the entrance to his tomb. The guests are staggering down a dirt slope, some on foot, some being carried standing up in litters.

Finally, everything gets coordinated, and at two o'clock the fun-eral is over. Moro's acting career is also at an end and he can now go back to being plain Mario Romagnoli, the popular and proper Roman restaurant proprietor. The five thousand dollars he was paid was little enough recompense for the suffering he had to endure on the set and at home. "*Porca miseria*! Wretched misery!" grumbles Moro, "I got lumbago from lying on the triclinium and bronchitis from going around half nude with the toga. Do you know how many hours I had to lie on that damned triclinium? Two hundred and fifty hours, from nine until one and from two until six every day! Do you know what strength it requires to remain in that posi-tion, first on the right side and then on the left? From my thigh to my ankle, I haven't a hair left on my legs. There is absolutely nothing. They are smooth as if they had been shaved.

"And you know my wife wanted to repudiate me," he moans. "She is very religious and didn't like my being around all those nude women. And then, my son-in-law used to help me in the evenings to learn my lines, more than two hundred pages. Imagine how tiring! Once, without our realizing it, my granddaughter hid behind the door and heard some slightly off-color lines. She went right away to her mother and reported that her daddy and grandfather were telling dirty stories in the living room. It was the end of the world for my daughter, and my wife put on a long face. She said to me, 'For seventy years you lived a clean life and now, in your old age, you have ruined your reputation and become a dirty old man, kissing boys!' "

Odds and Ends

March 10

Shooting resumed today after a two-week layoff. Salvo Randone, who is needed for two crucial scenes, has been ill. Since no other sets were ready, shooting had to be suspended. Max Born has also been in the hospital with pneumonia and there has been a strike at Cinecittà.

Fellini is dressed today in his Mephistopheles outfit: dark grey flannels, black sweater, and white shirt. The scene of the Pinacoteca, or art gallery, where Encolpius first encounters the poet Eumolpus, is being shot in Studio Fifteen. The gallery is a wide open space; on the rear wall are hung thirty-two paintings of classical origin: Greek, Egyptian, Sumerian, Persian, and Roman, in various states of ruin, prepared by Scordia and four assistants in four weeks.

Fellini particularly wanted an empty expanse like this to present the poet in contrast to the crowded scene of the dinner and, by showing paintings, to allude to the classical past of Rome. A huge bronze head in a crate with a stark white bandage running all around its face stares balefully into the camera. Another large statue, also crated, is set sideways in the center of the gallery. Tufts of grass grow between the flagstone slabs of the floor, an indication of how little visited the gallery is in this period of decadence and indifference to the arts. This scene, also, is taken directly from Petronius.

A plainly dressed woman is seated to the left, restoring fragments of Greek frescoes pasted onto a long net hanging from the ceiling in the foreground. To the right, another restorer works with the aid of a young boy who stands beside him holding a primitive sack of egg shells filled with paints. Fellini begins directing the restorer on the right, an extra named Rossi who has already appeared as a guest at the banquet of Trimalchio. Rossi's costume and makeup are changed but he looks vaguely familiar.

The director calls for a longer paintbrush and shows Rossi how to work on the canvas, then step back and survey his handiwork. "Madonna, Rossi!" he screams at him. "You haven't understood anything. You have to stick the brush in the egg, paint, then step back, look at the effect and then go back to the canvas again."

Antonio Scordia, on hand to survey his handiwork, laughs. "We did the exact opposite of the Institute of Restoration. Instead of repairing the paintings, we aged them." The painter has decided to leave the film for the time being. "I think I should do some of my own work and now 'The Garden of Delights' is all changed. Fellini didn't like the paintings and the measurements have been enlarged. The wall was to be thirty-eight feet long and now it's going to be around ninety feet. Everything is different."

After lunch, a new scene begins. The poet is wandering around the gallery inveighing against the decadence of the arts because of the greed for money. In a large square cut into the rear wall, slaves move silently past on a tiered scaffold. Where they are going and

Fellini directing one of Vernacchio's troupe in the theater episode. His mask is to protect his lungs against smoke effects used in this scene.

The two protagonists of *Fellini Satyricon:* American actor Hiram Keller (left), who plays Ascyltus, and British actor Martin Potter as Encolpius.

Giton played by Max Born.

At "The Dinner of Trimalchio," a mosaic of the host is completed while the guests gorge themselves.

Guests sip one of the delicacies offered at the banquet as musicians play in the orchestra pit.

Guests are bathed and massaged at Trimalchio's pool before the feast.

The widow of Ephesus, played by Antonia Pietrosi, keeps vigil by the corpse of her husband, accompanied by mourners.

French actress Capucine as Tryphaena.

American model Donyale Luna as Oenothea.

French actress Magali Noël, who is Fortunata, Trimalchio's wife, kisses Danica La Loggia, who plays her lesbian friend, Scintilla.

Lichas, played by Alain Cuny, embraces Encolpius after their marriage aboard his ship.

Ascyltus is slain by the boatman who ferries him and Encolpius to the house of Oenothea.

Ascyltus alleviates the torment of the nymphomaniac, played by Sibilla Sedat.

Fellini demonstrates to Wolfgang Hillinger, who plays the Soldier in "The Widow of Ephesus" tale, how he must attempt to kill himself.

Fanfulla, the Italian variety theater actor who plays Vernacchio, watches as Fellini shows him how to play a scene in "The Theater."

Salvo Randone, playing Eumolpus, the poet, mimics Fellini's movements as Martin Potter looks on during a scene in the Pinacoteca, or art gallery.

The Insula Felicles before its collapse.

Martin Potter chases Hylette Adolphe, a slave girl in "The Villa of the Suicides."

After he has been ejected from Trimalchio's feast, Eumolpus lies half-dead in a field and bequeaths a legacy of beauty to his young friend, Encolpius.

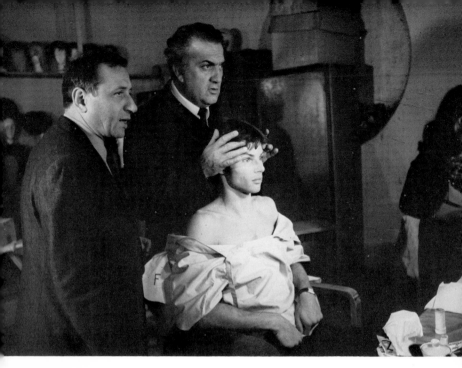

Fellini and Danilo Donati study Hiram Keller's face before deciding on the makeup and hair style for his role as Ascyltus.

Giulietta Masina, the director's wife, talks with her husband during one of her visits to the set.

Pasquale Baldassarre, the hermaphrodite, is displayed to the pilgrims.

Fellini demonstrating how to walk with crutches as some of the pilgrims in "The Temple of the Hermaphrodite" look on. At right is Antonio Moro, an ex-boxer, as a mutilated battle hero.

The Emperor, played by Tanya Lopert, is speared by the lances of Roman soldiers.

The thief, Gordon Mitchell, and Ascyltus and Encolpius fight ferociously after the death of the hermaphrodite, whom they have stolen from the temple.

Fellini wearing a black fedora like the one made famous in 8½.

where they have come from, no one knows, since this is not in the script.

Donati explains, "We had such fun one Sunday at Federico's house thinking up ideas for the Pinacoteca. We thought of putting a ladder hanging in a void as if there were people working outside, like a museum being set up. Then we thought of putting a hill behind the opening in the wall but decided that wouldn't do. Finally, we thought of having workers silently trundled by on a scaffold to give the idea of other people and other rooms behind the place where Encolpius and the poet meet. It gives you a start, doesn't it?"

Suddenly, as Fellini is setting up another scene, the set is plunged into total darkness. The workers are striking at Cinecittà. They have worked their normal eight-hour day but refuse to stay overtime and have turned off the power.

Since it was a short day, I wandered over to the makeup department to talk with Rino Carboni, the head makeup man, to find out how that crucial area behind the camera functions.

A calm, soft-spoken man who has spent twenty years in the cinema world creating makeup for at least a hundred films, including the *Toby Dammit* episode for Fellini, he has also worked in the theater and with Max Factor as a makeup instructor. To perfect his craft, Carboni studied osteology and myology, the sciences of bone and muscle structures, and became a painter, sculptor, and psychologist. He also has a tendency to look for a *filone,* or trend, in films, and is confident the *Satyricon* will be followed by at least eight or nine films of the Roman period, on which he hopes to work.

For the *Satyricon*, twenty makeup people were employed in all, twelve of whom were permanent and the rest brought in for crowd scenes. Half created the hairdos and half the makeup, working from six o'clock in the morning until eight in the evening. Each day, one test was made in the morning and one after lunch in addition to the six or seven makeups each person did daily.

The five thousand wigs used in the film, all made from designs by Tosi and Donati, were made in Carboni's own laboratory in Rome. Donati said the wigs were inspired by the Roman epoch on Mars. The cosmetics for the makeup were all prepared to order in two Roman factories and, by the end of the picture, about fifteen hundred people had been made up by Carboni and his assistants, working from a collection of photographs of Roman and Etruscan statues selected by Fellini. Tacked on the wall, they served as guidelines for the inventive capacity of the makeup artist.

Surrounded by jars of creams and lotions and cosmetics, wigs of all colors and styles, Carboni talked about the unique character of the makeup for the *Satyricon*.

"At the beginning of the film, Fellini made drawings. For example, he did a drawing of Vernacchio, but when I did the makeup as he designed it, he said, 'You must not take me literally. The drawing is only to give you an idea. Every character must have a hallucinatory aspect or a spectral look because all of them are seen as though through the smoke of a drug. All the expressions must be haunting.'

"So we devised a completely new system of makeup," he said. "Every makeup is done, not according to the character which the actor plays, but according to the exaggerated features of his face. Those that seem easiest are the most difficult to do. The makeup can take between three-quarters of an hour and three hours or more. If a person has a distinctive face, it can be easier. For example, an American girl had a high forehead which Fellini liked. We tried to persuade her to cut off some of her hair in front to make her forehead even higher. She refused, but Fellini got her to do it. He is not a personality but a type of magician. He seems almost a hypnotist.

"In other films," Carboni sighed, "it was always possible to foresee the categories of characters among the extras. The servants will be dressed in a certain manner, the coachmen will have black wigs with little tails, the infantrymen will all look more or less the same. Instead, here, Fellini wants delirious people who have something fantastic or weird in their faces, so the makeup is done according to each individual face. This means it may take twenty minutes to do one of the most important characters and an hour and a half for an extra. It took twenty minutes to do Moro and forty minutes to do Randone because Randone has a piece of latex on his eye to hold it closed. Who knows why? Others, who appear for only a few minutes on the screen, may take as long as two or three hours. It took two-and-a-half hours to make up the old pimp with the flowers behind his ears in the 'Lupanare' scene.

"Fellini sometimes sends types who seem anonymous; but when we begin to work, we discover they can be beautiful under certain circumstances. Fellini sees this right away. Often the makeup is done on the basis of a photograph of an actor. We start with an idea, talk about it with each adding his suggestions. Sometimes we make the actor walk or speak before we decide. Then, we show the actor to Fellini. Sometimes he will like the eyes, so we change the face and keep the eyes; or he may fall in love with another detail of the face and we have to bring that out.

"Fellini asks for such absurd things, but we always find we can do them. I must have noses, ears, eyes, chins, scars, and heads of various sizes, ready all the time," he laughed as he took me on a tour of his workshop. The hand of the slave which was cut off in the theater is there, as well as the mold of the nose of the boatman who slays Ascyltus. "He doesn't have a nose, you know, and we had to make five different ones before Fellini decided which he preferred. I also had to do five or six noses for the nymphomaniac before he was satisfied."

There was the mold of Lucia Bosé's face with her throat slit and the mold of Capucine's face with the scar. For her role as Tryphaena, Fellini has transformed the actress's finely chiseled features into a snakelike mask by hooding her eyes with copper paint and adding a disfiguring scar at the right corner of her mouth. "Fellini has had a bee in his bonnet for a long time about that scar," Carboni says, "and even told Capucine she should wear it all the time even though she would have preferred to be without it."

Two heads of defeated Roman generals to be carried back to Rome in the triumphal procession of the new Emperor are lying on the shelf. One head was made to look as if the man had been dead three months, another for only one month.

We went through boxes of noses in every size and shape, made by Carboni in latex, even one for a statue with a broken nose. There were patches to make eyes look old or pouchy, an eye with bubonic plague, and eyes to look like statues, open or shut. More patches simulated strange diseases or sicknesses, scars for the body or face, a cut lip with cracked blood on it. Others were designed to make people look jowly or double-chinned, to produce puffy cheeks or cauliflower ears.

At the end of the tour, I asked Carboni what he thought of Fellini and he answered, "His private life is simple. Working is happiness for him. It is here that he finds his life."

March 15

The film has now been christened "The Daily Miracle." The giant, an eight-foot-tall carpet merchant, arrived on a plane from Tripoli last night. Ali Suleiman Nashnush, a Moslem, refuses to be photographed or interviewed, but for five hundred dollars is willing to appear in the picture. Fellini had to take advantage of the weather to shoot the outdoor scenes he needed, and Ali got tired of waiting around and skipped off home. Fellini could have another giant from Rome, but he was a foot shorter; so Ali was tracked down and reluctantly brought back, because no one has the temerity to thwart the director.

On the set, Fellini is trying out the dawn with the fog effects.

The giant sits forlornly in his outlandish wig, his chest bare, a long skirt wrapped around him, and leather sandals on his enormous feet. Martin and Randone are still lying drunk in the dawn on the furrows which have been sharply re-etched. Maurizio is sent to make footprints in the furrows so the earth will be the same as the day before. The director is shooting a brief detail of Martin helping the poet to the little pool.

Bob Herrington is on the set and grouses that the BBC television crew waited around for two weeks while Randone was sick and went away with nothing. Herrington was repeatedly told shooting would start up any day. "I'm beginning to think Fellini is a compulsive liar," he sighs, "but I love him anyway."

This is a bit of a switch from what Herrington had said early on in the picture. "One day," he told me, "I said to Fellini, 'English gentlemen don't lie'; and he said, 'But I am a big liar.' I said, 'But you mustn't lie as you are an Italian gentleman; and English gentlemen always keep their promises and, since you are an Italian gentleman, you must always keep your promises.' Now he never lets me down." I could just visualize Fellini's expression as he listened to the earnest publicist instructing him in the rudiments of British, old-school-tie codes of conduct.

Fellini leaves the camera and goes over to inspect the giant. Capucine reports Fellini doesn't like the way the giant is costumed and the scene with him will have to be done on Monday. She wants to leave for Paris the next day and is terrified the giant will flee again. She wants him guarded. Fellini waits for the fog effect to be done properly, groans and looks glum with his head on his hand tapping the megaphone on his lap with restless fingers.

At long last, the director is ready for the scene with the giant and Tryphaena. It does not exist in the script, but Fellini invented it in order to get Encolpius from the banquet where Tryphaena first encounters him to the ship of Lichas where she plans to seduce him. It is an extremely difficult scene because of the many disparate elements involved: the dawn artificially simulated with lights, the chemically produced fog, the grains dropped manually into the pond, and the reluctant giant. During the first take with the giant, Peppino Rotunno explodes into a tirade directed at a prop man. It is so unusual for the gentle and unflappable Rotunno that a complete hush descends on the set. Even the director seems startled.

"All right," Fellini calls to the giant. "Walk in, Ali. Look at me and go down and pick him up." The giant only pretends to pick up Martin, who is lying unconscious on the ground, by spreading out his arms. During the second take, Fellini screeches at Ali in some language which sounds like Arabic; it is difficult to believe that Fellini knows Arabic—but maybe he *has* picked up a couple of phrases. It sounds good anyway, and Ali seems to respond.

On the fifth take, Fellini decides he wants the giant to smile with his mouth open but he makes such a frightening grimace that he reverts to his original idea, making him smile with his mouth closed.

"You have finished now, Ali," Fellini says. "Are you happy?"

The giant tears off his wig and costume and leaves the set as fast as his weak legs will take him. His two-foot sandals were found discarded in the men's room, and Ali probably went straight to the airport, never knowing he was to end up on the cutting-room floor. Watching his retreating figure, Capucine remarks, "Tryphaena certainly has some very strange friends!"

The Death of Eumolpus
and Other Tidbits

March 24

They've been trying to get this one off the ground for days but the elements have not been cooperative. The scene is being shot at Focene on the Tyrrhenian Sea, *Il Mare Nostrum,* as the Romans called it, not far from the Rome airport. On the seventeenth, the first day's shooting, the torn sail of Eumolpus' ship had to be repaired and the sky wasn't overcast enough for the scene. The next day, they were still waiting for the right skies. The nineteenth was a national holiday and on the twentieth, very little was accomplished except a brief scene of a Negro girl dancing in front of a strange fish suspended in the air with its mouth open, a vision Encolpius sees as he approaches the house of the sorceress Oenothea. Ascyltus has been slain in the marshes by the ugly boatman who takes the heroes to the house of the old Oenothea, but Hiram is always getting killed and is never dead. Fellini made him die at least four times before finally polishing him off for good.

Alberto Moravia, the writer, came to watch the shooting, vexing the director because he kept asking questions and then answering them himself.

On the twenty-first, I drove out to Focene following crude signs on fences or gates saying *Satyricon*. Fellini hailed me enthusiastically and beckoned me over to the camera. "Have you seen this Roman statue we have just found here? Right here. We dug it up. Maccari, what's the name of that professor who is coming out from the Antiquities Department to look at it?" While the camera operator fumbles for a name and Fellini cackles raucously, I look at the thing and say, "It doesn't look Roman to me. It just looks like a phallic symbol." He insists and I let him have his little joke. Fellini became very attached to that symbol and used it in a later scene. When Encolpius is thrown into the Labyrinth, the same phallic symbol stands at the bottom of the slope.

On March twenty-third, nothing was accomplished, waiting for the sun to disappear behind the clouds. Most directors wait for sunlight but Fellini waits for clouds. However, I suppose for such a macabre scene, it has to be a gloomy day, but these delays are costly. I bet Grimaldi doesn't have a fingernail left.

Today, the director is in his suede jacket, his customary fedora, bright blue pants, and rubber boots. "These are the pants of the sea, my sailor pants," he explains. The ship, riding in the waves in full sail, is a small, graceful craft with a thin prow almost like a bird's beak, but is hardly seaworthy. The sail is bigger than the ship. This is the ship which was to have carried Eumolpus, the poet, to Africa with a cargo of goods.

It is the final episode in the film and the most significant, the one in which Fellini states his message. There is the obvious analogy between pre-Christian Roman society on the verge of breakup and our own society in the throes of upheaval and a search for new values. In his film, the director is also commenting on the role of the artist in an industrial society and on the revolt of today's youth against traditional attitudes.

Fellini is intrigued by the character of Eumolpus. Perhaps the director, who is often called "Il Poeta" by his admirers, identifies himself with this tragicomic character whom he describes as "a poet who has a great many doubts as to the value of his mission. He's a rhetorician and at the same time, an anti-rhetorician; a pimp, yet when it comes to poetry, he reveals a certain dignity. When they go to the banquet of Trimalchio, Eumolpus adulates his host, calls him a poet; but when that nouveau riche of a Trimalchio begins to recite verses, then he rebels. Poetry must be respected and can't be bought with money. Even his end is significant. He disappears to reappear as a merchant who has become wealthy—a kind of Rimbaud of the era. When he dies, his last will provides that his heirs can claim their inheritance only if they eat his body! It's a formidable scene. Eumolpus lies there with an ironic smirk on his face, as though, instead of saying, 'Take nourishment from my body,' he were saying, 'Nourish yourselves on poetry!' And there is an analogy between Roman times and modern society. Eumolpus is like the man of letters today—cynical, dissipated, at the service of the powerful, with, however, a basic fidelity to poetry." Perhaps the poet's struggle to be faithful to his art reminds the director of his own efforts to remain a creative individual in the giant industrial complex of today's cinema world. Just as Eumolpus strikes out at Trimalchio for the sake of his art so Fellini battles money-grubbing producers, primarily interested in commercial success, to maintain his artistic integrity.

Placidi, the poet's stand-in, is lying on a bier trussed up like a mummy in white bandages. The bier is covered with a thin, gauzy cloth, decorated with a gold Oriental design. Various crates of assorted sizes and colors marked with undecipherable symbols are strewn on the beach. Scattered around are the passengers, Eumol-

pus' heirs, their faces made up like ghosts to match the colors of
their robes.

The captain, Carlo Giordana, has his hair dyed blond with a
blond beard to match. His crew are young and agile men, both black
and white, unlike the passengers, who are mostly old and decrepit.
The captain reads the bizarre will after which he and Encolpius and
the crew set sail while the old men carry out their cannibalistic
feast, which has also been likened to a symbolic evocation of the
Holy Communion. The young generation refuses to participate in
this affront to human dignity and departs for other shores where
hopefully a new and better life awaits them. Out of decay and
death comes rebirth and renewal. One civilization must die before
another can be born.

Fellini had told me, "If you want to understand this film, you
should read *La Mia Rimini, My Rimini,*" a book dedicated to his
native city, in which there is the following passage: "Life, in itself,"
he quotes Charlie Chaplin in *Limelight,* "has no meaning but one
must give it a meaning"; and then he muses, "But if the meaning
given to life up to now has led us to our present condition, it is
clear a new meaning must be found. In order to give life a new
meaning, it is necessary to destroy the old one. To delude oneself
that a sensible connection can be established between an old system
of life and a new one is simply impossible." Speaking of the current youth revolt, Fellini says, "I believe these young people are
finding their strength in going along another road which is theirs
alone and which, even if their long hair should fall out, is not
comparable to the brief dissoluteness of our student days. The
young today have really initiated another era. Theirs is a profound
rupture with the past." As the director once said speaking of *La
Dolce Vita,* but applicable also to the *Satyricon,* "This is a film
which in spite of showing moral decay gives a viewer a feeling of

being set free . . . free from the myths of our time, for the man of tomorrow must be a man without myths."

Fellini, unshaven and tired-looking, sighs and embraces me. "*Mi sono rotto le corna*. My balls are broken." To Roger Ebert, a journalist from Chicago, he jokes, "This is like a scene from a Fellini movie! We haven't decided yet whether there will be an actual scene of cannibalism or not. Some days I think 'yes.' Some days I think 'no.' "

While he is shooting the scene of the reading of the will, the journalist reports he has been to see Gillo Pontecorvo in Colombia where Marlon Brando has amoebic dysentery. Pontecorvo kept fretting, "I just hope we finish our picture before Fellini finishes the money." When I repeat Pontecorvo's remark later, Fellini replies, "We don't have any money problem here. We have already spent it. It was all gone over two months ago and now we are serene."

The journalist wants to know when the picture will be released.

"At Christmas. It will be a nize Christmas picture," Fellini says slyly. "It is just the right kind of picture for Christmas."

The journalist protests it might be a bit on the erotic side for that holiday, but Fellini objects, "It is not an erotic picture. It is very 'cast' if seen with virgin eyes, not as the Catholics see sex."

The journalist looks a bit perplexed and I say, "He means 'chaste,' not 'cast.' "

Fellini says, "That's what I said, 'tchaste.' "

Ebert, Bob Herrington, a French photographer, and I are invited to lunch in the director's drab trailer. Fellini is still on a diet and the fare is always plain and simple. "A poor Franciscan meal," Fellini describes it.

"When are you going to finish?" Herrington wants to know.

"This cheese?" Fellini asks.

"No, this picture."

"After we finish this cheese," Fellini replies with his puckish sense of humor.

Herrington announces he wants to get up a cricket team to play Dino De Laurentiis, the producer with whom Fellini fought so long over *Mastorna*. *Waterloo* is being shot at what is called Dino-città, the producer's huge, modern cinema complex outside Rome. "I think De Laurentiis would make a fine batman," Herrington continues, while Fellini looks puzzled. When I finally finish explaining what cricket is and what a batman is, Fellini beams, "Ah, *Satyricon* against *Waterloo!*"

Then he launches into a discussion of *Satyricon*, punctuating his remarks with, "It is a film made with cheap money." Each time he mentions money, Herrington, who is paid by United Artists, the financial backers of the film, rolls his eyes heavenward.

Discussing the *Satyricon*, Fellini declares, "This is my most difficult picture because I have to invent with my fantasy a whole new world and see it from a very narrow point of view. It is a foreign, unknown world. Who knows what the Romans were like? Nobody. This kind of jumping is very hard and very tiring. *Satyricon* has been the most challenging picture I have ever made because I look at this picture with detachment. It is a documentary on the customs and habits of the Martians. To be detached from your work is unnatural, like a mother who does not recognize her son.

"I try to forget the myths and weaknesses of the Christian world," he continues, "and to try to love that pre-Christian world. It is very confused, very chaotic, because it is impossible to understand the pagan world. They had different myths, different gods, a different kind of look. They have nothing of the Catholic desire and fear of sex which is considered impure. You can't go against your instincts and that makes the big contradiction. You are always taught sex is impure but you know it is a lie. So, in this pagan world, you are obliged to see sex with desire but cut off from the Catholic education.

"If you see things with an innocent eye, everything is beautiful," the director asserts. "For example, if you go to India and see that temple with all the statues making love in a hundred different ways, you don't think of it as pornographic, only as something strange and foreign, but apart from you. Pornography is in you, not in things. If we are not pornographic, then the film is not pornographic. That is the sense in which I try to keep away from my natural background.

"I don't like to be sneaky in erotic things," Fellini insists. "Otherwise, the picture should not be done. If I made the picture with Catholic desire and education, then it would be dirty and erotic. For that reason, the picture will disappoint many audiences who will go to see it thinking it is erotic; but it is not. The principal characters are asexual. They could be boys, girls, flowers even.

"This picture is in a different style. I have made no panoramas, no topography, only frescoes, and so the cutting is very fast. It has no real time. It is like riffling through an album. There is no psychological movement in the characters. Things in front of you are like frescoes. The rhythm is slow but also very fast. Everything is very different."

Herrington interrupts to comment that all Fellini's previous films have been autobiographical.

Fellini gives a beatific smile and says, "Yes, but this also is my picture. It is my idea. I am the actors, the ship, the wind, the waves."

I add, "And the god," and he smiles assent.

"This is my most demanding picture because of the necessity to change everything in a psychological way after having developed a style and a way of thinking and a technique," Fellini continues. "You have to become free from yourself, from your tastes, your technique and your tricks—in the good sense of the word—to try to see the story with new eyes, with different ideas and different money." Herrington's eyes roll heavenward again. Fellini notices and tries to rectify the situation a bit. "This is the first time I have done a film with American money although I have always had an Italian producer. United Artists are very nice people. They are the best in the States, I think. They are young and they love the fun of movies."

Ebert tells Fellini he has interviewed Marcello Mastroianni in London, who told him he had moved in with Fellini during the making of *La Dolce Vita*. "You were roommates," says Ebert.

"What is 'roommate'?" Fellini wants to know. "Does it have a sexual connotation, Eileen?"

After I have explained that peculiar Americanism to him, he giggles, "Marcello and I, roommates. Whatever will people think of us? It's true. Marcello moved in with me but because he had trouble with his wife. But after the film was finished, Marcello went back home and now they are happy again. But I see what you mean. Yes, when we made *La Dolce Vita* and *8½* Marcello and I were very close. We had to be, because in a way he was playing me."

This reminds him of something else, a story run in an Italian scandal magazine, purportedly signed by Flora Mastroianni, in which she allegedly said that she married an S.O.B. and that Mastroianni is in love with his secretary, Fred. "Another Fred," Fellini emphasizes, "not me." The director continues relating the story Mastroianni's wife is supposed to have written and ends up exclaiming, "It's terrific!" The journalist looks startled because Fellini has already explained the whole thing is a complete invention and he can't understand how things like this can be printed.

I interpret. "He means, 'It's terrible!' "

"That's what I mean," Fellini says as though he had said it all along.

Ebert inquires about the grotesque aspects of Fellini's films. The director replies rather heatedly, "Critics are always defining my pictures as grotesque but they are not. *La Dolce Vita* was a fresco of the society we live in. *8½* was a more restricted picture of the problems of modern man. *Juliet* exposed the problems of a Catholic woman which I think are universal." The journalist remarks that a group of priests and nuns in Chicago had seen *La Dolce Vita* and considered it a very Christian film.

I remind the director that the *Osservatore Romano,* the semiofficial Vatican newspaper, had accused him of turning the whole of Italy into a bordello with *La Dolce Vita.* Fellini well remembers and is infuriated. "It is the Catholic Church that made Italy a bordello," he rages.

The journalist begins to ask a question about directors and Fellini interrupts, "All directors are the same but it is their way of looking at things which is different. But critics have to say something because they use words instead of a camera and so they are forced to define and categorize. Just say Fellini is creating Fellini."

Ebert persists in the grotesqueness of Fellini's films. Fellini responds, "Well, maybe," and relates the difficulties with the hermaphrodite. "We had to make plastic breasts," the director explains.

"Plastic surgery?" the journalist asks.

Fellini says, "Yes, he had to be corrected," meaning he had to wear artificial breasts.

The journalist, still misunderstanding, clucks, "I hope he can have them removed."

"Yes, I hope so," Fellini says.

With that total lack of comprehension on both sides, which I didn't even bother to untangle, we returned to the shooting to take advantage of the cloudy sky.

Placidi's bandages have been unwound to leave him free to eat and Fellini is bellowing for him to be rewrapped. Old rubber tires have been lit on the beach to make dense black smoke and there is a terrible stench. A group of school children escorted by a little nun stand transfixed staring at the monstrous scene. The poet is about to be carved up. One guest has announced it is quite common in other races for the dead to be consumed by his relatives. "In fact, those who are ill are constantly reproved for spoiling their flesh." Another agrees, saying his stomach will follow orders if, after an hour of nausea, it is promised such a heap of good things.

Mastocotto, an old man, is sharpening serrated knives before cutting the poet's leg off while another passenger holds it up. Fellini orders, "Aurelio, talk with Gian Carlo, and Gian Carlo, say whatever *cazzo* you want but speak. Aurelio, come slowly around the table. Speak among yourselves. Mastocotto, action. Alfredo, sit down. Raise his leg up. Another one go around the table. Try to turn the body. Now, each indicate a part of the body. Now everybody touch the corpse."

One of the makeup men is gazing at the sea and musing, "I wonder why so many of Fellini's films always end up at the sea."

I recall the director's remarks in *La Mia Rimini*. "I was thin and I had a complex about it. They called me 'Gandhi' or 'canestalk' and I never wore a bathing suit. I lived a life apart, solitary. I looked for illustrious models to justify this fear of the bathing suit, this incapacity to enjoy myself like the others who went to splash about in the water. Because of this, perhaps, the sea is so fascinating for me, like a thing never conquered: the region from which monsters and fantasies come."

March 25

A friend of mine asked me to take three distinguished Protestant theologians, Harvey Cox, J. Robert Nelson, and Martin Marty (in Rome for a conference on atheism), to visit the *Satyricon* set and meet Fellini. I asked the director if I could bring them but he kept wondering, "Theologians, why do they want to see me?"

"I don't know, but can they come?"

Finally Fellini said he would see them the next day at Focene where they were still continuing with "The Death of Eumolpus" scene and having another go at killing Ascyltus off.

Dr. Marty couldn't make it so Harvey Cox and I started out in Dr. Nelson's car but had to turn back when it began to run low on gas. There was a service station strike, one of the many hiccup strikes in Italy which are frequent enough and long enough to be irritating rather than effective. We had to return to Rome to get my car, fortunately with a full tank of gas, considering the miles I was to travel that day. Fellini had promised to lunch with the theologians but by the time we arrived at Focene, twenty miles away, it was about one o'clock and I could see the crew leaving. I stopped Peppino Rotunno's car and asked him where Fellini was. "In the trailer," he said.

I accompanied the two theologians to the trailer, already knowing full well that Fellini would not lunch with them. He has a convenient knack of forgetting promises sometimes, and besides we were late. Sure enough, when I stuck my head inside the trailer and announced the theologians were there, Fellini, who had already begun his frugal lunch, looked sulky and groaned. "Take them to lunch at that nice fish place in Focene and then bring them to Cinecittà. I'll see you there." I could cheerfully have choked him. I had already driven twenty miles and now had to drive forty more all across Rome.

We went off to lunch at a *trattoria* in Ostia Antica and then set out for Cinecittà. By this time, I had discovered Harvey Cox was also a film critic for *Tempo,* the magazine of the National Council of Churches, and I thought this would tickle Fellini's fantasy —journalist-theologian writing about *Satyricon.* When we arrived at Cinecittà naturally there was no Fellini to be found. He was still in the production office. A night shot, the first to be done so far, was being set up on one of the lots outside Stage Two. It is the scene in Trimalchio's kitchen where Eumolpus is beaten by the slaves after having insulted the host.

Danilo Donati was running wildly around with his usual lament, "It's enough to make you cry. I had to do this whole thing over-night." In lieu of Fellini, I presented Donati to the theologians, a not very satisfactory substitute because Danilo doesn't speak a word of English, but he obligingly told me to take the visitors over to Stage Five to look at the gigantic erotic panels being prepared for "The Garden of Delights." The artists were still working on them, and after admiring them, we returned to the lot.

Fellini finally appeared, still looking like a big Teddy Bear in his suede jacket and black fedora. By this time, I only had one theologian, Dr. Cox, left, since Dr. Nelson had to return to Rome for a lecture. I introduced the theologian to Fellini, explaining, "Dr. Cox has come to Rome with the intention of seeing only two people, Fellini and Montini, and in that order. He is seeing you first and will see the Pope tomorrow."

Fellini glowed and was reminded of a story. After the furor created by *La Dolce Vita,* when half the clergy in Italy railed against the film as immoral and the other half praised it as a very Christian film, Fellini requested an audience with Montini, then Archbishop of Milan, to defend several of his Jesuit friends who had supported the film.

"Because of their support," Fellini related, "one had been transferred to Bangkok, one to the wilds of Sardinia, and another I don't remember where. After two weeks, I was granted an audience. I spent twenty minutes talking, but Montini said absolutely nothing, not one word. He is a tight man, inwardly troubled, not free."

By this time, it was dusk and the wind was coming up. Fellini noticed Dr. Cox had no overcoat. "Aren't you cold?" he asked. "I will give you a coat." He shouted for Bevilacqua and told him to go to the warehouse where all the costumes and props for the *Mastorna* film are still kept and get a coat for Cox. "Take a good look at him and be sure to bring back the right size." Then he said to me, "Take him with Pippia and Provenzale to the Institute of Light to see the Special [the hour-long television program Fellini had done for NBC on the preparation for *Mastorna* and the *Satyricon* which was shown in April, 1969, in the U.S.] and be sure and explain to him it has nothing to do with the *Satyricon*." Nothing would do but drive down to see the Special, which had been cut and dubbed since the first time I saw it in November. Both Fellini and Giulietta Masina spoke in English and some parts of it were rather amusing, others downright silly.

Back on the set, we are confronted by a wild scene. A huge fragment of wall has been built, with a staircase running up the left side, the rear of Trimalchio's villa. The walls are made of plaster and took two days to construct. To the left is a large mound of dirt and behind that, the staircase, visible only from the side. In the center of the wall a large arch has been cut with an enormous spit suspended inside. Giant carcasses of raw meat dangle from the spit, and tripes and entrails hang on the right wall.

Surveying his handiwork, Donati continues to complain. "Naturally, he asked for the kitchen the night before. Originally, the guests were supposed to visit Trimalchio's farm but then he decided to do some of the farm scenes here in the kitchen instead. I had to run to the country and buy threshers and ploughs and scythes. We had two hours to weld all the things together and make this huge spit. The film is always done the night before."

In front of the right wall, two grossly fat women sit behind a long, wide table littered with large pots. A Negro stands behind a wooden stump carving raw meat. Way back to the left an entire calf is strung up on a primitive tripod. In the left foreground is a wooden cage. Near the staircase, four large dogs—two German shepherds and two Doberman pinschers—strain at their leashes.

Behind the spit, the wall is being hastily painted reddish brown to match the walls of the villa. Three slaves, dressed in purple, yellow, and red, stand waiting for instructions. A slave has been put in the cage at left. The flame under the spit has now been lit, illuminating the scene in an orgiastic dance of madmen. The fire shoots up eighteen feet high from the spit, which is equipped with burners and special valves attached to gas cylinders. In all, 1,375 pounds of gas were consumed.

"Let's try a rehearsal with the dogs," Fellini calls. "Are the dogs ready?" The dogs, as if on cue, immediately start to fight amid much shouting and yelling.

"The two breeds don't get along," explained Pino Serpe, the animal trainer, "unless they have been raised together. Look, one already has his ear chewed off."

Fellini decides to work with the slaves while the dogs are being calmed. He is rather wary of animals. The slaves have removed their robes and are sprayed with sweat. They are stunt men, eight of them, who get paid forty dollars a day; but, "It's not very hard in this picture," one explains, "because Fellini doesn't like dangerous things."

By this time Bevilacqua has returned with the overcoat for Dr. Cox. For some reason it has no buttons but Fellini is very pleased with the fit. "Pippia," he calls, "put up a cord. All those not in the scene, stand behind the cord." He walks over to the slave in the cage and says, *"Mi raccomando,* mind you, laugh like a madman," then demonstrates to Randone's stand-in, in stunt man, how to run around in the kitchen pursued by the vicious slaves. Randone is waiting in a car for close-up shots, but because of his recent illness, Fellini doesn't want to use him until he must.

After the first take, he goes over to the two fat women working at the table and bares their ample bosoms. Getting ready to reshoot the scene, he warns the slaves, "Don't leap at him right away. It's a game, ring-around-the-rosy, *ragazzi.* Work, ladies, work. Carini," he says to the cook's assistant, "put the torch more under the flames."

On the second take, the flames roar and Fellini bellows, "Turn the spit faster." The slaves scamper around the poet. He fights them off with a torch while the slave chained in the cage cavorts like a monkey with Fellini urging, "Jump twice here and twice there."

"*Cicciona*, fatty," he calls to one of the hefty, perspiring ladies, "sit on the stool and stay curved," and leaves the camera to show her how. He makes her move again. "Stay bent over forwards. Turn to the left. Spread your legs open. Turn your body to the right. *Ecco! Brava!* Like that. Good."

It is now eight o'clock and Fellini has been up since seven and working all day. He shows no sign of fatigue even though he has been doing all the actions for everybody. Bevilacqua, who was to have had a part in *The Games,* being filmed in Rome, remarks, "I couldn't leave him," nodding at *il Dottore.*

Fellini asks Randone to get out of the car and come in for close-ups, calling for a coat to be put on him. While his makeup is being repaired, Randone carefully watches the stunt men go through the same actions they did with his stand-in. Fellini hollers for Bevilacqua but can't find him. He wants a blanket to put on his shoulders. It is blazing hot when the flame is lit, freezing cold when it is put out between takes—a nice way to get pneumonia. The director wants sweat sprayed on the slaves and screeches at Rossano, the makeup man, "There are thirty of you and I always have to call you at the last minute." His leg is bothering him. He has pulled a muscle and limps a bit. Randone is ready and they shoot the first take with him in which he has liquid poured into his eyes but manages to escape and staggers off.

By this time it was after nine o'clock and I drove Harvey Cox back to Rome. The shooting continued until eleven o'clock with Randone being chased up the stairs while the chained dogs barked madly and tried to attack him.

Before we left, Fellini, who had become rather intrigued with the idea of entertaining theologians, called, "Bring the theologians to lunch at Riano Flaminia tomorrow"—a village about twenty miles from Rome where a few scenes will be shot in a quarry. As we left, Fellini's hulking form was outlined in the flames. Earlier, Dr. Cox had asked, "You always have an angel in your films. Who is the angel in *Satyricon*?"

"I am," Fellini said solemnly.

By the light of the flames, he looked like the devil himself.

March 26

Luckily, before driving twenty miles out of Rome with the theologians, I called the publicity office to check on the day's shooting and discovered nothing was being shot at Riano Flaminia today, just a couple of brief scenes at the Colosseum in the afternoon. "The Colosseum!" I thought. "How is he going to work that historic monument into his hallucinatory world?" Maybe he's decided to do the gladiator scene after all, a scene everyone talked about as a vague possibility.

Ah, but then I remembered something he said once. "In spite of all the visits made to museums and Herculaneum and Pompeii, scrutinizing the secrets hidden behind the crusts of centuries, the only time I felt a shiver of discovery and of awareness of that remote Roman world was at night in front of the Colosseum, that lunar catastrophe of stone, that immense skull eaten by time set in the heart of Rome." Maybe he wants to shoot one scene there in memory of that one brief moment of kinship with the old Romans.

It's a sight to behold! The whole kit and kaboodle of them are in one of the outer passageways of the ancient amphitheater. Zambon, the set decorator, is calmly painting over the modern-day graffiti on the old stones, *"Viva Roma,"* "Yankee, go home," "Enough of American capitalism," "Go away, Nixon," and the hundreds of scrawled names and obscenities. False stones have been placed in the empty spaces of the old paving. A large crowd has gathered, attracted by the sight of Martin and Hiram and Max in their short tunics, and the four horses, two white and two black. The director is there, yelling and gesturing, and the tourists are having a real show—maybe not a gladiatorial contest but certainly a lot funnier.

Martin is seated on a white horse behind Hiram. I have no idea where they are going and I don't think they do either. They are riding bareback, and Martin, looking absolutely terrified, is clutching Hiram. Fellini calms him, "Martin, don't be afraid," and Martin's smile is sickly. Fellini laughs and asks, "Martin, you still want to become a movie star? Try to be very sure." As they do a rearview shot showing them going back down the arched passageway, Fellini calls, "Hiram and Martin, talk. Martin, say, 'I like horses. That will always be my natural way of traveling.' And try not to cover each other."

An AP photographer arrives looking shaken. He had spotted Max Born in his white tunic and curls. "I thought, 'That's a nice piece of cheesecake,' but I got a real shock when I discovered he was a boy," he shuddered. "I could have sworn he was a girl." Poor Max! Boys on Vespas keep riding past him, whistling and calling him a fairy.

Waiting for the lights to be changed, Fellini calls to me, "Eileen, where were you at lunch today with the theologians?"

Annoyed at the second misfired lunch, I say, "I don't want to talk any more about the theologians."

"But why you say that, Eileen? Wasn't I nize to him? Didn't I give him a coat? Why didn't you come to lunch?"

"Because you didn't shoot at Riano Flaminia so I didn't go."

"Ah," he insists, "but I was there and waiting for you." In one of those comedies of errors in which Fellini is constantly entangling himself and other people, he had indeed gone to look at the quarry site, but the publicity people didn't know it. "And where's the coat?" he adds for good measure.

They now do a scene of Encolpius and Giton walking along the same passageway. Fellini walks along with Max, demonstrating complicated hand gestures supposed to be some kind of sign language.

Fellini says to Martin, "Embrace him strongly. He is your fiancé. No, Max. I told you to cross over to your right, otherwise you will always be covered by the Hinglish actor." On the second take, Max skips ahead of Martin, faces him, and makes his funny little hand movements—which may have some meaning to Fellini but to nobody else—and then they kiss. On the third take, he says, "Martino, more affection, more sexuality. Action. Go fast."

At the end he calls to me, "What have you got on your head, a ricotta?"—my white fur hat reminds him of a cheese. Waiting for the lights, Fellini goes to sit by Giulietta, who is watching the shooting. A little girl comes up and asks for their autographs. When she tells him her name, the director writes, "*A Adrianna, Buona Pasqua,* To Adrienne, Happy Easter," and smiles sweetly at her.

It is getting windier, and one of the crew cracks, "The name of the film has just been changed to *Gone With The Wind!*"

Fellini wants to know how I liked the TV Special. "I enjoyed it very much, and I was amazed at Giulietta's English. It's very good." He beams his pleased smile and says, "Go and tell her. She will be very happy. And how was mine?"

"Interesting," I say.

"Ah," and he pouts.

When the shooting is over, Bevilacqua marches up and announces, "I've changed *il Maestro*'s name."

"To what?" I ask.

"To *il Faro,* the Lighthouse."

"Why?"

"Because everybody is in the dark and he's the only one who can shed light on anything." Bob Herrington grimly agrees. After I recount the story of the theologians, his only comment is, "I was in British Intelligence for five years, and I want to tell you it has stood me in good stead on this film."

The Garden of Delights

Fellini is back in a brothel again filming the episode of "The Garden of Delights" where the poet takes Encolpius to be cured of the impotence which overcomes him after fighting the Minotaur in the Labyrinth. The garden takes its name from the enormous painted panels which form part of the walls, on which every conceivable position of love-making is depicted. These are the murals, copied from Persian miniatures, which Scordia initially began on a smaller scale; they have now been blown up to grandiose proportions. The director deliberately put into the frescoes the pornography which he feared to portray in the film because of the stringent Italian censorship.

Originally, the Garden was to be shot outdoors with just a cracked wall for background. Then Donati proposed enclosing it within white walls with little windows. Fellini accepted the idea but wanted an additional big wall of erotic frescoes, which created another crisis. The panels were first tried on stucco, but didn't produce the desired fresco effect. Then tests were made on foam rubber, a unique technique, which produced a cracked-wall effect, exactly like an old fresco. The painters worked eight days, day and night, to finish them in time for the shooting, but had great difficulty getting the foam rubber to dry.

There were all kinds of other technical problems to resolve. The foam rubber panels, totaling eighty feet by twenty-six, had to be glued onto canvas which meant they had to be made in three parts and then attached to support frames. The construction shop made a mistake in the measurements of the frames, and during the night they had to be redone. Everyone thought the panels would break when they were pulled upright but they didn't, only because they were done in three parts.

The frescoes should have been made in the studio where they were to be shot to eliminate the necessity of transporting them, but Fellini was using it and there were no others available. When Donati finally got the panels assembled, the joinings were plainly visible and had to be camouflaged with other layers of paintings, as though the frescoes had been done over older ones. "In the end," sighed Donati, "*per miracolo,* by a miracle, it came out like the Sistine Chapel!"

In the center of the set is a big square sand garden composed in intricately traced geometric ridges and swirls furrowed with a specially constructed wooden rake. It has taken six men one entire night to make this section patterned after the Japanese gardens Donati saw in some books. The lines in the sand heighten the visual assault on the senses and also create the allusion to modern optical effects used throughout the film.

To the left of the garden, on the ground, against a low white wall, there is a large mattress in what appears to be an op design, but actually it is copied from an ancient Pompeian mosaic. To the right of it is a large blue swing, about four feet by four, with light geometric designs painted on its underside and odd-shaped holes cut into it. The swing is hung from the ceiling, and lying on the ground is a long blue cord to pull it back and forth.

An elephant stands in the far right corner of the Garden. Jenny, who is seven years old, was rented from a circus in Naples and is very shy. She will not enter the studio without the two other elephants who escort her to her place and then leave. Fellini is supervising the painting of bands of color on Jenny's head and orders her to "be good," then comes over to survey the panels with a smug look on his face, bragging, "I am all the men in these panels."

Waiting for the lights to be set up, Peter Ammann comments, "The elephant is a fertility symbol. Don't you see the long trunk?"

Hiram laughs, "Wouldn't it blow your mind to come into a brothel and find an elephant there?"

A scene in front of the panels of erotic love is just being finished. A little Neapolitan woman about three feet tall who looks like a nice little old granny is running along in front of the frescoes, screeching in Neapolitan dialect, 'Wake up, *ragazze*." A man's head appears in the little window cut into the painting of a horse on which a man and woman are riding off in an erotic but most uncomfortable position.

Finished with the take, Fellini ambles back to feed Jenny, the elephant, in her corner. When he returns, I show him a book written by a French critic and marvel at the long bibliography of books about him. "Does it surprise you so many books are written about me?" he asks in mock indignation.

Hiram, thumbing through the book, comes across a photograph of Anita Ekberg and remarks to Fellini, "I find her so incredible!"

"Why?" Fellini wants to know.

"Because she is so big," says Hiram.

"Ah, a Mama!" Fellini exclaims. "Everybody needs a Mama."

Perihan, an actress known as the Lollobrigida of Turkey, arrives on the set and is warmly greeted by Fellini. She was one of the anonymous guests at Trimalchio's dinner but is now going to have a bigger role. On her forehead and naked belly hundreds of tiny orange beads have been glued one by one in a geometrical design. It has taken three makeup men three hours to get her ready.

Perihan fainted in the makeup department when they began to paint her blue. "Apparently I was allergic to the paint," she says, "because I became paralyzed and my heart started to beat furiously. I had to have an injection from the doctor, who said if I had gone ten minutes longer, I would have been dead."

Fellini interrupts her story to make her demonstrate the belly dance she will do in this episode, after which the makeup man warns her not to take the beads off her stomach when she goes to bed.

"And what if I want to make love?" she asks archly. "Every day there is a change with Fellini," she remarks. "He is right to do everything he does, but he is swearing too much. I don't like that. We are not in the habit of hearing it in Turkey."

The director sets up a scene with two little girls, Paola and Liz, in front of the camera. They are the youngest prostitutes in the garden, and one of them has just learned of Encolpius' plight and is presumably whispering it to the other, although the little girls are ignorant of their actual roles in the film.

"Martino, would you be so kind as to stand by the camera?" he asks in the exaggerated English he sometimes affects. "All right, look at him," he orders the girls, then goes up to them again and gives them instructions, but so softly no one can hear. He calls for an extra named Sveva, and after much scurrying around, Maurizio finds her. She is dressed in pale pink, and he puts her standing behind the two little girls, who must run from their position in front of the camera and whisper Martin's shameful predicament in her ear. Fellini bends Sveva down like a puppet to the girls' height so she can hear, and makes the girls fall to the ground laughing. Sveva must throw her head back and laugh too, but she is like a stick. "What's the matter with you? Have you got a backache?"

"No," she answers sullenly.

"All right, do it then."

Giulietta, sitting on the sidelines watching, murmurs indignantly, "What patience he has with that delinquent! But he's like that. He has astonishing energy. I get more tired than he does just watching him."

On the first take, he calls for music and bellows at Sveva, "Wait until I tell you." On the second take, he whispers something in Paola's ear and laughs. On the third take, he calls to Paola, "Laugh, Paolì. Show your little teeth, 'Ooh,' " and laughs to prompt her. "Laugh harder, Paolì." On the fourth take, he's back whispering to Paola, "Turn to your right. Tease him," he says as she looks at Martin. "Say, '*O Dio, che buffo!* Oh God, how funny!' " Fellini stands behind Martin directing the child's every movement, then goes over and kneels down in the sand, bending up and down with laughter. For two more takes he plays this game with the little girls and then leaves with Giulietta, arm around her shoulders.

Sveva Eusepi, the twenty-one-year-old Roman girl who's given the director so much trouble, sits beside me and mutters, "Fellini always thinks he told you what to do but he didn't."

April 2

Today is whipping and swinging day in "The Garden of Delights." On the op couch, three ladies of the garden are supposed to be beating Encolpius on the backside with little switches. Paola is standing swinging incense in a brass censer like an acolyte in church. Sveva is in front of the camera. A new girl with a yellow dress and face has been added and Anna, the tiny Neapolitan woman, is peering through the railing shrieking, "Beat! Beat!"

Fellini keeps remonstrating with her, "Annetta, it's only a rehearsal and you don't have to talk," but Anna doesn't know what a rehearsal is and keeps on hollering until Liliana, the director's assistant, makes her stop. Three young gypsy girls, their long black hair streaming down their backs, are placed on the couch and given long thin sticks with blue and yellow stripes. Their faces are painted vivid reds and oranges to match their costumes. Jenny is quietly munching hay in her corner while Fellini runs through a practice session of beating. He wants a particular steady rhythm.

Before the first take, he admonishes Gloria Goelet, a member of a prominent New York family who is making her second appearance in the film, "Hit there, stronger, Gloria. Ferocious. Show me your teeth." Through the next two takes, while Paola swings the incense and a prostitute played by a male Roman hairdresser tootles a reed flute and the others whip away, Fellini is at Gloria. Disgustedly, he groans, "I say ferocious and you are smiling as though you were a baby. Spread your legs more and say always, 'Come.' Haven't you ever whipped anyone?" he demands and she shakes her head. "You know why you *must* whip hard?" he wants to know, and explains, "Because there is an impotent man here."

When the beating is over, the director starts the swinging scene lying on a mattress. Four gypsy girls, two dressed in bright yellows and two in bright pinks with faces to match, are placed on the swing and pulled back and forth by a grip. While Fellini fusses with them, explaining what he wants them to do, Clara reports, "They are very intelligent. You see, they understood Fellini immediately. But they have never been so clean. We had to give them baths. We had a terrible time getting them to take off their clothes but they still have bugs in their hair."

"Bugs!" Hiram yips. "I wonder if I'll get bugs. Maybe they'll use the same comb on me!"

The characters on the couch are still the same except that Fellini has placed a girl with a purple veil directly in front of the camera with two switches in her hands. He calls for music and the action begins. The gypsy girls are now pulled back and forth on the swing by two other gypsy girls chanting, *"Altalena dell'amore, altalena dell'amore"*—the swing of love—as if they were singing ring-around-the-rosy. They are all laughing and giggling and the director makes them put their feet through the odd-shaped holes so they can be seen as the swing passes above the camera. As the swing soars overhead, Fellini, still lying on the mattress, prompts the actors on the op couch to say "Pa-pa-pa-pa" as they beat. "Pa-pa-pa-pa" seems to be the principal line in this film. The director rests on his elbow watching the scene, sticking his tongue out at the purple-veiled girl to show her how to do it, as she beats in a staccato rhythm. Jenny snorts loudly. The hay has been taken away from her and she is annoyed.

On the third take, Fellini yells at the gypsies, "Scream more and stick your feet down in the holes. Giusetta," he calls to one of them, "holler and make a wild yell," but they don't seem to be able to imitate him. The swing flies giddily back and forth pulled by the two girls running up and down. It swerves perilously close to the purple lady's head but she imperviously continues her monotonous beating. On the fourth and fifth takes, Fellini is still trying to get the girls to imitate his wild yell but they continue laughing and tittering. The purple girl is made to open and close her eyes in the same rhythm as she is beating with Fellini saying, "Open them. Lower them. Open them. Lower them."

Now Fellini concentrates on Gloria. The man-woman prostitute is playing his flute and Paola is swinging the incense. Gloria's white eyelids make her look as though her eyes had been plucked out. To emphasize this, Fellini makes her sit on a stool, forcing her to bend over into the camera. "Say, 'Come, come, come,' and beat faster and stronger." He prods her through three takes, finally an-

nouncing on the third, "*È questa,* Norma. That is it." With Peppino pushing him, Fellini has a ride on the swing. This is not the
first time he's had a swing in his films. He must be hung up on
swings.

After lunch, the gypsy girls are on the swing. None of them is
older than fifteen but they work often in films, the swarthy man
who chaperones them reports, and they obey his every word. In this
scene, the swing is swung very high to show the strange geometric
designs painted on its underside. Giulietta Masina is sitting on the
set and Fellini brings one of the gypsy girls over to her, excitedly
announcing to his wife, "This one is called Giulietta." He directs
them through four takes, gesturing frantically with his hands and
shouting exuberantly, "Yell. Laugh. On your feet. Up. Down. Up.
Down," making them crouch up and down and then put their feet
through the holes while Adriano and a couple of grips push them
back and forth. Fellini is delighted with the swing, which he
thought of one night as a way of seeing the garden through the
eyes of a drugged or drunken person.

Hiram is placed on the swing and the trouble starts. He removes
his pink satin tunic and wraps the plum-colored sash around his
loins, leaving a long strip of cloth hanging behind like a tail. The
director rumples his hair and puts Tania Duckworth, a young half-
Ceylonese actress, lying on her back with her head hanging off the
swing. She is facing Hiram. Another girl, Irina, in an orange robe
and incredible bangles and headdress, is placed on the swing along
with two gypsy girls. Fellini tries to get the gypsy girls to hang
their heads off the swing too but they complain it gives them a
headache. Hiram must kiss Irina every once in a while.

"Do what you want, Iram. Scream. Holler. But then once he
come to you and once you come to him and kiss." Fellini is actually
saying Hiram must kiss Irina every once in a while and she must
do the same, but he has gotten his genders confused.

Hiram is swinging dizzily, bellowing at Tania, "I am going to fuck you."

Taking in the scene, the gypsy leader removes the girls from the swing and marches them and all the other gypsy girls off the set.

"I knew immediately what would happen," Giulietta remarks. "They are rigid and very prudish and puritanical."

Spoletini, the man in charge of the extras, follows to try to persuade the gypsy leader to bring the girls back. Bevilacqua reports the gypsy said it was a dirty scene, "*una cosa brutta,* a filthy thing," and the girls are too young; but Bevilacqua says it is only blackmail and what they really want is more money. "You'll see, they'll be back," he predicts.

Giulietta is very concerned. "Federico should throw them out. They are minors." She is also worried because the BBC has taped Hiram screaming at the top of his lungs to Tania, "I am going to fuck you." She confers with her husband, who says he doesn't give a damn.

The gypsy girls return and the two take their place on the swing. On the fourth take, Fellini reminds Hiram, "Remember to say, 'You're going to fuck *me, me, me,* not that bitch, Encolpius, *me, me, me.*' *Ragazze,* girls, laugh and scream. Tania, your head back. Kiss him now, *signorina,*" to Irina, "and, Iram, go down." Hiram crouches down the way one does to get a swing moving. One of the gypsy girls continues to sob because Hiram is kissing Irina and wants to get off. Fellini furiously roars, "Send them all home! Go, all of you!" The gypsy leader removes the crying girl and Fellini continues with the other. Evidently, the gypsies have gotten the money they demanded and are willing to stay no matter what goes on.

Now he has added to the scene an ugly old woman called Anna, who is taller than the tiny Neapolitan woman, and Giuseppe, the brothel eunuch, who are to turn the swing around and around. "Tania," Fellini says, "you have to extend both your arms to Hiram;

and Giuseppe, you say 'Heinema, Heinema, Heinema.' Wait, Anna, don't be stupid. Wait until I say 'Anna' to swing it." On the second take, Fellini shouts to Hiram, "Zmile, Iram. It's a joke! Turn, turn," to Anna, and she is knocked flat on the ground. The other gypsy girl has begun to weep loudly and is duly removed by the gypsy leader. Fellini calls for Marguerite, a Negro girl in white robe and yellow scarf, to replace her. Hiram is still yelling, "*Me, me, me,* not that bitch," and the gypsy girls helping Anna turn the swing lose it, and it twirls madly.

It's a mess!

On the fifth take, Fellini says to the gypsy girls, "Do whatever comes to you naturally. It's a game." Anna falls again and almost gets hit on the head. Maurizio grabs the rope to stop the twisting swing and is dragged along the ground.

On the sixth take, Giuseppe is knocked flat and his wig bounces onto the ground. Hiram loses his grip on the rope and almost hurtles off the swing. "Now kiss Tania, now Irina, now Margherita," Fellini croons to Hiram like a lullaby.

Waiting for makeup repairs, Fellini calls to Max Born watching from the sidelines, "Mox, you want to do this scene?" Max replies, "Yes, but in the nude," and Fellini laughs hilariously.

The bead necklace Max made himself breaks and while he scrambles in the dirt searching for the beads, the makeup man next to me remarks, "I don't know if this will be a success on the screen. People will go to see it for the bare breasts and asses, but to understand Fellini, you have to go to the variety theater where they are always putting on spectacles. I don't know if the mass public can understand this. It's just a series of scenes with very little dialogue."

Irina Maleeva, a twenty-one-year-old Bulgarian theater actress, who had a small part in *Toby Dammit,* leaves the studio saying, "It's amusing, really, but still it's not acting, because he can make a chair act. He does everything."

Some Visitors

April 9

Today, Hans Richter, the noted painter and avant-garde director of the twenties, is on the set with his wife. The eighty-one-year-old artist, who looks much younger, is in Rome to attend an exhibition of his works at the Museum of Modern Art. "Fellini wanted to meet me," he recalls, "and we met at De Laurentiis' studios when he was making *Juliet of the Spirits.* He asked to see all my films and when he saw them, said, 'But you have done everything!' Fellini is the most imaginative of all directors. He looks up to me like Cecil B. De Mille but I don't know why. My productions have always been done on a small scale as an artisan. That's why Fellini admires me, because he has to work with industry. But I can't understand why he needs such a big apparatus!" the painter marvels as he surveys the big set and the numerous crew.

Richter, who was the director of the City College of New York's Film Institute, where he had five hundred students, recalls, "I used to tell my students the essence of a film director is that he has to see *life* through his eyes. The story comes second. Everything he cannot create visually, story or no story, doesn't count. That's what I admire in Fellini. He changes the scene according to what he sees. Eisenstein once told me that to shoot the *Potemkin,* he took six points out of twelve hundred pages of script, and on these he built his story. Fellini doesn't do this in such an extreme way, but he creates the way he sees, not according to the script. That's why he is such a great director. First, you have to love to make films, and secondly, you have to be able to *see* and love what you see. The text doesn't matter. What you see matters. The action matters."

They are filming an intricate gold and silver wheel which is being whirled to create a hallucinatory effect. It has taken seven special-effects men to make the clouds massed in the background. This is one of the visions Encolpius sees as he wanders in a daze after the death of Ascyltus.

Afterwards, Fellini has an interview with a team from the French magazine *Lui.* "You come along," he beckons to me. "The more interviews you sit in on, the less I'll have to talk to you." I could hardly refuse such a gracious invitation, and trot along behind him up to his office in the production department.

He leaves to give instructions for the next day's shooting, and while waiting for him, I mosey around, since I've never been there before. A number of paperbound books are piled on a shelf, all dealing with ancient Rome and written in French by René Ménard and Claude Sauvageot, covering every aspect of Roman life from the family and funerals to hairdos, theaters, public feasts, and war. These must be the books Liliana and Norma digested for Fellini when he began the preparation of the film.

Hanging on one wall is a garish poster of the director's zodiac sign, Capricorn, and another on the wall behind his desk. On the desk are some strange drawings and some books, *Zoroaster and*

Religious Fantasy, The Heroes of Myth, and *Religion and Myths of the North.* There is also a pack of tarot cards with stylized faces painted on them which are used in fortune-telling. I remember somebody remarking that the faces in "The Garden of Delights" all look like the faces on tarot cards. Tacked up on the rear wall is a faded list of all the characters in the film with the names of the actors Fellini had in mind. As far as I could see, only two of them actually made it—Salvo Randone and Alain Cuny.

After whisking busily about, giving orders to various assistants for the next day's shooting, Fellini finally comes into the dimly lit office, preceded by the journalists, and announces, "This interview will be in English." The French reporter demurs and the director says, "All right, it will be in Italian," and continues in French. "There is no analogy between modern times and ancient Rome. At the time I decided to make the film, it was just to make a satire; but perhaps there is an analogy, although it is not calculated. I am making a film on the life of ancient Rome because I want to do it.

"I am not a cerebral artist like Pasolini," Fellini objects. "He has a rationale for everything, but I am not organized in that way. If I have a good moon, I can find a good explanation for everything, but after all, it is very silly to find an explanation. There is an analogy but it is not precise—that is, a society waiting for something new, and Christ came after that. This is the strange thing. They were pre-Christian and we are post-Christian and we are waiting for something new. And something new is coming! In that sense, the film is a justification of actuality or reality; but the human aspect is perhaps too difficult to judge, if you think fifteen thousand gladiators were killed by Hadrian in two days just to amuse himself—*quinze mille,*" he reiterates.

"The Romans were biologically different from us, born from a new day. We can't understand them because we are obliged to use our intellect, and this intellectual operation is what the younger generation does not want to do. I hope to have a point of view about the Romans but it is difficult to forget two thousand years of Christianity. I have had to forget my sense of sin in order to create this atmosphere, because it is almost impossible to imagine the pagan psychology."

Fellini insists he has tried to present Roman life without making a judgment. "To do it, I have been obliged to invent everything, a universe. It's a fantastic creation with passion. I wanted to look at it from afar—*un peu étrange*—a little alienated. I refuse to look at that world from a sentimental point of view. I look at it with detachment. To create is to be in love, to be involved. Detachment is to become cold and uninvolved. For this reason, *Satyricon* is my most tiring film. It is more anguishing than *La Dolce Vita* because that had the reality of daily life. This film is made from an unknown point of view. It's science fiction from the planet Rome—something which was destroyed and we have only the pieces left.

"*Mastorna* was a very autobiographical film," the director explains, "very unconscious, but *Satyricon* is not. For that reason, it is very difficult. There is nothing where I can recognize myself. Historians will dislike my picture very much but I always want to give the spectator the sense of strangeness, on fixed tableaux. It is the most difficult thing in the world to do, and I only hope you will have the impression that the camera is moving."

Fellini maintains the film is a documentary on an unknown race, like the Amazons, and will be very different from his previous films. "I have had to forget my style, which is a kind of autodestruction. The film does not have rhythm, music, psychology, characters. It's like a Japanese film and is against the most elementary rules of the spectacle. The only thing to do is to construct a story of a spectacle.

"It is not a sexual film because the pagans did not recognize the sin of sex," Fellini says. "This is an undefinable film. It is not erotic. It is my point of view of all the things the Romans did without a moral definition. If you were to go to Mars, you don't know what they will be doing there because you don't have the terms to define what they are doing. I think this is the strangest picture I have made and I have done everything in a mathematical way. I was obliged to do it because the picture wanted to be told like that. For a creator, the things create. A true artist is one who tries to materialize fantasy without interfering too much, nor does he try to intellectualize what he is doing. I don't feel I have chosen to be a movie director. Personally, I have the feeling of having *been* chosen —not of having chosen."

At the end of the interview, the French correspondent reads a quote from Alberto Moravia, the Italian novelist, playwright, and journalist, in which he claims that Fellini is, among other things, "a masochist, a sadist, a hoaxer, an *imbroglione*, or swindler, and has a mother complex.

The director is absolutely stupefied and finally says, "But Moravia is my friend. I will call him up and ask him." Moravia has been on the set several times and written articles for American and Italian magazines on the *Satyricon*. Still bewildered and a bit miffed, he turns to me and says, "Eileen, me an *imbroglione?*" Then he flashes his most disarming smile at the French correspondent and says, "Perhaps he thinks my pictures are like that. I don't think he is talking about me as a man. I don't think I am a sadist but I am not capable of judging my films. After twenty years, I am only able to say 'It is a good picture' or 'It is a bad picture'; but when I did them, I was sincere and candid and true to my fantasy."

The full implication of the quote has now hit him and he becomes indignant. "I will tell you something about Moravia. It is very difficult to be interviewed by him because he asks all the questions but doesn't ever listen to the answers. He answers the questions himself. He isn't interested in films. It is just a pretext to talk about his own things." Still rankled, he explains, "If you invent a world with its precise laws, you have to mystify things, to impose your passions, loves, and faults on it."

After forty-five minutes of French, English, and Italian—the French straining to understand the Italian, me straining with my rusty French, and Fellini groping for the English word which I finally supply—we conclude the interview with a drink of Scotch provided by Bevilacqua.

Fellini magnanimously invites the journalists back on the set the next day, although he'll surely give a heart attack to Bob Herrington, who has strict orders from the director to allow only one journalist and one photographer on the set each day. He even offers them a lift to Rome to clarify things even further. The quote from Moravia has obviously given *il Maestro* a jolt.

April 10

Walking along to the studio, I encounter Bob Herrington hurrying along with a desperate expression on his face. "What am I going to do? I had a letter from Japan saying ten top Japanese journalists wanted to see Fellini," he explains, "and they just showed up this morning. Ten of them, fancy! Ten! So I told them one or nothing and they said nothing. Now I've just gone to tell Fellini and you know what he said? 'But, Bob, why don't you bring them?' Can you imagine! Now I don't know where to find them."

Always unpredictable, our Federico. I arrive on the set to see a startling sight. Venus, naked as a newborn babe, is standing in the middle of a dust bowl, her left hand over her pubic area, her right hand over her breasts. She, also, is one of the visions Encolpius sees, and Fellini is saying to her, "Your leg is too bent. Turn toward me and bend your leg. *Ecco*, like that!"

While Adriano and his crew concoct the clouds that will make her appear to be half covered in a mist, I distribute the alabaster eggs I bought in Volterra at Easter to Clara, Liliana, Norma, and Gilda. Fellini, who never misses a thing, comes up, grabs one, and explains that holding the egg in the hand and rolling it around is an Indian way to concentrate. Norma reminds him the eggs come from Volterra, but the director continues with the Indian idea of concentration, "If you want to think about love or something like that, it is a very good way." Then he turns to me and crows, "Aha, you don't know what happened the other day when you weren't here!"

"Yes, I do. Ingmar Bergman was on the set." His face falls. Fellini is to make his next picture with the Swedish director, a two-episode film in which each expresses his views on love.

He goes back to Venus whose hand is giving him a great deal of trouble. A little of her breasts must show but not too much. At this moment, Bob Herrington arrives shepherding the ten Japanese like a brood of chickens. "I found them in the publicity office scrounging handouts so I've brought them all on," he announces triumphantly. The Japanese stand bug-eyed on the sidelines taking in the glories of Venus. The director is well aware they are there but ignores them and continues to give directions to Georgia Lillik, a pretty blonde Hungarian who appeared previously as the lame asthmatic pilgrim in the temple scene. "Georgia, smile and stay still. Look at me." The fog has risen round her and she is shrouded by the mist.

While the smoke is being spread again, Fellini strolls over to speak with the journalists, who are accompanied by an Italian-speaking Japanese businessman from Rome to act as interpreter.

Giulietta sits quietly in a corner watching and talking about Bergman's visit over the Easter weekend to discuss the joint film.

"What language do they communicate in?"

"English," she replies, "but nothing has been decided about how they will do the film."

"Maybe they could both be given the same script and see how they treat it," I suggest.

"Can you imagine Federico working with somebody else's script?" she snorts.

I can't.

I have been invited to lunch and Fellini swats me on the behind as we go up the stairs. The cripple, Giovanni—the chicken-like pilgrim in the temple scene—gets up from the seat where he waits every day and begs Fellini for more work. As he climbs laboriously up the stairs on his crutches after the director, Fellini's temper flares. "Stay there," he orders the man, "and I will send something down to you," but Giovanni persists. "*Li mortacci tua,*" Fellini curses, "Stay there, I said," and bellows for Bevilacqua to give him some money.

Bevilacqua sighs, "We've been feeding him every day for weeks."

Thinking about it afterward, I decided the reason Fellini got so angry was because he knows there is no other part for the unfortunate creature and he feels a helpless rage, not at the man, but at himself for not being able to give him work.

In his two-room suite near the production offices, Fellini excuses himself for a minute. When he returns, he asks, "Are you under a good moon?" His English is difficult to understand sometimes and I don't know whether he means moon or mood but he clarifies it by saying, "You look as though you have a good moon from your face. You look very well." Then he continues, "Ah, Eileen, I'm tired. I want to finish this picture."

I mention I will be seeing Sergei Bondarchuk, the Russian director, who is shooting *Waterloo* in Rome, and remark that he has a reputation for directing actors from a distance, very different from Fellini's technique.

"Ah, that idiot!" he snorts, "it will take him fifty years to finish that picture," and then bellows to Bevilacqua, "Tell those Americans I am at the table and if they want to come, then come, otherwise we eat."

I am startled to discover the guests are Saul Cooper, head of United Artist's publicity department in Europe, a French European distributor, and two publicity men from PEA. They are here to discuss the publicity campaign and I'm sure are wondering what I am doing at the luncheon. So am I, but Fellini always has a reason for whatever he does and it will come out sooner or later.

The meal is the usual plain fare followed by Scotch for those who want it. Fellini has some strange notion that Americans swig Scotch all day long. The luncheon is served by Bevilacqua (whom a German correspondent mistook for Fellini's brother, making some remark in his story that Fellini even had his brother acting as a waiter).

They start with a discussion of the sequestration of Gian Luigi Polidoro's *Satyricon*, which occurred the day before. This was the quickie version, also based on Petronius and undoubtedly truer to the book, starring Ugo Tognazzi, De Laurentiis' choice for Mastorna. Polidoro, plus the producer and the distributor, and four of the actors in the film were accused of obscenity, corruption of minors, and violation of the laws protecting the work of minors. They were subsequently acquitted of the corruption charge but received suspended sentences, which were appealed, and fines for having produced an obscene film.

They discuss what the title of the film is to be since Polidoro registered it first. Fellini has fought to use the name but has lost the case and the court upheld Polidoro's right to the title, *Satyricon*. "It must be *Fellini's Satyricon* in English-speaking countries," the director says, "but it may have to be changed in Italy. *Satyricon* must be somewhere in the title, but *Il Satyricon di Fellini* seems to me too presumptuous. There will be the same difficulty in all the Latin countries."

The French distributor asks the director if he will help publicize the film, saying, "There are no big names and it would be nice if you would go to various territories, especially the difficult territories, and help present the picture."

"Like what difficult territories?" Fellini wants to know.

"Spain, for one," the distributor replies.

"The picture will never come out in Spain," Fellini declares, and then continues with a twinkle in his eye, "I know you have not the courage to ask me, but what you really want me to do is to come dressed as an ancient Roman." Everybody laughs and Fellini explains, "No, I cannot promise because this is the hardest thing for me to do, to go into another country, speak another language, listen to other people. There is no money in the world that would make me do it." He stops himself and with a foxy smile, says, "But perhaps there is. Maybe we can fix a price. Besides, I cannot make a promise now. I shall be shooting another picture." To me he says querulously, "I don't want to do it. I make the picture. Why should I have to go?"

The subject of the publicity posters is brought up. Fellini suggests using a fresco of the main characters in the film similar to the panels of paintings in "The Garden of Delights" and they all seem to consider that a good idea. Someone brings up the subject of censorship in Italy and Fellini says indignantly, "I can't tell you how embarrassing it is to be a part of the Italian film industry. The pictures coming out now are shameful." This brings him back to the sequestration of Polidoro's *Satyricon*. "I believe it will be out again in a few weeks. They shouldn't pay so much attention to it. People go to see it because of all this publicity."

I sit there quite astonished. Before they came, Fellini grumbled, "I haven't had a lunch alone in five months," but now he is thoroughly enjoying himself and I think it is because he has managed to outfox the publicity people. With me there, he can't be pressured into something he doesn't want to do.

Saul Cooper tells about the shooting in Colombia with Marlon Brando on *Burn,* and describes the location as "hell at the end of the world about to drop off." Pontecorvo and Brando are out in the blistering sun for hours while the director does twenty and thirty takes on each scene.

Fellini is amazed and remarks, "I would never take an actor from Actor's Studio. They are too aware."

Fellini recounts the visit of Japanese journalists to the set. "I kept waiting for them to appear behind me but they were so dazzled by the sight of a naked woman they couldn't move. It was very funny."

Then he returns to the title. "Grimaldi can't decide about the title. One week, he says, 'Yes, we must change it,' and another week he says, 'No, leave it alone.' He is very insecure. My idea is to leave it alone. If the court forces us, we will change it, but somewhere *Satyricon* will be in it, maybe *Petronius' Satyricon*. Everybody knows it's *Satyricon* anyway."

(In the end, the title used in Italy was *Fellini-Satyricon,* the same as in English except it is hyphenated. Alfredo Bini, the producer of the other version of the *Satyricon,* later made a statement to the press belittling Fellini's talent as a movie creator who seemed to have run out of ideas. Fellini sued the producer for slander, but finally dropped the suit. United Artists bought the distribution rights to Bini's film for over a million dollars to keep it off the market until after the release of Fellini's *Satyricon*.)

Back on the set, the seventh take of Venus continues. Afterwards, Georgia Lillik, covered by a terry-cloth robe, comes to sit by me waiting for her close-ups. Fellini, whom she met in the Hungarian Embassy, has had her eyebrows shaved off. "It is very difficult to do a nude scene," she admits, "because of all the people around. I didn't tell my mother I was going to do it, but I didn't know myself. They only told me when I was being made up. I preferred not to refuse because it is useful for an actress to have an experience of this kind— even if I am full of complexes and inhibitions. I did it only for Fellini."

They all claim they only do it for Fellini. He could open the biggest strip joint in the world if he ever got tired of directing.

Fellini does five close-ups of just the top half of Venus sprayed to make her look dewy. Professor Canali, the Latin consultant, who is on the set, comments, "Lillik has a slight cast in her eyes. Italians call this *l'occhio di Venere,* the eye of Venus, and consider it a sign of beauty." Fellini probably chose her specifically because of this— but neither she nor any of the other visions filmed ever appear in the film.

When they break, I notice the sound man, Oscar De Arcangelis, examining some records with Liliana, and stop to find out what they are. A neat, unobtrusive man who always wears a peaked cap and sits way off in the background, he has known Fellini since *I Vitelloni*, which he recorded for the director.

"Music," he explained, "is played and recorded on the set very often without being heard, because it annoys him. In the 'Theater' scene, we played Henri Pousseur's 'Trois Visages de Lièges.' For the 'Theater' and also for the 'Dinner,' we used Anton von Webern's 'Five Pieces for Orchestra, Opus 10.' 'Margapati' music from Bali was used for the Greek dancers, and in 'The Garden of Delights,' Oriental music, 'Pansi Sereman.' All through the film, we've been playing Milton Babbitt's 'Ensembles for Synthesizer,' 'Electronics and Percussions—Five Realizations' by Max Neuhaus, and miscellaneous pieces of electronic music. I record everything that is shot, dialogue and music, and make a sound track which serves as a record of what went on and a guide for what must be cut; otherwise everything would be silent. The sound is necessary for the dubbing because it indicates what the actors said during the shooting and is important for the lip movements."

This, however, is not the music used in the film which will be recorded later.

"Fellini is very appreciative of the work one does and says so, but he is very demanding and expects all his collaborators to know their jobs."

Back at the publicity office, Bob Herrington is shocked: "I've heard Fellini uses dirty words on the set, awful words. I think I must speak to him about that. Gentlemen don't use dirty words in front of ladies."

I advise against it. Herrington might be able to get Fellini to quit lying and to keep his promises; but cleaning up his colorful vocabulary would be like putting him in a strait jacket.

The Labyrinth and
the Minotaur

April 12

Today begins the "Magic City" episode featuring the Provincial Arena and the Labyrinth. When I arrive on the set on a back lot at Cinecittà, I hand Fellini a copy of *Time* magazine in which the TV Special called "A Director's Notebook" he made for NBC is reviewed. There is an indignant yelp, and Pippia comes and says, "*Il Maestro* wants to see you."

Fellini is desperately trying to decipher the English. "What means *sponsor*?" he wants to know.

"The sponsor is the one who pays for the program," I answered.

"Who is the sponsor?"

"Burlington Industries. They didn't like your Special and withdrew their sponsorship."

"But why, Eileen? I don't understand."

"Well, after they got a look at the scenes of the prostitutes on the Appian Way and the transvestites in the Colosseum, they decided it was too racy."

"But why, Eileen? There wasn't anything terrible in it. It was a joke."

He reads the article very carefully wanting to know the meaning of *gambler* because *Time* said: "As a director, Fellini has always played with ideas and people and like most gamblers, he wins a few and loses a few."

"And what means *prime time*?" He is very upset and disappointed by the unenthusiastic reaction to the program.

Rino Carboni, the makeup man, is watching the shooting and says, "This is an African world, but an elegant African world. We gave the Africans very strong colors in makeup, and the whites, delicate colors, because the African culture is more striking, the European more bland." Fellini marches up to Carboni and angrily protests that the Proconsul's face is not as violet as it was the first day, and that it must be changed. The makeup man balks and tries to explain, but Fellini stalks off. "Every day," Carboni sighs, "he sees something," as he beats his head against the wooden shed which shelters the director and camera crew. "How can he see from this distance? It's at least twenty yards. It's incredible!"

Donati, who has just won an Oscar today for his costumes in Zeffirelli's *Romeo and Juliet,* laments, "I am destroyed. It took eight days for the costumes and the jewelry and the brass masks in the background. The brass plates on the breasts of some of the Africans are gold-painted radiator coverings, and the bulbs hanging off some of them are the floating balls from toilet tanks. It's true, Eileen," he giggles. "I needed something so I took those and painted them gold. They look rather good, don't you think?"

While the camera and lights are being moved back for a long shot, Carboni returns and says, "I discovered why the Proconsul's makeup is a different color. The first day, he was dressed in brown. Today, he is dressed in violet and this naturally influences the color of his face. Martin's face is different, too, because he is getting freckles. These are problems Fellini doesn't understand. When an actor loses weight, it affects the costumes and the makeup. Through six months of shooting, Martin has gained twelve or thirteen pounds. This changes his personality. We have to make his belly darker but Fellini doesn't realize these difficulties. Acid and greasiness of the skin affect the entire makeup too, changing it from day to day. Max is thinner by about twelve or thirteen pounds. He hasn't been working but it will be a disaster when he starts again because he won't be the same. We've warned him to stop smoking and eat and his girl friend, one of the makeup crew, is made to work every day so as not to tire him out."

Hans Richter and his wife arrive for lunch with Fellini and the director kisses Mrs. Richter's hand through the mask he is wearing as protection against the cement dust being blown in the air, saying, "Just ten minutes." Richter, whose best-known film is *Dreams Money Can Buy*, recalls, "Years ago, I wrote a story of a Minotaur and wanted Fellini to shoot it, but he can only do stories he writes himself. This is not like my Minotaur. This is a personification of a Minotaur who has become a human being, but perhaps Fellini still had my Minotaur in mind. I made a film called *8 by 8* and Fellini made *8½*. He says we have only the title in common."

During lunch in the restaurant, the ancient Romans are joined by cowboys and Indians, saloon girls and homesteaders in sun bonnets from the *Viva Max* production also being shot at Cinecittà. It's a ludicrous combination.

I lunch with Regine Blass, a scholarly German writer and professor from Cologne, who is writing a book on *Juliet of the Spirits*. "The young people in Germany do not like Fellini," she observes, "because they don't think he deals with social problems and has too much fantasy which they can't understand. Too many books have been written about Fellini. A myth is being created about him which prevents people from understanding his films. He has a message to tell and all these books only confuse things." I wonder if she isn't adding to the confusion, since she's writing a book. It seems a bit contradictory.

After lunch, Fellini spots Max Born, who has arrived on the set dressed rather conservatively—for him, that is. "Ah, Max, what 'appened?" he twits. "You are dressed normal." Then he saunters over to Hans Richter and announces, "She is writing a book," and points to Dr. Blass; "and she is writing a book," turning to me; "and he is doing a book," indicating Franco Pinna, the photographer; "and she is writing a book," looking at Liliana, his assistant. He is very pleased with himself.

Leaving the set, I come upon John Chevron, one of the Negro courtiers, in a white robe, brass coils, and orange and gold markings on his face sitting in a car playing Scrabble. An American actor from Los Angeles, he also had a bit part in "The Subura." "Fellini," he says, "is probably one of the few directors able to combine commercial and artistic success. This film and *La Dolce Vita* will be the two for which Fellini will be remembered. *Satyricon* is very similar to *La Dolce Vita*." Fellini would probably clobber him if he heard him, but it's not the first or last time that such a comparison will be made.

People are always making comparisons. Eugene Walter, Fellini's English language dialogue coach, told me, "Someone should study the young men in *I Vitelloni* and those in *Satyricon* to see to what extent *I Vitelloni* was an early version of *Satyricon*. It's the same story, the longing of the provincial to come to Rome. Well, here they are—and Rome is not seen in Fellini's films as it's seen by puritan America or England, as sexual liberty, the great orgy. Rome is seen as all the flavors of the world, all of the possibilities of the world. It's very important to insist on Fellini as a poet who is not of Rome. He's a man from the provinces in every good sense."

April 18

Shooting stops early because of the bad weather and Fellini introduces me to Vintila Horia, a Rumanian novelist and 1960 Prix Goncourt winner for his novel, *God Was Born in Exile.* "She is small, but a very important journalist," the director tells the visitor.

Horia is writing a series of articles on the creators of the world, people like Arnold Toynbee, Werner Heisenberg, Werner von Braun, and Marshall McLuhan, and has come to interview Fellini. "Toynbee is not crazy," he remarks.

"And is Fellini?" I want to know.

"I don't know Fellini well enough to say," he replies diplomatically, since the director is standing listening. "Toynbee is an interpreter of history, but Fellini is a creator of history."

Fellini demands, "Why aren't you writing that down, Eileen? You write everything else down."

Horia peers around the set at the ochre-colored wall with the queer sculpted figure of a man riddled with holes on the left, the other ochre wall on the right with three holes of various sizes and shapes, and the symmetrical greyish wall, in the center, and says, "These walls are the symbols of the interior life of Fellini."

The director looks incredulous and, glancing at the walls, protests, "But, Eileen, they are full of holes, like Swiss cheese!"

Fellini leaves and Horia continues, "The wall on the left represents man in chaos. The straight wall is harmony. This is very much like Jung. We are all full of holes, but through these holes you see many things. The dramatic dualism is all here. Those two side walls represent disequilibrium, the images of our unconscious. They are nocturnal. The white wall in front, with balanced symmetrical designs, represents the need for equilibrium. Fellini needs it like everybody else. In this way, Fellini works for us like a novelist. I find these three things incredible to understand. It is the mandala of Jung, interior equilibrium. Don't you feel happy and pure inside when you look at the white wall? You will dream of it one night," he assures me. "For me, Fellini is the greatest personality of the cinematic world. He is one of the greatest creators of the cinema and has made it into a great art, which it was not before."

"My God!" I thought, "the things you find out," and hoped I would soon dream of the white wall and get a little bit of that inner equilibrium I was beginning desperately to need, after all these months of smoke and dust, freaks and monsters, and ghosts and ghouls—the only things I ever dream about.

I stop by the office of Pasquale Lancia, the director general of Cinecittà. A big, amiable lawyer who has been in the cinema world for twenty years and head of the studio for seven and a half, he freely admits, "The *Satyricon* has been my most difficult film because it is a film where Fellini has left his fantasy completely unleashed. This time he is being rather faithful to the script, but, in Italy, the script is not so important as in America. It is the director who is important.

"Fellini is always asking me why it is more difficult to build his sets than others, like the Alamo we're now doing for *Viva Max*. We can easily construct the fort and chapel because they are realistic and traditional and we just copy the originals. Fellini's sets for *Satyricon* are far more difficult than those used in *Cleopatra* because they are pure fantasy and completely different from the standard ones.

"When we make American films," Lancia says, "we know everything before hand. The breakdowns are received and we operate on a very precise schedule. There are occasional delays, but there is always time allotted for these and there are seldom many changes. For *Satyricon*, it is quite another story—as for all Fellini's films—because here the director concerns himself with every detail.

"I did *Juliet of the Spirits* with Fellini and that was very difficult because the scenes were also strange. Fellini makes an image of himself in his films. He is the camera. His problem is one of spirituality, of sex. He says, 'They mustn't ask me what I am doing. I am good at translating what I see and read but not at translating myself.' But this is true of all great artists, just as all great artists live only when they work.

"Fellini creates a particular atmosphere on the set and this is very important," the head of the studio continues. "It is very hard to maintain a troupe without friction when a film lasts more than fifteen weeks. He gets mad at them, then he kisses them; and he is sincere but he is alone. I don't know anything about his private life but he feels alone. No one knows Fellini. In every one of his films, there is the problem of the spirit. I don't know what he will put in this film. He says it is pre-Christian, but he will end up putting something Christian in it."

April 21

I leave the set to talk with a visitor, Ornella Volta, an Italian who lives in Paris and writes on vampirism, magic, witchcraft, and mythology—subjects which fascinate Fellini. She has known the director since 1966 when she was introduced to him by Bernardino Zapponi, the co-scriptwriter of the film, with whom she had collaborated on a magazine devoted to bizarre themes.

In her opinion, the director is more interested in parapsychology than in magic, but was intrigued by her interest in magicians. "He even wanted to introduce me to one in Turin who he said could transform material things into apparitions," she relates. "Fellini claimed he saw little angelheads in the sky with wings like Della Robbia ceramics. He is convinced it is true. The magician in Turin sent beneficial emanations to help him get well when he was so sick. Fellini is always surrounded by strange types. But he likes magic too much not to believe in it. Even if he says he doesn't, I think he does. For him it's like a child going out into the forest to find a witch."

Miss Volta believes this inclination toward magic is connected to the director's interest in religion and that both are of an external nature, since Fellini is not concerned with the meaning of a symbolism, but more with the spectacle it presents. "He sees the processions and Masses and rituals as a spectacle," she says. "For that reason, his interest in religion coincides with his partiality for the spectacle or show. He likes the circus for this reason. It's a spectacle. Buñuel, on the other hand, has an interior interest in religion. Fellini's is a purely visual one and not profound, although he does have a sense of sin. He wants a world without sin in this picture, but he will create a world without a soul.

"He has a very infantile side to him," the writer continues. "Giulietta is like a mother. Before he was so sick, he was a boy. Now he is a man. Before he was Baroque. Now he is more concerned with the essential. He is sometimes persecuted because he tires of people very quickly. At the beginning, he is fascinated and gives the impression they are the most important people in the world; then he gets bored. It's a curse for him. The only way to maintain a friendship with Fellini is to stay away from him, to be detached from him."

Signorina Volta feels everybody knows Fellini but there is a secret part of himself he keeps hidden. "But if you were to know all the things each one knows and piece them together," she says, "you would see all of him, because he displays his mystery. He always says nice things because he wants you to like him but, basically, he is an isolated man. He has few friends, mostly his old school friends from Rimini, whom he still sees. He likes to see them because he is very attached to his childhood and carries it with him always. It is present in all his films. Even if he makes a film on ancient Rome and puts a phallic symbol in the place of Christ, there will still be the processions of his childhood.

"This is a new film," she adds, "because it is without sentiment. That's because Zapponi is cold and detached."

April 26

I made the mistake of handing him a clipping from a New York daily stating that Fellini's *Satyricon* had been sequestered by the Italian authorities and banned for obscenity. Moments later, I received the usual summons from Pippia. "*Il Maestro* wants to see you."

Fellini was livid. "Have you read this?" he asked me.

"Yes, but a week or so ago and I've forgotten what it says exactly."

"It says my film has been sequestered when I haven't even finished it yet. Run to Bob Herrington's office and tell him to have United Artists put out a retraction."

I objected, "Wouldn't it be more tactful to send one of your own people?"

He bellowed, "And you're not one of us by now? Run."

So I drove down to the Publicity Office and delivered the message, trying to soothe him upon my return with, "United Artists has probably already denied the story in New York," but he was dubious and furious.

At Bob Herrington's office, the publicist was marveling at a highly successful South African radio announcer and producer who traveled six thousand miles to see Alberto Grimaldi, who he had heard was Fellini's producer. "Just imagine," Herrington says, "he chucked everything and came all that way just to get a part in a Fellini movie. Fancy that!"

Several people have shown up with odd requests. A manufacturer arrived from the States and wanted sketches from Donati to launch a line of clothes inspired by *Satyricon* but Donati doesn't work from sketches; everything comes out of his head onto the cloth. Another man from London came and said he would open a night club if Fellini would make a psychedelic film for it. The man offered to settle for unused footage from the director's old films but the director doesn't own the rights to them. All the man has to do is flash the *Satyricon* on the walls every night and he'd have a perfect psychedelic film for his club.

I went off to keep an appointment with Nino Rota, a small, shy, skittish man who has composed the music for all Fellini's films and has the abstracted air of a man who is always listening to something—probably music in his head. Although born in Milan, he now lives in Bari where he is the director of the Conservatory of Music. "I stay in Bari," he explained, "to keep away from the world of the cinema in Rome."

An eminent composer, he studied at the Curtis Institute in Philadelphia but has a strong preference for England. "England," he sighs, "where even the chorus reads by sight!" Perhaps that's why he chose to meet me in Babington's Tea Room near the Spanish Steps.

Rota first began composing music for films in 1942 when an important musicologist with Lux films brought various musicians into the cinema to see if they could work in films. "It took courage," he declared. "Sometimes they made me do the worst pictures, hoping the music would save the film." By now, he has composed the music for at least eighty films.

The composer explained that music has the same importance in Fellini's films as all the other elements of his picture—the actors, the costumes and the makeup—although the director is not interested in music in the abstract or from an intellectual point of view, but only for its function in his films. Although Fellini feels music very strongly, he doesn't like attending concerts, just as he doesn't like going to art shows or the theater, or even to the cinema. The director amuses himself for hours working with music but will not tolerate music in a restaurant and will pay the musicians to go away. "He even loathes the radio," the composer said, "because it disturbs him. It's paradoxical. He'll gladly listen to me play the same tune two hundred times on the piano, but music irritates him in a restaurant. If he's not participating in something, it bothers him."

Fellini always uses music on the set while he is shooting, although it is not necessarily used in the film. In *La Dolce Vita*, only thirty percent of the set music, re-recorded, remained in the film because the director considered it a documentary of the moment he made the film. For *8½*, only ten percent was retained. "Fellini is not stubborn about music," Rota said, "so when I want to substitute a different theme from one already in the film, he will agree that it's better than what he selected. That's rare in directors, who usually are attached to old, familiar music and don't want to change. But Fellini is so sensitive that he realizes when music is good for the film, even if it is unknown and different.

"You must have an affinity of spirit to work with Fellini," the composer explained. "He gives the right suggestions so I can find the right theme. Sometimes you can introduce ideas you have already done, like the trombone theme I did for *La Strada*. I felt it was too affirmative but Fellini found it clear and beautiful. Other times, as in *8½*, my theme functioned well for half the picture, but he wanted it enriched with other things and we worked on it until we hit upon something better."

The composer's work begins only when the director has the film fixed in his mind. Before the film is finished, they find the principal themes. When the director discovers a theme which moves him and goes well in the film, he never changes and months later knows if a single note has been altered. "This is a great help to me," Rota said, "because I change all the time; but if he likes a theme, it always moves him—even if he hears it two thousand times—until he detaches himself and goes on to something else."

Fellini likes to work on the music at night because it relaxes him. Since he doesn't have a piano, the director works at the composer's *pied à terre* in Rome where he stretches out on the couch and listens while Rota plays. "He used to come more willingly when I had a comfortable couch," the composer laughed. "Now I have an antique one and he has to sit up and listen and he doesn't like it very much. After we have written the general musical idea, he gives a name to all the various themes—'Juliet,' 'Anita,' 'Grandfather,' 'Circus'— which I find written in a notebook; otherwise he complains I change everything. When we record the music, he knows it all from the first to the last note and we don't lose time. His feeling for music is so precise that during the recording, he draws the performance he wants from the musician in the same way as he does with his actors."

After the film is cut, a piano is carried into a moviola room and the director and the composer work on it a reel at a time, putting every detail of the music into place. For *Juliet*, they worked in the evenings—twenty reels in twenty evenings—with a boy to work the moviola or viewing box since neither of them understands the technical aspects of the machine. "This is why we work so closely," Rota said, "because Fellini wants to avoid putting the usual background music in his films and tries to use musical ideas which have a completeness in themselves. They can't be too short or too long or cut in pieces, but must seem made to the measure of the film.

"The music for the *Satyricon* was a great problem. One of Fellini's favorite themes, 'The March of the Gladiators,' which is in almost all of his films, could not be used because it was too obvious. *Satyricon* is macabre," Rota continued, "and shows the disillusion of life. Fellini is trying to return to the virginity of the pagan world without a conscience, and it isn't easy to understand. Just as he is trying to evoke a world which precedes our form of conscience, so the music must not be music as we know it. For us, this world is enigmatic because the scenes are not explained, nor does Fellini want them explained. Often, music in films tries to throw light on what is obscure, to clarify what is only implied. For *Satyricon*, you need music which explains nothing—a vegetable fact, sounds from a preconscience world, music at its origins rather than civilized.

"But, since Fellini is a man of the spectacle," the composer said, "he doesn't want music which causes physical annoyance. I don't know how we are going to reconcile not disturbing the ears of the audience and making music that isn't music. We also have to find the performers who can play it. The annoyance or physical appeal of the music must be considered throughout the film, otherwise the audience might leave after only ten minutes. The music must not emerge alone, but amalgamate the film, and is at its best when we are unaware of its presence."

At the end of August, I was back in Babington's Tea Room listening to Rota describe how he had composed the music for the film. "We threw out the idea of imitating anything tied to antiquity," he explained, "because that was the most uncertain method since we know little of ancient music. We know the theory and the representations of the instruments but it's difficult to reconstruct what the musical sensibility of that age was. Only fragments of Greek music have survived, but they don't give any idea of the enormous importance music had in that culture. For example, poetry readings and theater and athletic performances were given with music."

In the film, wherever musical instruments appear, the music is adapted to their sounds; flutes, percussion instruments, cymbals, tambourines, drums, and lyres. Besides evoking the sounds of these ancient instruments, Rota also listened to hundreds of Oriental records including an entire UNESCO series of all the Asiatic countries as well as other African, Iranian, and Indian recordings, taking pieces which could be useful in the film.

Two or three of Rota's musical ideas go all through the film played on the lute or lyre or flute, a kind of theme song. Giton sings it in the hold of "The Ship of Lichas." It is heard at the end of "The Villa of the Suicides," more elaborated with other percussion instruments during "The Dinner of Trimalchio" and again at length at the end of the film. Written in the modes of the ancient Greek scale, it seems almost to be of that epoch.

In some points, as in the hold of "The Ship of Lichas" when the boys are prisoners, music played on the gamelang, a sweet-sounding instrument especially common in the islands of Indonesia, is used to create a very tender and dreamy atmosphere. There are also many Japanese themes, and even the voices of Tibetan monks which are heard at various points including Trimalchio's entombment. In "The Garden of Delights," the music is African, made with percussion instruments. In "The Labyrinth," to create the rhythmical clamor of the crowd, an African record, "The Dance of the Monkeys," was used. Another African piece used is the lullaby heard when an old lady gives Encolpius a potion to drink before he sees Oenothea and is cured of his impotence. "It doesn't seem to be music," Rota said, "but the common Negro voice. Another piece we recorded was the 'Dance of Fortunata,' which can't be called music, but a concerted piece of percussion groups—percussion, brass, strings, and kettle drums. We also used a huge whip which makes a noise like a high wind or howl when it's twirled around."

The other source for the atmosphere of the film is electronic music to create cold sounds, reverberated with echoes and depth. It is used wherever there would have been a temptation to use sentimental music and is heard at the beginning of the film and in "The Villa of the Suicides" when the children depart. Instead of a romantic theme, Fellini preferred few sounds, almost static and dissonant, which, because of the contrast, evoke an unsentimental feeling.

"A lot of the music sounds electronic," Rota chuckled, "but we created it ourselves using the electric organ, percussions, and wild instruments of reeds and brass. When the Emperor is killed and the 'Cortege of the New Emperor' arrives, there are screams or wild horns with percussions and drums, and also when Trimalchio goes to the pool a shrill blast announcing the arrival of the owner. Another electronic effect is used when Eumolpus is thrown into the oven. We put the microphone inside the piano and from the scraping of the chords, achieved a more penetrating effect, like chalk scratching on a blackboard."

Since Rota is Fellini's most faithful and enduring collaborator, and one of the few people who know him well, I was interested to hear what he thought of the director. "Fellini," he said, " is moral because every problem is a moral problem for him. He doesn't do an audacious scene as an end in itself but to arouse the viewer's conscience. *Satyricon* will never have the shadow of pornography. However, it's difficult to know what his personality is because he has so many external peculiarities which can lead one astray about his true character. He has a great and substantial seriousness in his work, although it doesn't seem so because Fellini doesn't seem to be. He plays the part of a buffoon and kisses everyone, but he is very concentrated in his imaginative world. Maybe he acts this way to make things easier, but if he doesn't want to do something, nothing can make him do it. Fellini has had countless offers to work in the theater but he can't make that total commitment. He agrees only to make others happy, but he will never do it; and in this he is very honest."

The Ship of Lichas

April 28

We are back on the sea at Focene shooting "The Ship of Lichas" episode. This was to have been a very long sequence, full of perversities, but it was rewritten and considerably shortened, and in the end, Fellini condensed it into two interiors on two studio sets and scenes on the deck of the ship. Fellini's version, although it has its grotesque aspects, is neither as bizarrely erotic nor as ironically amusing as the episode in Petronius, perhaps because the director felt that the Roman satirist's account was too Fellinian and that enough eroticism had already been depicted in "The Garden of Delights" and the whorehouses in the Subura. By this time, the film was also getting very long, and he needed to shorten it.

Lichas is played by Alain Cuny made up with a revolting sightless eye. Among the collection of humanity aboard his mysterious ship—which never seems to touch land—are the three boys, Encolpius, Ascyltus, and Giton, who have been captured along with a group of other prisoners. Lichas, with his penchant for young and beautiful boys, selects Encolpius as his bride, and they go through a macabre marriage ceremony, but Lichas' pleasure is ended when the Emperor is assassinated and the soldiers of the new Caesar board the ship and behead him. Lichas' head, with an expression of shock and wonder, sinks below the waves.

The ship is built in two sections, one facing the sky and the other sloping downward. The ship exterior, made of wood covered with tar, resembles a big raft or airplane carrier and is about a hundred and thirty-two feet long and sixty-five feet wide. It has deliberately been designed in a contemporary form to conform with Fellini's intention of making a parallel between the modern and the ancient, but with an air of mystery that makes it impossible to imagine from its exterior what is inside the vessel.

When I arrive, it is cloudy but warm, and Fellini is sitting in a camp chair way back from the beach surrounded by his crew, waiting for the weather to clear. The director has exchanged his black trademark fedora for a yellow straw hat. "Ah, Eileen!" he greets me, "come and sit here," indicating his lap. "Maybe the American journalist can settle the question." There has been a long discussion about how many times a woman can have an orgasm in one night.

"Oh, well, a prostitute could easily do it thirty times in one night," I venture.

"No," he demurs, "we're not talking about prostitutes. We're talking about a normal woman."

While I ponder this question (a bit like how many angels can dance on the head of a pin), Clara, the seamstress, declares, "As a woman of the people, I say five or six times, no more," and everybody laughs.

Max Born's father, a pharmacologist, arrives from England looking for his son, who isn't at Focene. While he is being introduced,

Fellini keeps asking, "Why doesn't he have a beard? He had a beard at the beginning of the picture. Why doesn't he have one now?"

I try to explain to him that this is Max's real father and the bearded man who accompanied him at the beginning of the picture was his stepfather. Max's father wants a private chat with Fellini and the director takes him to one side and listens intently, nodding from time to time. When he leaves, Max's father remarks, "He needed something like this!" Apparently he has not been too happy with his son's hippie habits.

When it becomes evident the weather isn't going to clear, several of us leave to lunch at Fregene and in the car the director is still perplexed. "He said the same thing the stepfather did—that Max regards me as a father and I must think about him and take care of him. He said Max is more important than the picture; but the picture is more important to me as a director. Naturally, from a human point of view, if I can help him, I will. It's funny. Max has two fathers and they're looking for a third."

He complains about how difficult it is for him to learn English. "The people I see are mostly Americans from the film world and their language is not very cultural or intellectual. It's as though you were to try to learn Italian from a peasant. The peasant misuses the words and they are always very simple."

This brings him to the subject of the NBC Special. He is still smarting over the mixed reactions to it in the States, and boasts, "NBC wrote me they have received 640,000 letters about the Special. Naturally, they didn't tell me whether they were for or against. Originally, I only intended to do an hour interview but they kept asking for more and more things like how I prepared a film and how I cast them. Anyway," he complains, "they never should have shown it to forty million people at ten o'clock. It was intended to be an intellectual program and the mass of people didn't understand it was a joke.

"And now," he continues, "NBC wants eight more prints. And

who is going to pay for them? We contracted to give them four and we have already done that."

I recall Ingmar Bergman's visit to the set and ask him how it went. "He was very exaggerated in his reactions," Fellini replies. "He's a very Gothic type, very romantic. I feel as though I have known him for a very long time. Like any true artist, he is genuine and simple. But I haven't even thought about the picture I'm going to do with him." After months of talking, the project was abandoned.

We arrive at Fellini's lovely villa in Fregene to pick up Giulietta, and Fellini changes from his working clothes into a suit. It is extraordinary how utterly transformed he appears in a suit, elegant and rather dashing looking. It seems to slim him down, making his large frame less bulky and burly than it appears in his working clothes. We lunch at a nearby *trattoria:* Liliana, Gilda, Peppino— who is on a diet because of his colitis—Norma, and the driver Nando, whom Fellini keeps twitting, telling him he will have to pay the bill. He just might, because Fellini rarely carries any money with him. The director orders for everyone, is very merry and writes out a dirty poem in dialect by Gioacchino Belli, a famous Roman popular poet, illustrating it in my notebook with some explicitly graphic drawings.

After lunch, we drive to Cinecittà because there is to be no shooting today and Fellini is going to work on the cutting which he and Ruggero Mastroianni, Marcello's brother, have been doing almost simultaneously with the shooting. Driving along, I ask him about Moravia's remarks which the French journalist had cited. "Ah," he sighs. "He was not talking about me. Moravia is a good friend. He was talking about the men I create in my films—Marcello in *La Dolce Vita* and 8½."

I didn't say it, but I was thinking it—the men in these films *are* you.

April 29

The episode of "The Ship of Lichas" begins on the section of the ship sloping upward. A huge black-pronged anchor lies on the upper part of the deck and behind it is a strange square copper apparatus which resembles a primitive kind of radar. Donati explains, "It's a *specchio ustorio* or burning glass, a weapon of war, based on a principle of Archimedes. The mirror in the center caught the sun and when it was directed at another ship, it could be set on fire. It can even open and turn around."

Donati has another tidbit. "Federico asked for a whale tomorrow. One day when he was in the cutting room, he saw a picture in *Life* magazine of a dead whale being hoisted up. He said, 'Look how beautiful this is!' and added he wanted one just like it. You're supposed to see it way off. I haven't got it yet, naturally, and Production never helps. When have they ever done anything for me? No, I'm going to kill myself because I can't go on any longer. I have already told Fellini I was just here on a visit on my way to Rimini. And then he wants a procession of the victorious Emperor. It will be done after the film is completed but you can be sure he will want applause afterwards." Then he hurries back to Cinecittà to make a whale.

At lunch Bob Herrington talks about his experience with Fellini. An engagingly whimsical but proper Englishman, the only one Fellini has ever had as a publicist for any of his films, Herrington churned out reams of copy on *Satyricon* as well as coping with hundreds of foreign journalists who arrived from the four corners of the globe.

"Fellini can smell phonies a mile away and while I may not radiate warmth, he knows I respect him," Herrington says. "He thought I arrived from Mars, that I was either an idiot or a super-intellect, and was a bit awed by me. The first time I met him, I was very apprehensive."

Herrington spent a good deal of time worrying over the director's forgetfulness about appointments for interviews and his tendency to invite everyone on the set. "He forgets," the publicist sighs, "but he keeps his promises, so you have to tell him every day. Now he comes to me each day when he sees me to ask if he has an interview. I can't change his memory but it's a challenge to get him organized.

"One has difficulty separating the truth from reality with him; but when he says something, he means it at the time. Fellini has never told me any lies at all. He is one of the most truthful men in his work and as a man. I can't be cross with him no matter how he behaves. He apologizes to me on the set when he loses his temper. Fellini feels I must be one of those British types with a stiff upper lip and that I don't approve of such antics—but he has to explode. He's not an antiseptic Englishman like me.

"Directors usually run to a mold but Fellini's technique is different," Herrington continues. "He has everything tucked away in his head. Any efficiency expert would be impressed. And he is one of the most money-conscious people in the world. I would despise him if he weren't. You have to work for money. If he is only an artistic success, that doesn't help the people who finance the picture.

"But Fellini is a gentleman. He has the three qualities needed for success: energy, ability, and integrity. A man is no good if he lacks one of the three. Just to watch Fellini working with ordinary people has restored my faith in human nature. Whatever he did in life, he would have been a success. If he'd been a politician, he would have been president of Italy.

"Fellini asked me," he recalls, " 'Why don't you call me Federico?' I told him, 'I call you Mr. Fellini because I want to be courteous.' 'But I call you Bob,' he said. [Baub is the way Fellini pronounces it.] 'Am I not courteous?' So, now I call him Federico and he gives me a big bear hug. Dear, dear Federico, I think I'll take him back to England as a souvenir of Italy."

After lunch, the cast is strewn all over the beach and Fellini is waiting for Alain Cuny's blind eye to be inserted. "It's a contact lens of a cornea," Rino Carboni, the head makeup man, explains. "I made it in one day. Cuny didn't want to wear it. He still thinks of himself as a reigning matinee idol in France, even though he's fifty-five years old. Fellini told him, 'Wear it or go right away to the airport.' Cuny insisted it be the right eye because he photographs better on that side. He won't even look at himself in the mirror. I even had to raise the shape of his head because he has a flat, square head."

After a long wait, Cuny arrives dressed in black with a gold waistband, instead of in the orange robe he was first wearing. The white, staring eye makes him look terrifyingly cruel.

There is a high wind but Fellini ignores it and shoots a close-up of Martin, also dressed in black, and Cuny with their backs to the camera. The polystyrene snow is all over, in everyone's eyes and mouth. On the first take, Cuny fondles Martin, kissing him on the neck; and then Fellini shows Cuny how to rest his head on the back of Martin's neck so his white eye is always turned to the camera blindly gaping off into the distance. His other eye is almost closed and slanted downward with patches of latex. After each take, it requires four makeup men and hairdressers to put Cuny and Martin back together again. Fellini is hatless today and his thinning hair blows wildly in the wind as he explans in French what he wants Cuny to do.

On the fourth take, Cuny screams in French, *"Plus vite les rameurs,* faster with the oars," in a harsh, grating voice, then turns and kisses Martin lasciviously on the neck. They go through several takes of this and Fellini finally calls, *"Très bien,* Alain," and cuddles Martin's face in his hands.

May 2

I have lunch with Alain Cuny, the French actor who played the role of Steiner, the enigmatic intellectual in *La Dolce Vita* who inexplicably kills himself and his two children.

"At the beginning of April," Cuny tells me, "Fellini phoned me in Paris and talked about a part that would be violent and cruel but without naming it. I came because I had confidence in Fellini. I trusted him, and by doing so, proved I am an incorrigibly naïve person, because, although Fellini is trustworthy, everybody here is not. Later, I learned I should not have been so blind, because all human beings are *canaille*, rabble." Probably he's bitter about the dickering over his salary and the false eye he detests. Cuny wanted ten thousand dollars and the production only wanted to give him eight.

"Is there a connection between the characters of Steiner and Lichas?" I ask.

"One explanation of Steiner's character is that he doesn't accept himself as he is." Cuny replies. "I believe Steiner was a homosexual who married only to give a certain legitimacy to his position, but he was an unconscious homosexual. Lichas knows he is a homosexual and is happy with it, and that is the difference between the two civilizations. Even today, you can be a homosexual, but there is more repression than in those days. You have to know what you want to do and do it and be at peace. Do you remember the line of Steiner, 'I am a professional among the amateurs and an amateur among the professionals'? This explains Steiner's character. Among the people who seem to know, they think he is intelligent. In the same way, he is a homosexual among the married with a wife and children, but he hates his wife and regards her as a penance. Lichas is the forerunner of Steiner, whom every man would like to emulate. But how many men have the courage to live the way he did?

"I would play any part for Fellini without knowing what it was,"

the actor adds, "but I would prefer to play the part of Lichas rather
than Sainte Thérèse de Liseux. But it doesn't matter which part,
because Fellini has all the talents and all the charm. What do I
think of him? That's like asking St. John what he thinks of the
Heavenly Father."

While the camera and lights are being prepared, there is terrible
confusion on the set. After sitting calmly through the bedlam, Fellini returns to Cuny and explains what he wants him to do. "Martin," he says, "go to your previous place so Alain can look at you."
Then he explains a second time in French what Cuny must do.
Cuny grunts and groans with voluptuous pleasure as the slaves
massage him. "Silvestro, three times with the right arm, then go in
back and take both arms and go up and down." He shows the
other slaves how to tie his helmet on and massage the actor's stomach while he moans ecstatically. On the second take, Fellini is
directing in three languages. Cuny laughs diabolically and circles
Martin like a cat, murmuring, "*Ma petite colombe, je t'aime*, my
little pigeon, I love you," then makes a terrifyingly abrupt gesture
and a harsh noise like a Japanese Kabuki actor. On the third take,
Fellini changes the action a bit and tells Cuny, "You can talk to
yourself like a madman." At the end the director calls, "*Va bene, è
questa*." But the fight is repeated twice more from a different angle
with Fellini calling for "a rehearsal without violence." The set is
eerily silent for once, but out of habit, Fellini bellows "*Silenzio*,"
then puts the actors through their movements laughing like a child.
When the two takes are finished, he asks, "Martino, did you hurt
this time?"
Martin, who now has a deep cut in his thumb from the sharp
edges of Cuny's metal breastplate, angrily mutters, "Making a man
fight with a thing like that is like making him walk on a bed of
nails."
A new character arrives on the set dressed in a blue robe, curly

blonde wig adorned with copper bands on her forehead, and long earrings dangling onto her reddish face. She is an American actress, Tanya Lopert, the daughter of the European head of production for United Artists. "I don't know what I'm doing," she marvels. "I've worked with other strange directors but I've never been in a lunatic asylum. I was terrified when I saw Capucine with that scar. I've known her a long time but I didn't recognize her. When they told me who she was, I asked her if she had an automobile accident. I don't know what I am or where I am. I have to take a tranquilizer."

May 3

Lichas and Encolpius continue their fight in the darkened interior of the ship, while the slaves and sailors run towards them, egging them on, clapping and chanting. Lichas has Encolpius on his back, pinned to the floor, and is staring into his face. Fellini, dressed in a blue shantung shirt and grey trousers, calls to Alain, "Make gestures of love, whatever you want. Martin, when I say 'stop' you remain still and look to him stupefied because you realize he loves you."

This has just been a rehearsal and now Fellini calls for *l'occhio fritto del capretto*—the fried eye of the kid, his name for Cuny's false eye. Everything stops while Cuny has his eye inserted, and in the meantime, the director calls to a young man whose very prominent teeth and glittering brown eyes make him appear a bit mad when he smiles, "Alfredo, smile always." On the first take Alain ends up kissing Martin on the mouth and smothering him with kisses down to his stomach. Fellini teases the embarrassed Martin and calls to Capucine, sitting in the background with the passengers, "What do we have here, Capucine?"

Peter Ammann remarks, "Fellini didn't expect him to go so far. You can see Cuny has gotten freed by his stay in Japan."

"Martin," Fellini says, "when I call, if your knee is up, put it down slowly or we will not see the unbelievable thing involved. Are you Protestant?"

"No."

"Catholic?"

"No."

"Pagan?"

"No, nothing," replies Martin.

Why he is interested is beyond me. Fellini did not demonstrate this action to Alain as he normally would have done. He told Cuny what he wanted him to do, keeping Martin in the dark so he would get the astonished reaction he wanted from him.

Everyone agrees this is the first really erotic scene in the film and after the take, Capucine yells, "Martin is finished with the girls. We've lost him forever!"

The camera is placed on the floor near a strange looking fake-onyx statue for a close-up. Fellini directs, "Alain, you smile and kiss him and embrace him. Martin, always look to him in the breast, not in his eyes, because you look as though you have your eyes closed. Martin, you have to kiss him for real. I am very sorry to ask you to do it, Martin, but it is the exigence of art," he says, articulating the last three words very carefully. "Martin, raise your head slowly and try not to excite him too much," he jokes. In the next second, Fellini explodes. A makeup man is spraying Martin with brilliantine as directed. "When I say, 'Dirty him,' you don't have to dirty him all over. Do I have to tell you all the time?" he complains. "We are still in the same scene in the same movie. After a fight, he would be dirty. Norma"—he turns to the script girl— "you have to take care of these things."

Max Born is looking on and complains, "If Cuny gets to kiss Martin, I'm going to kiss him, too. I made love to him but didn't kiss him. It's ridiculous."

"Martin will belt you," I say.

He disagrees. "He won't be allowed to."

Cuny must return to Japan in a week and Fellini is rushing. Normally, shooting ends around three o'clock on Saturdays, but this is an exception. Cuny, still pursuing his theory that Lichas is the forerunner of Steiner in *La Dolce Vita,* tells me, "In *La Dolce Vita,* I played the organ. Here I am playing the harp, and Martin is Mastroianni."

I object, "But the difference is, you are not going to commit suicide. You're going to have your head cut off."

Cuny insists, "I am unconsciously arranging things so I am going to die."

Meanwhile Donati sends his assistant to get me. He has something to show me.

Down in the Saloon, a set from an old western where Donati works, a monstrous whale made of foam rubber covered with black anti-noise paint is hanging from the ceiling. Donati's whale is forty-three feet high and a hundred and sixty-five feet long and weighs about half a ton. The teeth are made of rubber, and the whole thing is constructed in sections—otherwise it wouldn't fit under the bridges on the road to Focene. It has taken five men three days to put the whale together, and Donati is very proud. "If the fish eat it, they'll get indigestion," he laughs. "Oh, Eileen, *che fatica,* what drudgery! Fellini never gives you time to make anything. I was furious when he asked for the whale, but I made it," he sighs. "It's crazy. You can't ever make a mistake."

May 10

When I arrive, Luisa, the calf, is stretched out cold by the ramp leading up to the deck. A sacrificial victim, she was supposed to lie down in readiness for the whack on the head. It took six men to wrestle her to the deck, and in the end she had to be given an injection to keep her quiet. (The poor beast spent all day recovering from her performance.)

"Eileen," Fellini declaims in exaggeratedly precise English when he catches sight of me, "ziz buk you are writing must have an apotheosistic ending." I look a little puzzled and he clarifies, "A glorious ending."

"Well, if you want to go off in a blaze of glory, I'll be happy to write about it," and he laughs and goes off to shoot a close-up of Max and Hiram as they watch Tryphaena officiate at the marriage of Lichas and Encolpius. It is one of the longest speeches in the film and the only time Capucine speaks.

"Look sad," he says to Max. Fellini sneers and Hiram sneers. "Zmile more, Mox. More vivid, the eye. Don't shake your head like that, Iram, because that is a little bit too American. Look to me, Iram, to Mox, to me. Go down with the eyes. Turn away."

Max should look sad. It was he who got cheated, because originally Giton was to be married to a little girl while the passengers peer through the keyhole and watch the consummation. The marriage of Giton and the girl is pure Petronius, but the Italian censors might have frowned on the idea of a child bride.

I left to find Liliana Betti, the short, squat, and unassuming young lady who has been Fellini's assistant, shadow, and confidante for six years, ever since she wrote him a letter from her native Bergamo explaining she wanted to be a director. He replied and they continued to correspond, and after about a year, she came to Rome to work for *il Maestro*. Liliana probably knows Fellini better than anyone else except his wife, Giulietta.

"My time with Fellini," she declared, "has been the fundamental encounter of my life, and for him too. He's been like a father to me. It will always be a great friendship. I would have had a different life if I had never known him. I was twenty-three when I met him, a girl from the provinces. Federico is an extraordinary human being. He drew me out of myself but if I stay with him, he will castrate me. It's inevitable that I detach myself from him. I stayed with him four or five years, every day, always together, and he revealed himself to me.

"Before," she said, "it was nourishment for me; but I have to leave the father figure, otherwise I can't lead my own life. Fellini is mature and has his own life, but he is very egotistical, very possessive, and wants to monopolize you. A person must stay only with him.

"He is a man alone, with no personal life. His life is his work and his friends are there. His collaborators are always his friends, but when the collaboration is finished, the friendship is finished. My collaboration has always been a modest one, and therefore our friendship can go on. Each of his friends gives him a different element. Norma is very gay. She revitalizes him.

"But our relationship was destined to end," Liliana said. "I decided to break it off and at first he resented it but now he understands. This is perhaps the first time such a thing has ever happened to Federico. He is still infantile and there is no middle road for him. I am more mature because I understand that I am no longer a daughter and that we cannot have a father-daughter relationship but a mature friendship. Besides, I prefer a modest position which is my own to being in his shadow. Fellini offered me my first opportunity to write and I am now writing a book on the years I spent with him, which is perhaps a kind of liberation. It's almost finished, and he read it and objected to a few points he didn't like; but you must also show a person's defects, not just the best side. That is a realistic friendship, a mature friendship.

"Why didn't I become a director?" Liliana laughed and answered, "Because coming into contact with reality, I knew it was not the road for me."

The Baths

May 14

Encolpius is searching for Giton and runs to the baths to find Ascyltus, who has absconded with the boy. This is a scene in the very beginning of the film, right after Encolpius gives his lament by the wall. It is the only time where anything resembling the traditional concept of ancient Rome appears, because Fellini's intention was always to show the Rome of the people, not the monuments and official buildings.

The baths are a vast open space built in Studio Five. To the right are arches and pieces of marble and ducts, for water to pour into the thirteen small pools and two large ones. In the right foreground, steps lead to the second level, which has many tiny chambers opening off a passageway. On the lower level, leading off to the rear, is a suggestion of a long marble corridor. It is closing time at the baths and they are almost deserted. Mounds of used wet sheets are piled on the floor.

It has taken all morning to set up the scene and now Fellini puts on his unctuous tone and says, "Martin, may I have the pleasure to have you in this scene? Where is his sign?" Maurizio runs in to show him and slips on the wet pavement. In the background, three slaves are playing a rough game of ball.

"Angelo," Fellini calls to one of the players, "go forward, still more. Put a sign there, Maurizio. Go, Martino, very fast, to your sign." He is made to enter from far on the left and walk into camera range. "Go from that point to the second sign. Go very impetuously and then to the third. *State zitti,* shut up a minute," he yips at the ballplayers. "Come on, go, Martino." Fellini, looking through the camera, calls, "Go to your left, Bucci. Whoever throws the ball and whoever receives it must not move a single step. Ah, *cafone,* boor," he snarls at Angelo when he loses his balance and moves. "When I say, 'Begin,' yell, 'One, two, three, four,' the yell violent but short and harsh." Martin enters the scene as the ballplayers throw the ball saying, "I must find you or I am no longer a man."

The director places Giovanni, a bald-headed old man in a grey tunic, behind a pile of sheets on the steps to the right. He makes him wring out a sheet again, and this time wants him to walk down the steps sideways, screeching at him, "Do what I told you. Fling the towel over your shoulder." Then, in despair, he changes everything, replaces Giovanni with another extra, putting the old man in the back near the marble corridor to do another action. "Giovanni," he says, "go further back. Come forward slowly. Now come to the pile of rags.

"Vingeli," he says to Giovanni's replacement, "when I call, come down slowly and say your lines descending the stairs. Giovanni, come. Maurizio," he calls to the assistant director, "put a pile of rags on the ground. Open them so he has time to pick them up." His temper rises because a new shade has to be placed above the camera. "Why always at the last moment? I don't understand.

Maurizio," he bellows, "when Vingeli begins, make Giovanni start too.

"Go to your first position, Martin, and don't walk like Donald Duck. Maurizio, make Giovanni start from behind the column. Put Vingeli further back. When I say 'Vingeli,' come slowly. When you see Martin at the second sign calling 'Ascyltus,' start your lines. Adriano, how much time for the steam?"

"Five minutes," comes the answer as the special-effects crew begins to place dry ice in the pools to create vapor. (Each day, thirty-three hundred pounds of dry ice is used to maintain the steam effect in the baths.)

Fellini surveys the scene, hands on hips, palms outward and fingers pointed down, a common stance for him which always strikes me because it was so unusual. "There is too much smoke in front. Adriano," he complains, "I don't want it. *Andiamo,* let's go, *a posto,* in place. Everybody out of camera range, everybody. A complete rehearsal. Maurizio, tell that *cazzone,* that big prick, not to march in like a soldier. Come slowly."

On the sixth take, he hollers at the ballplayers, "Stop! You played like *tre bambinetti,* three little babies. You must remain immobile and then with great violence, throw and yell."

On the seventh take, he exhorts, "Scream like wild men. *Fate stronzati, così.* Act like shits. Yes, like that. Stop. *Va bene.*" But the camera operator wants another. On the final take, he says sarcastically, "Bucci, don't stand there like a baby expecting his Pablum." With that elevating remark, he finishes for the morning.

On his way to his suite up in the production office, he is besieged by two young men who claim they are divers and can work underwater. "Go see the production," he tells them, "but I can't promise." Fellini's had a string of odd visitors lately. Yesterday, two young English students hitchhiking around the world stopped off at Focene to ask for jobs. A German sculptress arrived and wanted photographs of the young girl who played the devil in *Toby Dammit* so she could sculpt her.

The strangest visit of all was an eccentric professor who came to tell the director that he was in touch with Petronius and Nero. "He kept beckoning me," Fellini laughs, "and I went over to him and he said, 'I talked with Petronius and Nero and they are pleased because you are not saying what has been said in other films about ancient Rome. You know, of course, that Petronius was Nero's lover. They are very happy you are making a film from a pagan point of view, but you mustn't forget the music. They sang the music for me which you must use.'"

Maybe there was something to it. Later the professor wrote a letter to Fellini describing the music, and it is remarkably like that used in the film.

May 16

Yesterday was a holiday and there was no shooting. Fellini is now working on the second level with the small rooms opening off the corridor. It's an enormous set for the little shooting they will do here. He must have planned to do much more because there are many extras waiting around in sheets and wigs, but none of them appear in the scene. Finally, he tells them all to leave. Maybe, as he sometimes does, he wants them on hand just in case he gets an idea.

Clara changes Hiram's loincloth while he complains. "At the end, they make me up perfectly. The scenes I'm supposed to look good in, they don't care. The ones I'm supposed to look terrible in, I look perfect." Then Martin's loincloth is changed. "Can I start, Clara?" Fellini demands as she wraps the cloth around Martin; then he turns to Hiram and says in mock seriousness, "When he hits you, jump back and hit him very hard. Don't be afraid, because we have finished the picture and we don't need him any more."

Max Born joins the crowd on the set in a navy blue polka-dotted shirt open down to the front, exposing his bare chest, and flowered satin pants. "I'm going up to see my chick in makeup and I'll be back." I think he's wearing her clothes again. I often see her in the same things.

Another close-up of the fight with the stunt men is shot and then a retake with Martin and Hiram. Fellini bellows *"Silenzio"* at the top of his lungs, seconded by Pippia and Maurizio. "Go, Martino." Hiram has been on top of Martin. Martin turns him over and begins to strangle Hiram until he tells him where Giton is. Martin leaves. "Iram, get up. Touch your neck," Fellini orders. *"Va bene."*

Two more takes and the fight is finished. Hiram comes off the set weary but exultant. "I've loved it but I'm glad it's over," he says. "It's not anything like I thought it was going to be. For one thing, we've been working so long, I can't tell the difference between working and living. The work has now become more real to me. Don't you think it's more normal for us to be with only freaks and people in costumes? But maybe that's the point of this film. It's all so much out of his imagination. How could one anticipate what it was going to be like? I had dreams in New York before I left. I dreamed I was walking down an old Roman street in costume. Since we've been here, I've dreamed every night. When I wake up, I don't know if I am waking into reality or if the dream is a reality.

"When I first came," Hiram says, "my only preconception was of Fellini's greatness and his reputation. It's a very scary thing for a twenty-four-year-old boy to face working in a film for the first time with him. I was so scared that when he yelled at Norma, the script girl, I started shaking. I told him after a couple of weeks and he said I shouldn't pay any attention; so I stopped, and I got to know him more as a human being. He gives the same amount of attention to each person, but I'm extremely jealous if he pays more to anyone else. I'm not jealous by nature but there is something about being around him. You want him to notice only you."

Martin is as jealous as Hiram. Max doesn't need to be. He is Fellini's pet. *"Un saggio,"* the director described him, "a wise old man, calm and serene and the most intelligent of the three." Fellini certainly does have this capacity to arouse jealousies and rivalries, and he plays on it to keep his collaborators on their toes and himself the center of attention, much as a woman might do to hold her husband's or lover's interest.

A night shot is being prepared of a passageway in the Subura. Since they are still setting up the scene and nothing much is happening, I go off to look for Max Born, and find him outside one of the sound stages swigging champagne.

"You want some?" he asks. "Let's go!"

"Where?" I ask.

There are buckets of it over on the *Viva Max* set so we go there and while we sip champagne, Max talks about these long months. "The whole thing seems so much like a fairy tale," he marvels. "It seemed predestined. Although each thing is a new and incredible surprise, I seem quite used to it. I thought that I would have a lot more difficulty doing what he wanted, and also that my part would involve a lot of dialogue.

"I can't imagine an easier director to work for," he declares, helping himself to more champagne. "I'm going to have trouble with other directors. The hardest thing I had to do was work outside with no clothes on, but I liked the actual work. I feel myself working with him and it's a game I want to do; but I don't like the set game, which is the usual social rat race. I know you can't make a film without all these people around the place, but it's a drag. They are more distant with stars; but with me, if they can get through at all, they're always at me. I have no barriers. Everybody sees this and they're always asking me for something. There are two different parts to this—work, and the cinema world. I dig the work like I thought I would, but the world I don't dig at all.

"I've gotten a whole lot out of this," Max confides. "It's taught me basically that I could go into the outside world and conquer anything if I wanted to. If I decided to be the richest man in two years, or the top politician, I could. I really want to be an actor and lots of things. I want to act but not *be* an actor, like I want to paint and not *be* a painter. I want to *do* those things, not be *it*. I'm always making up fantasies about my future and about the choices I have. Now I've got something to lose which I didn't have before. I started at the top in this so if I'm careful, I can pick and choose. This was outside me. It came to me. Now I've got to make decisions, which is difficult.

"This film will really grab everybody," he says, "because it is one of the first films where Fellini didn't compromise with his vision. There is nothing about it anyone can explain to anyone else. It is purely visual. Up to now, all films tended to be second-rate. The director tried to make them easy for everybody and ended up with nothing for anybody. This is a mind-opening thing, not a mind-closing film. Fellini thinks of himself as a father figure for me. He calls himself my 'third father,' but to me he's just a very open person of ever-widening thought and action. I haven't met many old people who are still open, especially Italians. I find that amazing!"

Wondering what Fellini would think to hear himself described as an old man, I wandered back to the lot where they were shooting, but not much progress seemed to have been made.

It's a good thing I didn't stay. They worked on until two o'clock in the morning, because Fellini suddenly decided he wanted a huge statue raised off the ground.

The next day Donati grumbled, "He is quite capable of saying, 'Raise the house,' but he doesn't understand you need time."

The Death of the Emperor

May 19

The troupe left Anzio at 11:25 in the morning on the hydrofoil bound for the island of Ponza, about thirty miles off the coast, to shoot the scenes of Lichas' sailors capturing the three boys and the slaves for the Emperor, and the death of the Emperor. It's a beautiful sunny day, and Fellini, who normally suffers from seasickness, enjoys the fifty-minute trip immensely—fortified with a pill. "It's only when the sea is rolling gently that I get sick," he explains, "not when it's rough and choppy."

We arrive in port and the troupe is dispersed in various hotels. I am lodged with the director and his key crew members at the Chiaia di Luna, a new luxury hotel on a hill overlooking a sparkling blue bay. In the afternoon, Fellini, Giulietta, and others take a trip around the island in a motorboat looking for locations, since Fellini doesn't even know where he's going to shoot. A sailor reports that there is a sirocco, the warm wind from Africa. "Is it dangerous?" Fellini inquires anxiously.

We make a complete tour and return to port. Known as "The Island of Silence," Ponza is a wild and enchanting place still unspoiled by tourism, although beginning to be discovered. The cliffs of the island rise straight out of the incredibly clear water as if they had been sheared off with a knife. The houses are mostly white and pastel blue with rounded roofs, and remind me somewhat of the white walls of "The Garden of Delights" with their tiny windows. The island has a long history. The Phoenicians stopped here, and the Greeks and the Arabs; and in Roman times it was called Pontia and used as an island of exile.

After dinner Giulietta and Fellini retire fairly early, but the director returns to continue a conversation he had begun earlier with Gideon Bachmann. The director is displeased with the independent television documentary Gideon has been filming for the past six months on him and the *Satyricon*. Fellini has seen some of the footage and is irate. Gideon insists he is trying to discover the interior Fellini by showing him in different situations including his private life. "I want to portray the essential Fellini," he reiterates.

"That is an essential that can never have an answer," Fellini responds. "I can only be understood through my films."

They go round and round the subject and Fellini is in turn amused, exasperated, and disgusted. "An artist," he declares, "can only be understood through his work. You can study an ant for years, photograph it in every possible way and never understand what an ant is."

Gideon recalls that years ago Fellini used to stroll around every day in the Via della Croce, a busy street in the center of Rome, and greet his friends.

"But I don't do it anymore and I refuse to do it for your documentary," Fellini says. "If you want to show that, why don't you write a script and get an actor to play the part? You would have to prepare a procession of elephants and have someone fall out the window at my feet for something to happen. What are you expecting to happen?"

Gideon remembers another incident when he and Fellini went to the zoo and the director became fascinated by the skeletons of some animals.

The director retorts wearily, "You are citing two examples that happened in the course of eight years and trying to make them an essential part of my life. What you are trying to do," Fellini continues, "is very pretentious. If you want to get inside me, the real me, you should put an electroencephalograph inside my head."

Gideon explains he wants to show how a director can function inside an industry and still remain an individual—which Fellini clearly has been able to do.

Fellini objects, "You can find others. Bergman can make a movie with three people. Your whole point of view is wrong," the director maintains, "because a documentary claims to be objective and yet can distort reality. You have shown me directing for three hours, all those pictures of me gesticulating and screaming. I might be flattered to see myself on the television screen for so long, but the spectator would just turn to another channel."

Fellini persists that Gideon should interview more people from the film, and can't understand his resistance to the idea. "You should do what Eileen did, because *this* is my world. You have been repeating the same thing over and over—always with someone covering me up anyway, Bevilacqua or Peppino—so you can never get at the objective truth. You should be more modest. Maybe there would be some justification for doing a film of this kind on the Pope or Buddha or Christ, but not on me."

The discussion continues until one o'clock, which is very rare for Fellini, and it is clear that he is not only annoyed and disappointed but definitely does not want to be dissected by a camera. By now, it's too late for Gideon to begin photographing the world of Fellini because the filming is almost at an end.

Hiram and Max have joined the group and Hiram remarks, "Why do you have to understand how he did it? That destroys the magic. Why can't you just be satisfied that he did it?"

May 20

The next morning, Fellini returns to the discussion of the night before, complaining, "*Che stronzati* does he want to do? What fucking thing does he want to do? What private life do I have? *C'ho il mio lavoro e poi scopo,* I have my work and then I fuck."

Today the prisoners are going to be captured and taken in small boats to the ship of Lichas. How Encolpius, Ascyltus, and Giton have gotten to this place is never explained. The shooting is to be on the beach in the semicircular bay way down below the hotel, appropriately named Chiaia di Luna, or Beach of the Moon. On the right side are sheer stone cliffs whose surface, eroded by wind and waves, resembles a lunar landscape. On the other side green cliffs abloom with vivid yellow juniper bushes rise up from the sea to our hotel.

The equipment, crew, and actors—including Hiram, Martin and Max—are strewn all over the beach. Walkie-talkies are used by the production staff, to communicate between the hotel high on the hill above, and the beach and the trucks on the road. Maurizio reports the shooting can't begin with the boats for half an hour because the tide is high, the water is choppy, and the port commander claims it would be too dangerous. Fellini, sporting a little beige straw hat, shrugs. "It looks calm to me." The sky is grey and it looks like rain.

Waiting for calmer waters, he sits sketching a caricature of Liliana, which he then tears up, promising to do another one. He often does this, and it's quite maddening to have it in your hand only to have him snatch it away and destroy it. Giulietta arrives with a picnic hamper of snacks—the prosciutto Fellini loves so much, and cheeses—followed by Bevilacqua bearing a basket of mineral water and thermos bottles of bitter black espresso.

I go over to join Hiram and Martin a little way off and Fellini comes over, lies down on his stomach, and asks the boys to let Gideon interview them; but they refuse.

When he leaves, Martin complains, "He's been around for seven months. Why does he leave it until now. Why should we make money for Gideon Bachmann?"

Hiram objects. "Just as Fellini doesn't want to be dissected, so I don't want to be. I don't know what I think about this experience now. Maybe in two or three years, I will."

Fellini returns to plead: "Please do the interview, otherwise he crucifies me and makes my balls big." They finally agree to do the interviews if the director will ask the questions. "I don't want to ask the questions," Fellini begs off, "because I will only ask dirty ones. Eileen, you must ask the questions."

"Me? What have I got to do with it? I've already asked a million questions!"

Gideon begins an interview, but Martin is irked and walks away. Max and Hiram turn it into a joke and say whatever foolishness comes into their heads.

The sun begins to shine, the water is calmer, and the shooting with the prisoners and sailors finally begins. The director lies on the beach looking through the camera. Hiram, in chains and wearing a greyish woolen tunic, and Max, covered with a black shawl, are being prodded with other prisoners into the first boat. Further down the beach, the prisoners peer through the bars of the cage on the second boat. Fellini walks up to it and makes some of the prisoners kneel down.

The captives are being dragged along and shoved into the boats, the last one of which is about three hundred yards down the beach. "Look back, Iram, before you go into the boat," Fellini commands.

"Wet the panties. They seem new," Fellini tells a makeup man, "and wet the boats. Iram and Max, don't walk straight, walk hunched over, and pull the chains hard. Have you understood, Max? Before you get in, look up, desperate."

After four takes, the first boat is hauled up on the shore for a close-up of Max and Hiram, with the camera aimed down into the boat at the two boys squatting among the other prisoners.

After shooting, we all gather in the salon before dinner. The director strums Cynthia Pettigrew's guitar or makes deft caricatures of the people around him while the young actress plays. Fellini wants to hear "Tea for Two," "Summertime," and "I Am an American," none of which she knows. The generation gap is sadly apparent. Gideon arrives and begins filming these activities, but it irritates Fellini and he gets up impatiently and stalks off.

May 21

There was no shooting this morning because Fellini was out on another scouting trip around the island looking for a location to kill the Emperor. The director kept saying to the captain, "Stop here, now a little bit to the left, now a little to the right," all the things you can't do with a boat, as though he were directing an actor.

Danilo Donati arrives after a three-hour trip on a ferry boat. "I am destroyed. I've been seasick all the way," he moans. "This is the first and last time I will ever get on a boat. There were ten passengers on the ship, all sick. Four old ladies dressed in black kept sucking lemons, and every time I looked at them, I got sicker. I had to hang onto a pole all the way. I couldn't even sit down."

Along with him is another newcomer, Dana Benjamin, weirdly dressed with a band of beads around her head, hippie style, and black hair trailing down her back. Her face is long and rather masculine looking, her voice deep. "I was on my way to Calabria," she announces, "but missed the plane, and then discovered the production office had been looking for me because Fellini wanted me to come to Ponza."

"Who's she?" I ask Rino Carboni.

"The Emperor," he replies.

"The Emperor! If she's supposed to be the Emperor, what are they going to do with her breasts?" I want to know.

"Take them off," Carboni deadpans. "Donati will be delighted to remove them."

With that chilling thought, I go off to find Martin Potter. His is the most important role, since the figure of Encolpius is the very fine, practically invisible thread which holds the film together. It is a lot more pleasant sitting on the sunny flower-bedecked terrace than the last interview I had with him in the tomb of Trimalchio, and he is more relaxed and less reserved than usual.

"The last two months have been more like what I imagined," he says, "because there has been more of a departure from the script, whereas in the beginning, the script was there and he followed a preconceived pattern. 'Lichas' was a complete departure from the script; Fellini suddenly decided to shovel snow all over the ship and have us come out and look at it like children."

Speaking about his role, Martin says, "Encolpius is a kind of classical hero but he's not a film hero. You can't get your hero impotent. He's an aesthetic hero. What we have now is a character in a given age, probably between sixteen and twenty-four, at a certain period of his life. We get an idea that Encolpius may well be different when he is older, but he is now *very, very real.*"

At five o'clock, after he finished shooting more of the captives being loaded on the boats, Fellini went directly to the small room where Donati and Carboni had been making up both Tanya Lopert and Dana Benjamin as the Emperor. Fellini had still not decided which one he wanted. He finally chose Tanya who is ecstatic with joy. The Benjamin girl is to be the Emperor's sister, a part which does not exist in the script.

No one knows why Fellini chose Tanya Lopert or even why he wanted a woman for the role. Perhaps it was because of Tanya's father's position with United Artists, and he thought it prudent to give her some kind of part after she had waited around three weeks doing nothing. But it is almost impossible to push Fellini into doing something he doesn't want to do. Dana Benjamin believes she looked too feminine. ·

Carboni says, "Fellini wanted someone who resembled the make-believe Emperor in the theater episode and Tanya looks like him."

Donati's version: "It's a mystery. He would have chosen the brunette, but at the last moment, he saw Tanya Lopert and used her. However, they were always two women. Fellini always wanted a youth as the Emperor, an albino with white hair, a little like the hermaphrodite, not like the one on the theater stage. That one looked sick. He wanted a really washed-out looking Emperor, not monstrous like the hermaphrodite, but bloodless, the fruit of a marriage between relatives. Perhaps a feminine element was already nearer, without redoing the albino."

Only Fellini knows.

Donati, still suffering from his trip and thinking of the return voyage tomorrow, keeps lamenting, "I want to die. I want a poison. I am of absolutely no use here. I came because Federico needed to have me always near to calm him. It was a great sacrifice for me to come. I'm already in pieces. Just think, after a year! But I had to come, otherwise everything will go badly because he will make it go badly if I'm not here." I sometimes think Donati missed his vocation.

Fellini abruptly suggests, "Let's go down to the port and spit in the water. That's what we used to do in Rimini." What he really wants to do is to inspect the Roman galleons anchored in the port ready for tomorrow's shooting. He is dressed in a dazzling white trench coat and I twit him, saying he looks like a foreign correspondent. We drive to the village with Giulietta and Liliana, see the Roman boats incongruously anchored next to battered old fishing boats, and then saunter through the streets, stopping to buy some of the local wares. Federico buys seven hats for Giulietta and the rest of us, and a captain's hat for himself. After all, he's going to command the Roman fleet tomorrow. As he is buying magazines and comic books to show Donati, Fellini rounds on Gideon, who is following his every movement with the television camera. "*Ma che cazzo fai?* You embarrass me and make a fool of me."

At dinner, Dana Benjamin announces in her deep voice, "I think I shall call you Fred. You look like a Fred." There is total silence. Only Fellini's closest friends and collaborators call him by his first name. From someone who has hardly set eyes on him before, her audacity is embarrassingly brash.

Cynthia asks Fellini if his inspiration comes from the Bible, and he looks startled.

While he gropes for an answer, I pipe up, "He ain't never read it."

"Oh, yes I have," he retorts, "but only parts of it."

The mayor, who is also the island doctor, arrives to pay his respects to the director and his wife. Fellini rises to greet him, but the mayor, a portly man, objects, "No, sit down, I see you are almost as fat as I am." Fellini's face falls. All those grapefruits he's been eating to lose weight obviously haven't produced any visible effect.

May 22

Down at the port, the crew assembles to be transported to the location where the Emperor is to be killed. The soldiers of the new Emperor triumphantly carry the body aloft on their lances off to sea, where they encounter Lichas' ship. Originally, the soldiers were to have boarded the Emperor's ship, tossed him overboard and clubbed him to death with oars, but the entire episode has been changed, probably because Fellini decided when he got to Ponza it could be done better on land. In addition to the role of the Emperor's sister played by Dana Benjamin, he has introduced another new character—the Emperor's attendant, played by Cynthia Pettigrew.

The three Roman warships set out to sea to the cheers of the troupe, and we board a launch. En route, Rino Carboni prepares a dummy of the Emperor which Fellini has asked for at the last minute. Clara had to run frantically around the village buying the materials to make it.

Tanya is exultant and gushes, "Fellini reminds me of a combination of Max Ernst and Bosch."

Cynthia's eyelids and face are painted orange and her own Afro hairdo is left as it is. She wears a simple green robe and nothing under it. Her guitar rests beside her as she reads the Psalms of David from her Bible. "I read the Bible every morning," she says, "but I forgot this morning. How did I get in the picture? I just came to see Fellini and asked him if I could work for him."

Dana Benjamin cuddles a black kitten she has adopted, which she calls Fred after Fellini, although it's a female. She is in a tan robe with no jewelry except for a small copper plate on her black hair, which streams loose around her yellowish face. A twenty-two-year-old theater and pantomime actress from New York who has lived off and on in Italy for twelve years, she raves, "He's so beautiful, he and Giulietta."

Giovanni Serboli, who is to play the part of the Emperor's tutor, keeps asking on the trip, "Am I a Mongol or a Chinese?" because his face is painted yellow. An ex-government employee, he looks so much like Mussolini that he has played the dictator three times during the ten years he's been working in the cinema. He is the man who gave so much trouble to Fellini in the baths by picking up the sheets before Martin and Hiram began to fight. "I'm happy to work with Fellini," he says, "but not very pleased with the pay. Twenty dollars a day is just niggardly."

We pass the Chiaia di Luna, where they shot yesterday, and arrive at the location, a peninsula of stark white limestone with sheer, molded cliffs looming high up. It looks like a set dreamed up by Donati. All around, the water is very clear and blue. A large two-masted sailing vessel is anchored offshore with most of the crew and extras. Almost all are seasick, since they have been waiting two hours tossing in the choppy sea. Another smaller fishing boat is anchored in the cove to the right, with the Emperor's delicate little golden Japanese-looking boat sailing alongside. A small motorboat brings a few of the crew off the large boat. Raffaele, one of the prop men, lolls with his head hanging over the side, sick as a dog. Fellini spies him and jokes, "Raffaele, you have to sail right back to port to get a nail."

He chats by walkie-talkie with Giulietta, who has remained at the hotel. "*Ciccia,* pudgy pie," he tells her, "we'll be finished by three." What a joke! If we get off this rock by five, we'll be lucky. The Roman boats have still not arrived, although five fishing boats and several rowboats are now scooting about every which way. (The Roman boats never arrived that day because the sea was so rough one of them almost sank, and they returned to port with everyone aboard seasick.)

Fellini decides to shoot a scene of the soldiers who land and kill the Emperor, but the soldier's breastplates have not yet been transferred to land from the big boat. In walkie-talkie communication with the fishing vessel, still pitching violently up and down in the water, Adriano asks for their shields but they can't be found. Meanwhile, the camera is moved for the third time before Fellini finally settles on a slope. He sets up a scene of soldiers in black uniforms and helmets, a startling contrast against the dazzling white rocks.

In the background is the bleak island of Palmarola, like a prehistoric monster rising out of the sea. Half the soldiers are still not fully costumed, but he makes the other half hide behind a ridge on the right and run into the scene as though they had just landed.

Bucci, one of the ballplayers in the baths, is placed in front of the camera with his back to it. Cynthia is stationed in front of the Emperor, who is dressed in a tan robe with a square brass piece holding her cloak together over her bosom, which has been bound tightly to make her look flat-chested, but it is plainly evident she is a woman. Over her ash-blonde wig Tanya wears a helmet of copper strips through which the curls can be seen. Her eyebrows have been shaved off and her face made up in a sickly pallor. Fellini is beginning to get nervous. "Move the crowd back, preferably to another island," he calls to Pippia.

Cynthia is made to lie on her back in front of the Emperor, then turn over and crawl agonizingly on her hands and knees, fall into a crevice, and then turn over, her face up. Then the director decides she should die with her face downward. After making her run through this several times, showing her each movement, he changes his mind and doesn't shoot. Cynthia has to wait until tomorrow to die. Fellini goes off and sits alone in a camp chair looking out to sea with his captain's hat on backward. There is complete chaos. It is almost noon and nothing has been shot yet. Nobody knows what Fellini is going to do and he isn't telling.

Finally the spears arrive, but there are only four shields and nobody knows where the rest are. Someone finally recalls they are aboard the Roman boats which are now on their way back to port. Adriano is frantically calling by walkie-talkie ordering the shields attached to the Roman boats to be detached and transported to the location in another boat. The situation has now become almost farcical, with Fellini glowering in frustration. It's a typical lack of planning. No one has even considered the possibility of a rough sea which would prevent the clumsy Roman boats from arriving.

Fellini, making the best of an impossible situation, decides to begin the death of the Emperor.

On the first take, he starts off patiently enough, "Tanya, look in profile. Look to the right side, then to the left. Run." The soldiers dash in and surround her. "Lower your head, Tanya. Say 'One, two,' and then go." He doesn't like the way her cloak hangs and places her hands inside holding it so that it sticks out like a sculpture. On the third take, he changes a bit. "Open your leg to the right. More bent over in front. Look terrified. Tanya, look here." She is getting very rattled and he goes to explain what he wants quietly.

Cynthia remarks loudly, "If only he'd use actresses, then he wouldn't have so bloody much trouble."

On the fourth take, Fellini places Tanya exactly where he wants her, saying, "Leave your clothes alone now. Stand up. Look dignified. Are you tired, Tanya? Tanya, when I say, 'Look there,' look, but scared like a beast who wants salvation. Now. Go. Run! Run! Stop! *Va bene, è questa.*"

The camera is moved to the right side of the rock where the Emperor's tiny golden boat is floating in the cove. A rudder in the shape of a half moon has been attached to it and orange cushions placed on the seats. A fishing boat starts to tow it away. "Ma, *che cazzo fai?* What the prick are you doing?" Fellini yells to Renzo Gronchi, Donati's assistant, who is vainly trying to row the boat back to shore. "Find some way to tie it so it won't move," Fellini orders, but he is working on solid rock and it is impossible to tie it to anything.

"Tanya," Fellini calls, "go sit in the place of the Benjamin girl without falling into the water. Benjamin, go to the rudder and throw that cigarette away," he bellows. "Those who aren't in this scene, go to the other part of the island. We've been in a mess for two hours. Dana, hold the rudder with both hands. Throw those umbrellas away. No, give one to Cinzia. Cinzia, go on the other side. Put the umbrella over Tanya. Higher. Dana, turn the rudder towards us. Giovanni"—to the Emperor's tutor—"make believe you are reading and count to a hundred if you know how to count. Read, Giovanni. Cinzia, smile. Hold the umbrella straighter. Let me see your teeth. Count, Giovanni."

Reflectors have been placed back of the cameras to reflect water onto the boat as if it were really sailing. The tiny boat turns crazily in the wind in spite of everyone's efforts to keep it steady. The camera has to be moved to a lower point and is practically in the water with the waves spilling around it. To the right of the camera, frogmen are trying to tow in a boat with three pieces of a prow to be used for tomorrow's shooting, but can't get near the rocks.

"Why don't they just float them in?" Carboni wonders. "It would be so much easier."

The first take of the Emperor and his entourage in the little boat begins with the director saying, "Lower your head, Tanya. Smile slightly and then turn your head and be surprised because you see the Roman boats coming. Cinzia, when she turns her head, you turn yours. Giovanni, count to two thousand. Smile, Benjamin. Count loudly, Giovanni. Lower the book. Then, get up, Tanya. Cinzia, you get up, and Benjamin, you get up. Stop. *Daccapo*. From the beginning."

The camera is moved back to where the Emperor died for a close-up of Tanya before the soldiers surround her. Fellini shows her how to hold the dagger after pulling it out of her robe, wave it from right to left and then plunge it into her stomach. "Do it well, Tanya," he admonishes her, and shows her again. He is becoming very impatient with her. "Look to the left, then to the right," then takes her two hands, holds them up with the dagger and plunges it. "No, look at me," he yells, when she doesn't do it right. "Have you understood or not?" He is furious and goes back to show her again and again. *"Silenzio,"* he bellows to everyone. "Tanya, with much force," then snatches the dagger from her and demonstrates again. "You mustn't force it into your stomach. It will hurt you. It's only when you plunge it that you must use force."

On the first take, he says, "What I do, you do, Tanya. Breathe, Tanya, strongly. Look around. Look to me, slowly, very dignified. Down with the dagger. Did you understand or not?"

"I understand," she quavers.

"Then do it."

At the end of the third take, he yells to Tanya, "Go down on your knees, otherwise we do the same thing for twenty minutes." His patience is exhausted. On the sixth take, "Breathe, Tanya. Strongly," he bellows infuriated. "Stop, *va bene, è questa.*"

That evening as we are strolling outside the hotel, Fellini is almost boyishly gay and I ask him, "How does it feel to be at the end of the picture?"

He looks at me very seriously and answers, "A film doesn't finish all at once. It dies little by little. I already finished a month ago."

May 23

Fellini is talking through a walkie-talkie. He and the crew are going out to sea to shoot the arrival of the Roman boats at the rock, while the Emperor and his retinue sit in the fragile golden boat and watch. "When I tell you," he is advising the men with the walkie-talkies on the Roman boats, "have them raise the oars," then moans for an umbrella. "Who has a drop of water?" he pleads.

It is dreadfully hot and there is the usual turmoil. The camera crew leaves, with Fellini ensconced in a chair on a little raft attached to the stern next to the camera. The electricians follow in another boat. Fellini orders, "Sit down and push with your asses."

"Pippia," he bellows to the production inspector, who is on shore with a walkie-talkie, *"che cazzo ha quella barca dietro?* What the prick is the matter with that boat behind?" The crew is still trying to get one of the Roman boats in motion but the battery is dead. "Hurry up," he yells. "The light will go away. Pippia," comes his crackling voice, "as soon as we go away, everybody out of sight. Who has the radio telephone? Have we got it or not?" They have it and Fellini mutters, "This is a fleet!"

He is still perched on the raft rigged onto the back of the boat. "And what if it breaks?" he wants to know. "We have to go a little further out in front of the Roman boats," he orders. "Stay in the back and sit on your behinds. Bevilacqua, push with your ass. What's your name?" he asks the captain of the boat.

"Umberto."

"Umberto, the prow must be turned more toward the land." He whistles happily and then orders, "When we are turned, stay still. This boat won't ever go," he complains. "Still a little more turned, Umberto."

The two boats with the director and crew are now facing the land. An orange umbrella provided by the ever-thoughtful Bevilacqua shades the director, who orders, "Throw the anchor down. We stay here. Maurizio," he calls through the walkie-talkie to the assistant director, who is also ashore, "the Roman boats must stay here in front of us. Is this boat anchored?" he asks the captain. "We have to turn off the motor. The three boats must pass us and go in to land. Maurizio, does that other boat move?" he wants to know. Maurizio burbles a rapid explanation into the walkie-talkie. "I didn't understand *un cazzo,*" Fellini complains.

Maurizio, enunciating very clearly, explains, "The battery is still dead."

"Enzo," he screams at one of the Roman boats, "make it turn towards us." The Roman boats put out to sea with Fellini asking, "Can all the oars go together? This one here has to pass in front of the camera. Umberto, a little farther from the other boat, otherwise we will hit each other." The other boat with the electricians bumps into the command ship and Fellini moans, "We haven't done it in time. We are lost!

"Pippia," he asks, "do you see me? The rudder towards there. Put the boat horizontal towards this one. Benjamin," he screeches to Dana, seated with the Emperor and the other attendants in the little golden boat in the cove to the right, "stay seated, and Tanya and *la negretta,* like you were yesterday. When I wave my handkerchief, do like you did yesterday."

"What do they have to do?" Pippia asks through the walkie-talkie.

"Like yesterday," Fellini bellows back. "Umberto," he complains to the captain, "I explained to you. We have to stay further apart," then whistles and sings "Boo, boo, boo. Pippia," he calls. "No, Pippia, I am not Maurizio. I am Fellini. Don't you recognize my voice yet? Gideon [who is filming on the rocks and is in camera range] must go to Rome; and Pippia, you hide in a grotto. Umberto, what are you doing? This boat is turning around and around!

"Pippia, in two minutes we shoot. Tell those in the Emperor's boat when I wave the handkerchief to get up. We're ready to shoot right away. Come," he calls to the Roman boats. "No, make them stop. When we shoot, turn them toward our boat as much as you can. *Qui!*" he screeches in frustration. "Here! Maurizio, don't they have a radio?"

"No," Maurizio replies, "we only have five."

"Give me the megaphone," Fellini orders. "Ready," he bellows to the two Roman boats. "Go toward the golden boat. Row. *Che cazzo!* Maurizio, get out of there. We are shooting.

"Maurizio," he shouts, "who is at the second oar? Speak slowly, Maurizio. I can't understand you. Arena? He rows like a crazy butterfly. They must all row together."

Maurizio yells through the walkie-talkie to the soldiers, "You don't have to row like the thighs of a woman. Row together!"

Fellini's voice comes on his phone saying dryly, "Don't try to be literary, Maurizio. Just get them to row together."

Fellini comes ashore and wants a shade put up over the camera and crew. "Now, let's do the *negretta*. Where were we yesterday?" Cynthia lies down on the rock on her back. "Tell me when you are ready," he says. "Cinzia, start agonizing. Wet everything all over, her dress, her face, her lips, her behind, a bath of sweat. *A posto,* Cinzia. Start. Breath fairly strongly. Go. Try to get up. Crawl. Go down. Cinzia, again. Try to go in this direction, up, not down. Wet her again. Try to get up and then you remain like a dead leaf. Wet her little fanny. Don't be afraid, Cinzia, if we see it," he soothes her, as she squeals when the brilliantine is sprayed on her. "It's a nize little fanny." On the second take, he chants, "Breath very strong, very quick. Go. Try to get up. Make more strange gestures, like a crazy cat, a cat who is drunk. Down. Stop. Cinzia," he says and tries to explain how he wants her to "breathe," but he mispronounces the word.

Finally, I can't bear it any longer and yell "Pant."

He says, "What?"

And I say, "Pant like a dog."

He gives me a chilling look and snarls, "You've been here six months and finally you pull out a word. After three hours you tell me."

Tanya Lopert sighs. "He's beautiful today. Why is it all of us here want to be loved by him, to feel good with him? He's a god! He has a magnetic force!"

We lunch on the rock and Fellini remarks to Cynthia, "For somebody who died this morning, you certainly have a good appetite."

Cynthia replies, "I feel good, but if I don't make love, I don't feel good."

Everyone is burned from the sizzling sun and some have had a swim in the crystal clear water.

"Why don't you go for a swim?" I ask him.

"I can't swim for a year because I had pleurisy; but I can take a bath," he replies whimsically.

It takes over an hour to pack up all the gear, probably longer than the Allied landing at Anzio. On the way back to port, we pass Commodore Fellini, steaming along perched on the makeshift raft at the back of the boat, shooting the island of Palmarola for the end of the film. Chugging along with him are the Roman galleons with the soldiers sprawled all over, basking in the last rays of the sun.

We visit the mayor's office as Fellini has promised, sip an aperitivo, and sign the Golden Register. The director tells the mayor he had chosen Ponza from a picture in a magazine without ever having seen it. Afterwards we stroll through the streets of the port. Giulietta stops to shop in a store, making her husband very fidgety. Walking along the streets, he gaily greets the stunt men, whom he is very fond of, and the extras. He stops outside a pastry shop, carefully reads all the names of the pastries they make, inquiring about each and sniffing the bakery aroma. "It reminds me of my boyhood," he remarks, then asks me, "Which do you think was the most beautiful girl in the picture?" Before I could come up with a name, he says, "Georgina Lillik?" I suggest Antonia Pietrosi, the beautiful brunette who plays the bereaved widow in the "Widow of Ephesus" tale, but he doesn't agree. Fellini apparently prefers blondes.

The next day on the hydrofoil back to Anzio, Fellini remarks, "I am very grateful to you, Eileen. You 'ave kept your promise and not pestered me. You 'aven't asked me any stupid questions; but zen, you 'aven't asked me any intelligent ones either. Just remember, ziz buk must be very funny, except when you write about me. Zen it must be glorious!"

Finale

July 10

It took a crew of thirty people an entire day to sink the head of Lichas in a specially constructed pool on the back lot where "The Labyrinth" was filmed. Rino Carboni made two heads, one light enough to float for a short time and the other heavy enough to sink, but nothing worked. Either the head sank to the bottom immediately or it bobbled in such a way that the face couldn't be seen clearly. Red fluid from a tube inserted underwater to simulate blood spewing from the severed neck didn't squirt at the right moment or spurted too much, muddying the water and blurring the face.

I got bored watching, and left to talk to Danilo Donati, who by now is referred to as "the echo of Fellini" because they are both on the same wave length. The forty-three-year-old designer, who planned to be a painter, studied fresco painting at the Academy of Fine Arts in Florence before drifting into designing in the cinema

and theater. During the past decade he's spent as a cinematic de-
signer, his best known films have been Pier Paolo Pasolini's *The
Gospel According to Saint Matthew* and *Oedipus Rex,* and *The
Taming of the Shrew* and *Romeo and Juliet* for Franco Zeffirelli.
Fellini Satyricon is the first film for which he has designed the sets
as well as the costumes.

"I absolutely didn't want to do the sets," he said plaintively, "but
Fellini made me do them. Now I'm grateful to him because Fellini
discovered a potential force in me which I held inert, and gave me
the courage to confront it."

We were in the Saloon next to Forrester's Market where Donati
worked like a magician creating the most imaginative things out
of bits and pieces of odds and ends. In the shop all the elements
to be used in the *corteo,* or triumphal march of the new Emperor
on his way to Rome, were being assembled: a mammoth polystyrene
statue on a crude wooden cart, the medallion of the Emperor, plastic
bodies of dead captives hung grotesquely on Latin crosses, giant
trumpets, brass and copper Roman Legion insignia on long poles,
spectral helmeted and armored skeletons of vanquished generals.

"I was running out of bones," Donati quipped, "and thought I'd
have to start robbing graveyards."

I was thinking to myself, Fellini is not only going to have one of
those processions he so dearly loves, but he's also going to have
crosses, which he said he didn't want in the film.

Donati took me outside to show me the carts with more helmeted
corpses in wagons shrouded with colored gauze—a ghastly sight—
and a huge white statue of a head with a gold crown, and mouth
and eyebrows rimmed in gilt, with golden tears running down its
face.

"Not real, just imagined," he remarked, giving it a satisfied pat.
"We are behind, as always," he moaned. "I have a terrible headache. I took some aspirin but I think I'll just give myself a hit on
the head and it will go away."

As he scurried from one chore to another rat-a-tat-tatting orders at Renzo Gronchi, his assistant, and the half-dozen craftsmen who worked with him, he explained how he came to be employed by Fellini. The director had wanted him to work on a couple of his other films, but Donati was always busy. They met finally on the stairs at the PEA production offices.

"He liked my shirt," Donati recalled. "It was actually a dreadful shirt, but we became friends. We talked for a month before beginning the film, and I finally worked up enough courage to undertake this thing. Fellini didn't explain anything to me. It was never a relationship of that kind.

"I read a phrase of Picasso's at the beginning of the film and realized that it was the key to my relationship with Fellini," Donati said in his staccato Italian. "The line goes something like this: 'A painting is never a complete thing in the mind of the artist beforehand, but evolves as he paints it.' This is the motto I adopted to serve Fellini. It was like walking on the edge of a knife blade. The problem was always the same, for a face, a head, a cart—to rediscover a remote and virgin world. Everything had to be made on the spot. We had models and designs in our heads which we couldn't forget, but to create this ancient world we had to obliterate our knowledge.

"Another difficulty was to create a spectacle which ran parallel to the world of today, because you can't present the public with a world they cannot understand. For this reason, Fellini has always called the film science fiction—a past so remote and incomprehensible that it becomes the same as a future equally mysterious and unintelligible.

"How did I know what Fellini wanted? You must never listen to Federico, only interpret," the designer said. "If you listen to him, you only arrive at madness and alienate yourself from him as well. Interpreting him is the only way to be close to him. I had to try every day, every hour, every minute to follow the changes and nuances of his conversation. There has never been a practical discussion with him and the script doesn't serve any purpose. You have to prepare only what is needed for each scene. To make costumes usually doesn't require any great effort, but with Fellini you must be able to stop yourself at the exact point in which his idea has taken shape and is what he has been searching for. Therefore, it was very difficult for practical purposes. Every episode had its particular problems and requirements which had to serve the characters of the sequence, but the general discourse remained intact. Everything was inserted into Fellini's grand scheme."

Generally, the relationship between the director and the set designer is more mechanical. The director usually asks for something and the designer tries to do it as best he can, following his own ideas. "With Fellini, it is quite different," Donati said. "Fellini departs from an idea—the base of what he wants. I would try to add something. Then the problem would shift and become another. He accepted or rejected what I did, but this opened other possibilities and we would start over again, until we reached what he was after. Most things happened like this, either during a ten-minute chat or at dinner or in a taxi.

"Picasso once said he made a blue picture because he didn't have any red paint," Donati continued. "It was a little like that here. Customary materials are not always useful. In this film it took some of the wildest things to render the desired image—anything that could possibly work well in making a particular object at a minute's notice. It was like this throughout the film, working twenty hours a day. It was a complex of multi-media art, and my greatest problem was time."

Restless, Donati muttered, *"Dio mio!* I'm going crazy here because now I have nothing to do. I have never taken a vacation in ten years. I die when I have no problems to solve," and went off to consult with one of the workers.

While he was gone, I looked around the room and my eyes fell upon a note scribbled in a familiar scrawl on one of the huge work boards, which read: "*Daniluccio caro,* dear little Danny, I came to say 'hello.' I am going to the recording studio. I'll call you later. I embrace you and thank you so much for the splendid gift. *Bacioni,* big kisses. Federico."

"What was the gift you gave to Federico?" I wanted to know when he returned.

"Oh, perfume from the pharmacy of Santa Maria Novella in Florence. Fellini likes perfumes. He says they guide his dreams.

"Where were we now, the costumes?" he asked. "Fellini told me to do whatever I wanted, but I understood from the first day he needed something timeless and unreal. The fundamental thing was to destroy any reference to factory-produced clothing, mass production. I made a basic form to suit everybody, changing the materials and colors yet still allowing the faces of the characters to remain the dominant factor. In this film, it wasn't possible to distract the public with stupefying things. The great challenge was to remove everything, leaving only the metaphysical. Nobody knows exactly how many costumes were used because the film was not programmed. They were done as needed. Half were made in a shop outside and half at Cinecittà. The important thing was that we had to dye the costumes from one day to the next and had to have a whole range of dyes ready from day to day.

"*O Dio,*" he groaned again, "I don't know which was the most difficult costume, because I never worked on just one at a time. We saw the whole thing. I did exhaustive research of the Greek and Roman periods, but the only thing I used was the tunic which is still worn in Africa. People think of the Romans as they were painted in the seventeenth century, but the toga was not generally worn. It was an official costume donned to go to court or the tribunal and took two hours to put on with the help of a slave. It was like a man wearing tails today, very uncomfortable and impractical, and for this reason went out of fashion."

Fellini and Donati designed the models for the sets together at the PEA production offices in forty days, working all of July and half of August in 1968, creating the visual part of the film. As soon as the creative work was finished and sketches were made, the technical part got underway—the plans, the constructions, and the architectural realizations of their ideas. At that point, it became a question of translating the ideas into new materials, exactly as had been done with the costumes, so as to avoid an erudite or scholastic approach.

Donati glanced at the diagram of the *corteo,* all neatly plotted out on a big board, including four elephants with towers, camels, and dromedaries. "Of course, it will all be changed tomorrow," he sighed and left to go outside and supervise the painting of some big trumpets muttering, "When I hear *Fine,* The End, I shall drop dead from relief."

After this momentary diversion, Donati confided, "Fellini wants me to do his next picture with him. He keeps saying, 'We are like *due fratellini,* two little brothers,' but I told him, 'Yes, we are like two brothers; but *you* are Cain and I am Abel.' He keeps asking me what I think of him. It's a big trap. Of course," he shrugged, "there are always two brothers. One dies and the other lives; but who knows who's alive and who's dead? Perhaps I was dead and Fellini resuscitated me. I must say it was an overwhelming experience!

"What do I think of Fellini?" The designer gasped incredulously. "It's the end of the world! It's impossible to describe how certain things are achieved with him. I've always been sure he was a magician. He simply falls into a trance when he's shooting. He's nervous and hysterical, and afterward becomes very sweet. I don't recognize him when he's working on the set; but when he's preparing, he's very intelligent, open to any experience or experiment. Working with Federico is never easy," Donati sighed for the last time. "He's a man riding a tiger, and he can no longer get off."

July 11

The new Emperor's procession, barely visible through the dense black smoke spewing out of large torches, was shot very quickly. True to Donati's prediction, there were some changes. No dromedaries or camels made the scene, but the four elephants were on hand and stampeded madly over the lot. In the afternoon, they were to shoot the collapse of the model of the Insula. A crew of eight had been working for six weeks on the model, intricately wired with small charges of gunpowder, to fall exactly as the original tenement had, but because of technical difficulties, the collapse was postponed until July 26th, the very last day of shooting.

On July 25th, the final scene of the film was shot. Fellini changed the ending. Originally, the director planned to end the picture with Encolpius wandering aimlessly around after the death of Ascyltus, seeing visions of gods and goddesses and other hallucinations. Then he decided to show frescoes of the film's principal characters, on the walls of a ruined villa, which slowly fade and disappear. The wall, already constructed at Nettuno near the sea by Donati's crew, had to be knocked down and redone by Antonio Scordia because as Fellini told him, "I cannot finish the film with such a squalid thing." When Scordia, curious as to the significance of the two walls which begin and end the film, asked if the first one signified history and the final one a re-entry into history after all the fantasies in between, the director replied, "Yes, it's a little like making a detour which then returns into reality."

When it was all over, I went to see Gideon Bachmann, the bearded, bespectacled writer and award-winning documentary film-maker, who has known Fellini since 1956 when the director went to the United States to publicize *Nights of Cabiria*. Fellini was little known in the States at that time and Bachmann was the first American broadcaster to interview the director and guide him around New York. The film-maker has spent several years collecting extensive material on Fellini, taping interviews with the director, his family, friends, and collaborators, as a result of which he has a perceptive insight into the working of Fellini's complex character.

Bachmann worked on the entire shooting of the film, producing seventeen hours of color film and twice as much sound in thirty-three days spread over the six-month period, to prepare a one-hour television program and an hour-and-a-half documentary for theaters. "In our film," said the multilingual Bachmann, who has now lived in Italy for five years, "we have attempted to show how Fellini works, who he is, and why he makes the kind of films he makes. Fellini intrigues me as an absurd remnant of another time transplanted into our century—a circus director in the industrial age, a minstrel in a factory, an artist who has managed to remain totally himself in a medium that is completely collective."

Bachmann claims that "After thirteen years, I've finally gotten to the point where I like Fellini, and this has not been an easy struggle for me. He's like Italy. You go through a first year of total enchantment and then four or five years of total disenchantment when you realize that nothing works. However, if you stay long enough and give it enough of a chance, you begin to appreciate the deeper aspects, the more delicate and poetic things that Italy has to offer. It's the same with Fellini. You work through the weaknesses that bug you, disturb you, or make you hate him from one minute to the next—all those insecurities that make him unreliable, for example, or the stories that make him lie. But you get to the point where everything is explained in terms of the basic human being, and that human being I don't presume to understand. It would be a sort of sacrilege to say I understand Fellini because understanding is the one thing he fights all the time. At least I realize he doesn't want to be understood, and maybe that's part of knowing him."

The documentarist maintains Fellini is very different now from what he used to be when he first knew the director; but the changes are external. "A great deal of strictly physical maturing has occurred," he said, "not that he's gotten older. He's not talking on the surface anymore. He doesn't make that many jokes, and when he does, it's all more transparent. I don't think it's because he's not afraid anymore. That is still one of the basic characteristics of the man. His strength is to have been able to live with this fear all his life and to create things out of it and with it and to use it as an artistic discipline. But he has empirically learned those fears aren't that basic and that important. After all, he's had twenty-five years of success. That's the reason why it is difficult for him to take criticism, but success hasn't gone to his head. He builds on it. It is important to him that it shouldn't end, and, in a sense, it's a safety thing because he can always rest on his laurels. But success has not made him any different or changed him or made him do things knowing that people would accept them from him but not from somebody else.

"Four or five years ago," Bachmann explained, "I was beginning to feel the pangs of doubt about Fellini's character. I saw what he did to people; and there is no doubt that he is absolutely ruinous to many people. I don't know if he does it consciously because he fears people may discover too much about him. I think it's only the basic defense mechanism of anyone who is insecure, but Fellini has always been the boss in any human relationship starting from when he was a kid in Rimini. His basic insecurity is strangely juxtaposed to this external capacity to control every situation. There is no need for insecurity. But once he gets out of his element, the world of the cinema, he feels very insecure, which is maybe why he doesn't do anything else. There is no Fellini when he's not working. There just isn't. Nothing goes on between films.

"I don't know if he is really interested in people," Bachmann mused. "Maybe he's just involved with himself a great deal unless you have influence in some sphere of his life. But I know he is interested in enough things and in enough people to pass as a normal human being. We demand so much of an artist of that caliber. We demand that he be socially engaged. We demand that he be 'interested in people.' We expect all the things which we don't ask of the cobbler down the street—who may really be concerned about people—but these are all judgments that we impose. His 'interest in people' may take a wholly different form. It may take the form of using them up. And who knows if to use them up isn't the most natural, atavistic, basic, and original form of 'being interested in people.' It's a sort of social cannibalism, artistic cannibalism, if you like; but maybe it's the same as loving them. Fellini is very destructive to insecure people but renounces very quickly doing anything to those in whom he feels some strength or even acting subconsciously upon them in such a way as to impair their capacity to continue.

"In that sense, I think this business of being cruel to people, which he can be, is really the same as his creative capacity—namely to bring out in the person more strongly that which he already is. If the person is weak and self-destructive, he brings that out, and the person gets destroyed. Since most people in the cinema world that you are likely to come into contact with, if you are a film director, are insecure, he's more apt to ruin more people in the cinema world than if he were a cobbler or in some other element where people are not necessarily neurotic. I've seen many people who, all their lives, have fought against being a certain thing, like a homosexual. Fellini throws one look at you. He knows right away what your basic weaknesses are and if he can use them in the film, he will make you be what you yourself have been afraid of being all your life. Suddenly you see yourself on the screen and you are that and you can never get out of it. That's part of the reason why he's always making only one or two films with the same person."

Discussing the many accusations leveled against the director, particularly by the Italians, Bachmann objected, "Fellini behaves more like most people than a lot of other great artists in history have. Okay, so he lies. But he's certainly less of a swindler than a lot of other Italian film directors I could name, or producers or writers or whatever. He just does it much better than most Italians. That may be a recognition of the force of their own characteristics carried to the *n*th degree. They see themselves reflected in him, only better. Since Italian society is entirely based on self-reflection—which is why it takes place in the street—and not on self-realization, everything that is on the order of recognition or association is of prime importance and everything is a threat."

I asked Gideon if Fellini has many friends. "He's always talking about having friends," he replied, "but I don't think has *any* friends. Rota is a friend but Rota has always been there. He's security. Rota is like a dressmaker for a beautiful woman. When you have washed and fixed your hair and put on your makeup and really done all you could, Rota comes, puts the dress on you and everything goes out into the world. Rota dressed the Fellini pictures in music. At a certain point, this magic of Rota-Fellini piano-playing sessions would start. Out would come *8½*, which was as much music as it was film. And Rota doesn't spend that much energy. That's the friendship with Rota."

Did he think Fellini has succeeded in doing what he set out to do in the *Satyricon*? "My first impression was that it's one in a long row of experiments in self-liberation," he said thoughtfully, "because that is the theme of his life. Here it might have been from the strictures of having to represent things that really exist which, in all his other films, have been clothed in what he called 'a topography of the contemporary.' For years, I've always said Fellini's next film would be science fiction, and this is science fiction. I remember seeing *8½* cut but without the dubbing and music, and really not having a total impression. Again, I felt it was a flight of fancy of some guy who was trying to get out of responsibility, which it is, but it is a responsible flight of fancy and I think the *Satyricon* may be a little bit less so in terms of involvement with real life. Certain critics on the left will say that *Satyricon* is not socially involved. It does deal with a social problem, the breakup of a society, but they would want to see him facing the problems confronting our society. I don't think, even in terms of Roman society, the *Satyricon* tackles the essentials.

"There is no doubt this is the first historical spectacle that is also a work of art and also a real film," Bachmann asserted. "But there are aspects in Roman morality and society and the passing of Roman times of which I, from reading nothing more than Flavius, get more of a sense of reality than I have from watching *Satyricon*; or maybe a sense of difference from us. I never understood the 'absence of Christ' in this film, in the sense that he says there is not an exclusion of Christ but an 'absence' of Christ. In the things he has written or said about the film, he's always said there's no 'conscience of Christ,' in this film. Therefore, it's a whole view to another *Weltanschauung*. In a sense you have a feeling there are different values, but I don't think he's gone all the way. It's not a sexy film. One thing I don't like about it is Encolpius in the loincloth on top of Ariadne or the boys in bed. Why couldn't he have gone all the way? This is the presence of Christ we've had for two thousand years, of looking, not executing. And all that licking of the lips! Maybe this means something to him or is his idea of sex. It could be done with his kind of imagination and courage—or with his kind of imagination, *and with courage*."

Epilogue

The last time I heard Fellini talk about himself and the *Satyricon*, I had gone to the International Recording Studios where the director was dubbing the film. He made two versions, one entirely in Italian and the other with certain parts in Latin. For the

Latin, he wanted a guttural accent, and hired German actors and also two seminarians from Rome's Pontifical Gregorian University, which is run by the Jesuits but is under the direct jurisdiction of the Pope. The seminarians were not very keen to know the content of the film and I wondered what the Pope would think about his seminarians helping Fellini out with his pagan pan-erotic romp. The director didn't particularly like the German actors because their Latin sounded too harsh but he left himself open to two possibilities and in the end used Italian mixed with Latin, as well as a few other strange languages, dialects, and accents thrown in.

Fellini was seated in a small glassed-in room, and an Italian actor was dubbing the part where Encolpius begs the Minotaur to spare him, panting and repeating the same lines over and over ad nauseum. He must have done it twenty times, and I decided I couldn't stand it any longer. As I was leaving, Fellini came out of the recording booth grumbling, "How tedious to be locked in that room for hours!" I really had to sympathize with him, because the dubbing is agonizing.

The director insisted I come to lunch and I soon discovered why. He had an interview with an American journalist and wanted me along to translate, even though Mario Longardi, the Italian publicist for the picture, was there and speaks perfectly competent English. The interview was almost aborted on the first question. "Are you the big liar everyone says you are?"

Fellini scowled but quickly regained his good humor. "This is one of those stupid legends propagated by the press," he laughed. "I don't think I am a liar. If a producer asks me if I can make a picture for a certain amount of money and I say 'no' and he asks me again and I say 'no' and then he asks me again and I say 'yes,' is that a lie? And then if an actor comes to me and begs me for a part and I say, 'No, there is no part in this picture for you,' and he pleads and I say, 'Well, maybe,' to make him happy, is that a lie?"

I chided him for blaming the press for fostering the myth of his lying. "It is you who have created this legend. I remember the first time I ever interviewed you in 1960. I asked you if your reputation for lying was true and you answered, 'I tell lies all the time. Even when I don't have to.' "

He made a face and went on to another legend, his improvisation. "That's another myth. I always leave myself open. I am like a mother. I make love, get pregnant, and give my creation what it needs but I don't know what the creature will be like until it is born.

"In the *Satyricon*, there is an analogy between modern times and pagan times," he stated. "They were in a state of breakup as we are now, waiting for something. Their something was Christ. We don't know what ours is, but we have to go ahead because the old obscurities, the old ideologies, don't serve any longer.

"No, I can't say I have completely departed from my autobiographical pictures," he asserted. "An artist can never leave behind his fantasies, his memories. Nor can I say which of my pictures I like best. That is like asking me which do I like, my marriage or my military service? It is all part of my life."

I thought it an odd comparison for him to make since he never did any service in the army.

"What do I think about pornography in films today in Italy? The education we have had in Italy is at fault, and this is the reason people want to see these films. Maybe that is good because it gets them away from the bad education they have had; but the thing I object to is not the pornography in the films, but that they are badly made," he said heatedly. "They are crude and vulgar and made for commercial reasons. I would like to see good teachers who can really teach the young all over the world, because what I dislike most in this world is stupid authority and stupid violence.

"Maybe going to the moon will change things, but I don't think I would like to go myself," the director mused. "It's not necessary for an artist to actually see. He is a child always and see things with childlike wonder. This is what makes him an artist."

Asked what advice he would give a young director embarking on his first film venture, Fellini paused and responded with that naughty smile of his, "Ah! That's like asking me how to make love. I would say, *so make it!*"

Afterword

Since beginning my book, I have so often been asked what kind of a man Federico Fellini is. I don't really know. He has a chameleonlike character which thrives on ambiguity and ambivalence, a shifting, elusive nature which defies instant analysis or easy definition. As Eugene Walter, Fellini's English dialogue coach and translator and the only American in his entourage, says, "No two people say the same thing about Fellini, and he is completely contradictory about himself. He has been called a madman, an archangel, the power of evil, a clunk, and even, as he points out, 'a fairly good director.' "

Fellini is a mystery, even to those who have known him a long time, maybe even to himself. He clothes himself in a variety of guises that change from moment to moment—the flamboyant showman, the artful persuader, the raucous buffoon, the ironic poet, the shameless huckster, the clown-genius. He is a man made for hyperbole. At the age of fifty, Fellini has become a legend—a largely self-created one—and he is as much a prisoner of that legend as he is the expounder of it. By now, he has said so many different things about himself that it is difficult if not impossible to distinguish where fact ends and fantasy begins. "One musn't believe too much in what I say in my interviews," he has cautioned. "I have a tendency to be rhetorical and to let myself be carried away by my imagination."

Certainly he is gifted with a baroque imagination, a galloping fantasy, an uncanny insight into people, and an unerring instinct for the visceral. His boundless talent for intuitive directing is balanced by an indefatigable energy, an almost fanatical attention to detail, and a ruthless insistence upon perfection. Though notorious for his impatience and driving demands upon others, Fellini brings to the set an astonishing vitality, enthusiasm, and freshness, almost as if he were a novice director making his first film.

On the set, as he clowns and cavorts, mimes and acts, shouts and curses through scene after scene, a variety of Fellinis emerges. The myriad facets of Fellini's personality shape and reshape as he runs through a virtuosic display of histrionics and directorial skill. In rare moments of repose, the jowly Byzantine head is sunk on his chest, the large eyes hooded in concentration, the expressive hands mute, the heavy frame relaxed but ready to spring into the graceful posture of an Italian dancing or fencing master. He can bellow like a drill sergeant, cajole with the caressing voice of a Siren, shoot off shafts of withering irony or convince with insistent sincerity. His expressions run a gamut from the scowling displeasure of a petulant baby to the exultant rapture of a saint in ecstasy. But whatever the mood of the moment, Fellini thoroughly enjoys what he is doing.

Fellini's public façade of convivial jocularity masks a man of magnificent paradoxes, a lonely fearful man with demons on his eyeballs nurturing his morbidly sad vision of life in the midst of compulsive camaraderie and controlled confusion. I saw not one Fellini but many with one constant and striking note running through all of them. What Fellini has is a charismatic quality, a magnetic charm even in his most outrageous moments, that compels attention not only from his devoted coterie but also from those who don't particularly like or admire him. He is accustomed to dominating the scene, to evoking uncritical adoration from his collaborators, among whom he creates a remarkable *esprit de corps,* and to inspiring a certain respectful familiarity in his actors and the hundreds of anonymous extras who besiege him for work. On the set, Fellini reigns supreme, a stern but benevolent paterfamilias, the captain of a ship on an uncharted route, whose confidence is unlimited, whose authority unchallenged, and whose genius is unquestioned.

Even off the set, Fellini has enormous popular appeal. In Italy, as elsewhere in Europe, film making is the prerogative of the director, from the initial concept of the story through the scriptwriting and its translation to the screen. Generally, the director, not the star, draws the public and sells tickets at the box office. At the Venice Film Festival, where the *Satyricon* had its Italian premiere on September 4, 1969, Fellini demonstrated his stellar quality. Accompanied by his wife and several of the most important actors in the film, *il Maestro* proceeded down the Grand Canal like a conquering hero. At the Palazzo del Cinema on the Lido, a feverish public, many of them holding tickets bought from scalpers at eighty dollars each, awaited the arrival of the director and his entourage. By popular demand, to satisfy disappointed spectators unable to squeeze into the first showing, a second showing was held at midnight, an unprecedented event in the Festival's thirty-year history. As one Italian journalist wrote, *"Fellini Satyricon* is living proof that the star system still exists, the only difference being that the place of the star of yesterday has now been given to the director."

A fair share of this anticipation and curiosity about the film had been shrewdly generated by Fellini himself—he is undoubtedly his own best press agent. Before, during, and after the shooting of the *Satyricon,* the director, in interviews to journalists from all over Italy and the world, unleashed a steady barrage of words about himself and the film. "I've said a million things about this film," he declared. "I'm almost ashamed of myself. I said, for example, 'It's the story of another planet, a science-fiction film, an epoch in history seen in another dimension.' Everything I said at the beginning of the shooting was frivolous, vague, delirious, and presumptuous on my part. I said anything that came to mind about the Romans. Before setting out on a new 'voyage,' I feel the need to talk." On other occasions, Fellini has ingenuously confessed that he rarely says the same thing twice in interviews, not because he is a liar or inconsistent, but simply to help each journalist get a different story.

Fellini, who once was a journalist, has a high regard for the power of the press and keeps close tabs on what is written about him. He carefully scrutinized the reams of press clippings and also, in spite of a backbreaking schedule, found the time to peruse the hundreds of publicity stills taken daily on the set. Those which focused too clearly on the dismaying signs of middle age—the bald spot on the back of his head, the flabby chin and the tendency toward paunchiness—were immediately eliminated. Fellini was somewhat of a dandy in his youth and still has a good healthy vanity about his appearance.

Still, in spite of these understandable foibles, Fellini is surprisingly uninterested in collecting memorabilia. He destroys everything, including scripts and photographs, claiming he feels like a thief or an assassin and doesn't want to leave any tracks behind. His films are his tracks but he is oddly indifferent to them once he has finished them. "I never view my pictures a second time," he revealed. "It's a narcissistic, masochistic, and imbecilic operation. I know perfectly well that, should I see them again, they would show me spoiled aspects, deformities. Then I would discover their humps, goiters, and club feet. Why should I stay there and feel myself judged?"

In a certain sense, Fellini's endless press briefings on the subject matter of his film and his intentions and message paid off handsomely, because the director came away from the first judgment of the *Satyricon* at the Venice Festival comparatively unscathed. Though the premiere audience sat in benumbed silence, too stunned even for applause or the customary bravos, the critical reaction was generally enthusiastic and the film was hailed as "a magnificent film of overwhelming stupefaction," and "one of the most exciting and important films of the year and a considerable step forward for the Italian cinema." Although various critics took exception to some aspects of the film, the unanimity of the response even prompted one reviewer to suggest, "Fellini is a siren, a hypnotizer, a magician with the power to dictate from afar the words a critic will write without the critics realizing what is happening." Another remarked, "It's a film which has nothing to say but it says it superbly." But, as the following excerpts from some of the Italian reviews indicate, though the film provoked discussion and a reexamination of Fellini's artistic message, it did not provoke the uproar that many expected.

Gugliemo Biraghi—*Il Messagero*: "The portrait of society dissolves into an orgy of ghosts because the inhabitants of Fellini's fantasy are no longer Romans but rather beings who belong to no time or place and who, merely by chance, have been reclothed in the robes of a certain historical period. . . . The film is superbly uniform in its ever-present magical, dream-like atmosphere. Fellini has spoken of 'enigmatic transparency' and 'undecipherable clearness.' Truly after seeing the film more than once these rather contradictory statements somehow seem mysteriously appropriate."

Giovanni Grazzini—*Il Corriera della Sera*: "Fellini's Rome bears no resemblance to that we have read about in books or studied in school or the Rome we have seen in previous films usually characterized by chariot races. It is rather a place pertaining to no particular era in history, located somewhere in the subconscious, in which the tales of Petronius become those of Fellini's ghosts. . . . Any attempt to transform *Satyricon* into a direct allegory between antiquity and life today, equally decadent and thirsting for pleasure, is soon evaded. Fellini's *Satyricon* is a journey through the fairy tales of adults."

Angelo Solmi—*Oggi*: "Although I cannot say that the film is quite so 'chaste' as Fellini claims it to be, I must emphasize the fact that, despite its crude subject matter, it never exceeds the limits which separate it from morbidity and pornography. Homosexual love is reduced to a minimum and, generally speaking, it has a certain sober austerity about it not to be found in other films of this genre. Even if not the best of Fellini's films, *Satyricon* has to its merit the fact that it never becomes vulgar, finding a happy medium between good taste and pictorial needs, between rhythm and style."

Leo Pestelli—*La Stampa*: "The difference between Fellini and Petronius is that the latter is a refined writer who purposely amuses himself with a vulgar subject matter (the deadly corruption of the Neronian society) while Fellini has assimilated this same baseness into his film as a purpose of art. . . . Generally speaking, the prominence of the characters in *Satyricon* is not quite so vivid or profound as in other Fellini films which were directly concerned with the abnormal. . . . I do not wish to imply that Fellini is an outdated director but rather that his position is at the periphery of modern cinema, giving the impression of having by now said time and time again all that he has to say."

Ugo Casiraghi—*L'Unita*: "In this fragmentary, phantasmagorical work (in the end somewhat stifling despite the frequent air vents of inventiveness and the frenetic outbursts of genial imagination), Fellini reflects the decadent Roman world . . . in a disfiguring and always ephemeral mirror of his own personal obsessions which invariably reemerge even if, in this instance, Fellini has done everything to set them aside and conceal them. . . . But one can't always believe everything an artist says. Fellini promised a film about pre-Christian, or rather post-Christian, society and has, indeed, made *Satyricon* swarm with crudeness and lust, infernal gorges and physical monstrosities, abnormality and cynicism, dreary skies and imminent apocalypses—that is, what has always been the Christian idea of that era without God."

When the film opened on March 11, 1970, in New York, critics were sharper and more divided in their reactions, although audiences were more sympathetic and applauded more than the Italian viewers. As Fellini had predicted, the film had particular appeal for the young who regarded it as a mind-grabbing, mind-blowing, experience and viewed it with the reverence of devotees awaiting a revelation.

As Richard Schickel noted in his review in *Life* magazine, "The work can only be understood I think as ritual, and in fairness I should note that on the night I saw it, many in the audience assumed attitudes of near-religious veneration. But," Mr. Schickel continued, "ritual, of course, implies celebration and so we must ask what Fellini is asking us to celebrate—his own virtuosity or his vision of decay? The first is impossible, for however powerful his images, they are not enough to sustain us for the length of the picture. That leaves us with his vision—and with the contradiction I have mentioned. If the film is no more than the dredging operation in his unconscious, then we are forced to the conclusion that he is a man without sufficient wit or intelligence to hold us long. If, on the other hand, we are to accept his insistence that there is an analogy between his imaginary world and our own, we are forced to the conclusion that his vision is severely limited, for there is more to the world than the repetitive nightmare he insists on showing us."

Time magazine's critic, who called Fellini "the cinema's greatest living satirist," wrote, "There have been hundreds of Freudian films; *Fellini Satyricon* is probably the first—and certainly the most important—Jungian one. In the course of two hours and seven minutes, images, totems and archetypes rise and burst like hydrogen sulfide bubbles from the marsh of the collective unconscious. The unsynchronized sound track has the timbre of racial memory, echoing some eternal dream time. The film's devices are, in fact, so frenzied and eruptive that they tend to obscure an artlessness of thought or substance. Perhaps it is just as well; the *Fellini Satyricon* is manifestly made for the eye's mind, not the mind's eye. 'Faces are my words,' says the film-maker, and he manages to make them speak an epic."

Newsweek's Joseph Morgenstern said, "It's repetitive and surprisingly solemn, as if Fellini were mainly interested in the past as a club with which to whack the present. Until I saw all those sadfaced satyrs debauching more and enjoying it less, I thought decadence was at least its own reward. . . . As long as Fellini took some characters, incidents, a title and the idea of a mock-Odyssey from Petronius, why couldn't he acknowledge, as Petronius did, that there's genuine humor in the human comedy, that the most seductive side of vice is delight, that the Golden Age has always been one that nobody is alive to remember?"

Writing in *New York Magazine,* Judith Crist said, "*Satyricon*, a vision of the orgies of man amid materialism, sees the cycle of human survival and destruction in eternal terms. . . . It is the work of a master, a further enlargement upon the basics he has been considering and reconsidering throughout his career. And its value is in the essential heartbeat that brings the painted flesh to life and retains the sense of life on a fragment amid ruins. It is another step toward the ultimate Fellini."

Vincent Canby, the *New York Times* reviewer, called it, "Fellini's Magical Mystery Tour,' and described the film as "a hallucination of man in a chaotic world, a world ruled by chance, without government, without values, without faith and almost totally without conscience. As if to obtain his ultimate revenge on the Roman Catholicism he has satirized in so many of his earlier films, he has imagined a world without Catholicism and, ironically, come up with a strong argument for it, or at least something."

The New Yorker's Pauline Kael dubbed the film "Il Mondo Trasho" and wrote in her acerbic review, "The idea that sticks out in every direction from *Fellini Satyricon* is that man without a belief in God is a lecherous beast. I think it's a really bad movie—a

terrible movie—but Fellini has such intuitive rapport with the super-
stitious child in the adult viewer that I imagine it will be a considerable success. . . . I'm sure there are people who will say that it
doesn't matter if Fellini's movies are based on shallow thinking, or
even ignorance, because he uses popular superstitions for a poetic
vision and makes art out of them. The large question in all this is:
Can movie art be made out of shallow thinking and superstitions?
The answer may, I think, be no. But even if it's yes, I don't think
Fellini transformed anything in *Fellini Satyricon*."

As Wanda Hale succinctly put it in the New York *Daily News,*
"A few intelligent people who have seen the picture ask what the
hell it's all about . . . I'm glad I saw it because it's going to be the
most cussed and discussed picture of the year."

Satyricon is a controversial film, one that viewers are apt to
loathe or love. Certainly it is not an easy film to watch, and it needs
to be seen more than once to take in all of Fellini's mind-boggling
imagery. It is too long and the links between the episodes are very
often nonexistent or so tenuous that it is sometimes difficult to follow. And what is it about? Fellini has insisted, "It's not a film of
ideas but of images. Its dimension is purely visual. It must be contemplated."

After having contemplated it at least a dozen times, I still find it
a film of stunning visual impact, sometimes of breathtaking purity,
as in "The Villa of the Suicides" episode. More often it is horrify-
ingly brutal and terrifyingly grotesque. Fellini has dug deep into
his troubled fantasy and shoveled out a harsh world of unremitting
dreariness, a somber and lugubrious no-man's-land in which masked
phantoms awakened from the dead stare mindlessly into the camera,
dart their tongues in and out like snakes in a pit, or rivet the eye
with absurd alien gestures. The director's ultimate faith in man's
perpetual regeneration out of corruption is almost obscured by a
stupefying fresco of decay painted in murky mists and peopled with
monsters, cripples and freaks, witches and wizards. Endless con-

trasts assail the eye, giants and dwarfs, the old and the young, the beautiful and the ugly. The miserable squalor of the pitiful pilgrims in the temple of the hermaphrodite and the wretched tenants of the Insula Felicles mocks the sumptuous splendor and ghastly gluttony of Trimalchio and his gruesome guests. It is a long, horrid nightmare, fragmentary, incoherent, repetitive, beautiful, startling but fascinating. Like a nightmare, it ends in mid-sentence, and the viewer is left to finish the dream himself—or maybe Fellini intends to finish it for us in another film.

Fellini has repeatedly said, "What I have to say, I say in my work. My work can't be anything other than a testimony of what I am looking for. It is a mirror of my searching." The *Satyricon* mirrors a world obsessed with death and impotence, a world without a shred of joy, compassion, humanity, or humor. It's as though Fellini decided that these were Christian monopolies and that any portrayal of pre-Christian Rome must necessarily exclude the more humanizing aspects of life. But even his main source, Petronius, or Apuleius' *Golden Ass* and Ovid's *Metamorphoses* which he delved into for inspiration, are far funnier and more joyous, less bleak and oppressive than the director's concept of "Rome before Christ after Fellini," as the ads for the film fatuously proclaim. Surely human beings of two thousand years ago could laugh and cry and even feel pity for the sufferings of others.

Still, one of the most extraordinary things about the *Satyricon* is that it was not conceived by a young man but a middle-aged one. Youth is the time of innovation, yet, as one critic wrote, "On the funeral pyre of his Satyricon Fellini has burnt every rule of film making." And on that pyre he has also burnt his autobiographical cycle of films. If Fellini's films mirror what he is searching for in life, then perhaps he is trying to recapture a lost youth through the young protagonists of his film, a youth that he would have liked to emulate. Identifying with the three hedonistic vagabonds of the *Satyricon,* he can vicariously relive a freer adolescence than he had in

Rimini, without the repressive restrictions of his Catholic upbringing, more like the unfettered wanderings of the modern hippies he professes to admire so much. At the beginning, it occurred to me that the *Satyricon* might be an attempt to purge himself once and for all of one of the great themes of his life, the preoccupation with his Catholicism.

And yet, watching the *Satyricon*, it becomes apparent that while Fellini may have left the Church, the Church hasn't left him. Nor has Fellini changed many of his other themes; he has merely transferred them to a different time and terrain, which he calls ancient Rome but which is largely a figment of his monumental imagination. There is still the same pervasive preoccupation with sex, but instead of the lusty abandon with which Petronius' rascals scamper from one sexual encounter to another, Fellini inhibits them with puritanical loincloths. Nor can Fellini quite bring himself to perversion or pornography on the screen. The feeble attempts at orgies and sexual deviations occur mostly in "The Ship of Lichas" episode, where he contents himself with showing Tryphaena fondling a mouse or bathing in a tub. Lichas exchanges the only homosexual kiss in the film with Encolpius, and the two do marry, but Fellini makes Alain Cuny play the bride in such a coy, simpering manner that he appears more ludicrous than lecherous. Of all the episodes, this was intended to be the most erotic, but Fellini shies away from explicit eroticism. What was actually filmed is such a watered-down version of what was written in the script that it almost leads one to believe that Fellini gets rid of his sexual fantasies by writing them down on paper.

Fellini also vowed to get rid of his old tricks in this film, but he has clearly carried the whole kit and kaboodle of them right along into *Satyricon*. There are echoes of the religious processions of his childhood, the hope for miracles, the mountainous whores, the stoic suicide, the mysterious statues underwater, the monstrous fish, the baskets, the carts, the swings, the willow trees, the raft with the grotesque beasts. Questioned about these recurring symbols, Fellini responded with his usual disarming candor, "It's natural. How can one not be oneself? A man is born with a certain myth and continues to revolve around that, to reflect, to question himself, to anguish over it, to ruminate. Obviously *Satyricon* hasn't changed my destiny, but it has given me a new sensation. I seem to be a machine to reproduce images, images referring to any kind of story, even one far removed from my own experience."

What Fellini will do next is a matter of conjecture, although he has often talked of doing *Orlando Furioso* or Dante's *Divine Comedy*. Now that he has got his feet wet with his first costume film and resorted to an outside source for the first time, other than for the short *Toby Dammit* episode, it doesn't seem likely that he will return to the autobiographical phase of his career. The new season of Fellini's life is likely to be focused on the supernatural or on science fiction, where his mastery of imagery can flourish unrestrained by reality, even his own.